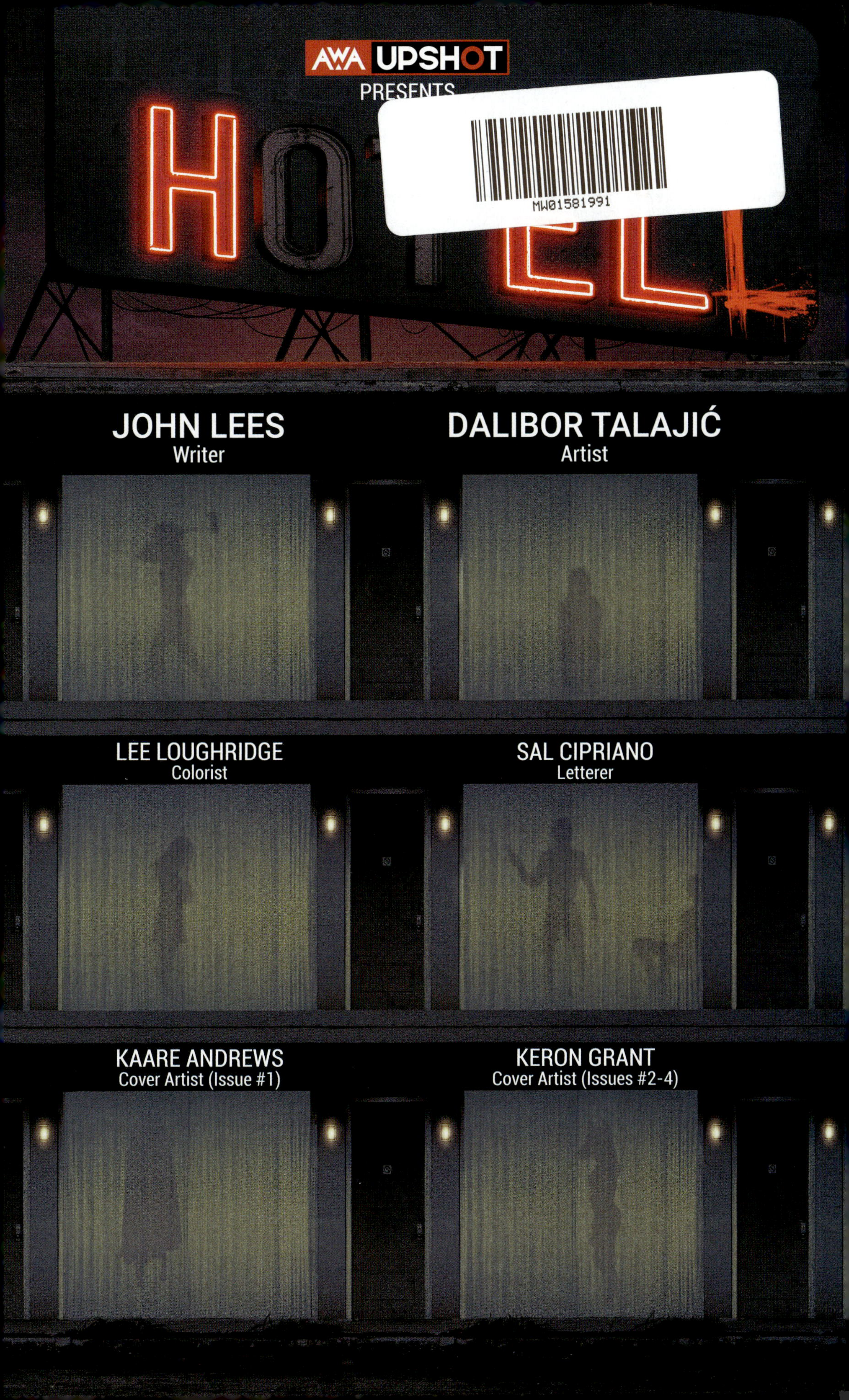
AWA UPSHOT
PRESENTS
JOHN LEES
Writer
DALIBOR TALAJIĆ
Artist
LEE LOUGHRIDGE
Colorist
SAL CIPRIANO
Letterer
KAARE ANDREWS
Cover Artist (Issue #1)
KERON GRANT
Cover Artist (Issues #2-4)

  AWA_studios  AWAstudiosofficial  UPSHOT_studios  UPSHOTstudiosofficial

Axel Alonso Chief Creative Officer
Chris Burns Production Editor
Stan Chou Art Director, Logo Designer
Michael Coast Senior Editor
Jaime Coyne Associate Editor
Frank Fochetta Senior Consultant, Sales & Distribution
William Graves Managing Editor
Bill Jemas CEO & Publisher

Amy Kim Events & Sales Associate
Bosung Kim Production & Design Assistant
Allison Mase Executive Assistant
Dulce Montoya Associate Editor
Kevin Park Associate General Counsel
Maureen Sullivan Controller
Lisa Y. Wu Marketing Manager

HOTELL, VOLUME 1. October 2020. Published by Artists Writers & Artisans, Inc. Office of publication: 1359 Broadway, Suite 800, New York, NY 10018. © 2020 Artists Writers & Artisans, Inc. or their respective owners. All Rights Reserved. No similarity between any of the names, characters, persons, and/or institutions in this magazine with those of any living or dead person or institution is intended, and any such similarity which may exist is purely coincidental. **Printed in Canada.**

10 9 8 7 6 5 4 3 2 1

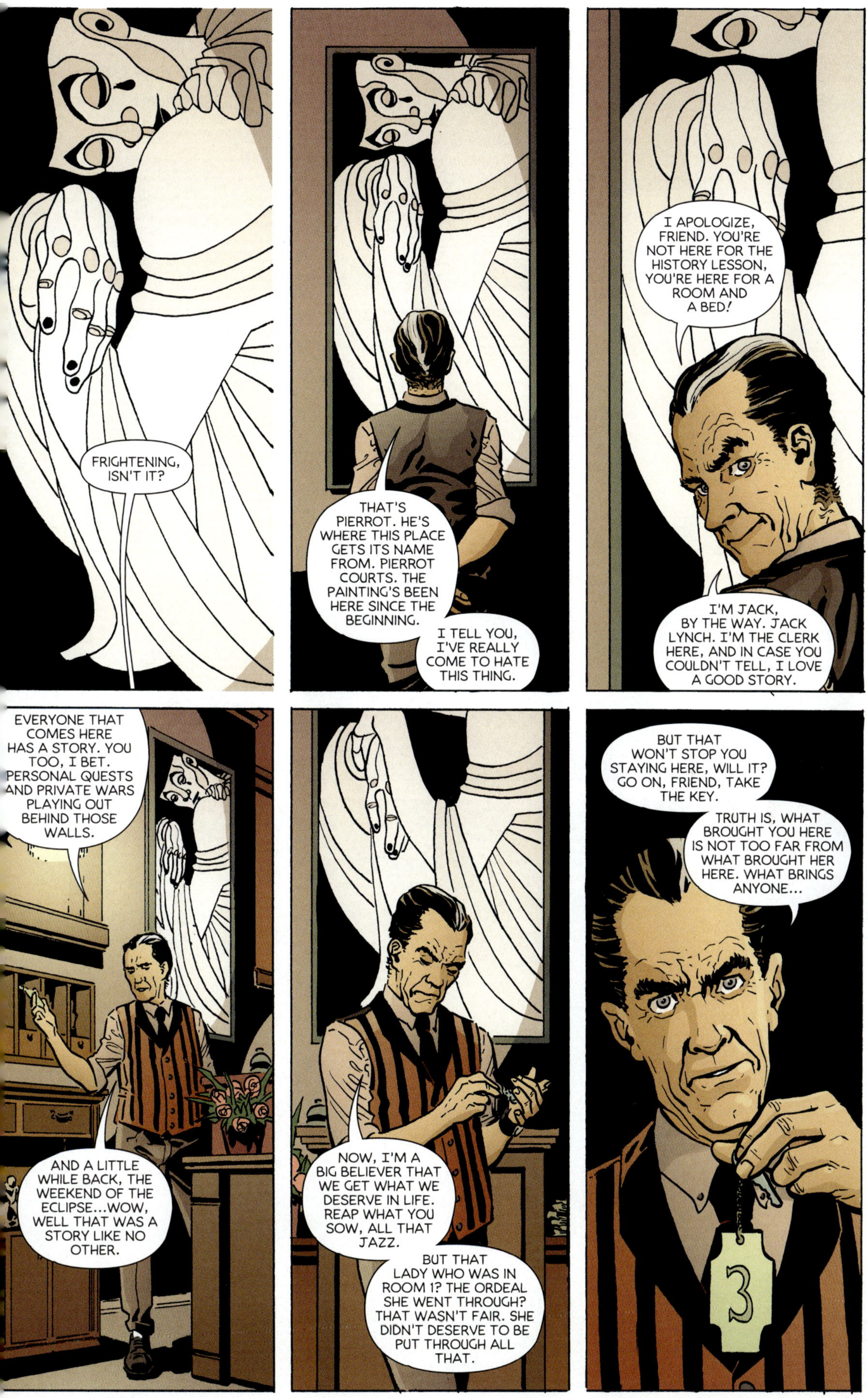
FRIGHTENING, ISN'T IT?
THAT'S PIERROT. HE'S WHERE THIS PLACE GETS ITS NAME FROM. PIERROT COURTS. THE PAINTING'S BEEN HERE SINCE THE BEGINNING.
I TELL YOU, I'VE REALLY COME TO HATE THIS THING.
I APOLOGIZE, FRIEND. YOU'RE NOT HERE FOR THE HISTORY LESSON, YOU'RE HERE FOR A ROOM AND A BED!
I'M JACK, BY THE WAY. JACK LYNCH. I'M THE CLERK HERE, AND IN CASE YOU COULDN'T TELL, I LOVE A GOOD STORY.
EVERYONE THAT COMES HERE HAS A STORY. YOU TOO, I BET. PERSONAL QUESTS AND PRIVATE WARS PLAYING OUT BEHIND THOSE WALLS.
AND A LITTLE WHILE BACK, THE WEEKEND OF THE ECLIPSE...WOW, WELL THAT WAS A STORY LIKE NO OTHER.
NOW, I'M A BIG BELIEVER THAT WE GET WHAT WE DESERVE IN LIFE. REAP WHAT YOU SOW, ALL THAT JAZZ.
BUT THAT LADY WHO WAS IN ROOM 1? THE ORDEAL SHE WENT THROUGH? THAT WASN'T FAIR. SHE DIDN'T DESERVE TO BE PUT THROUGH ALL THAT.
BUT THAT WON'T STOP YOU STAYING HERE, WILL IT? GO ON, FRIEND, TAKE THE KEY.
TRUTH IS, WHAT BROUGHT YOU HERE IS NOT TOO FAR FROM WHAT BROUGHT HER HERE. WHAT BRINGS ANYONE...
3

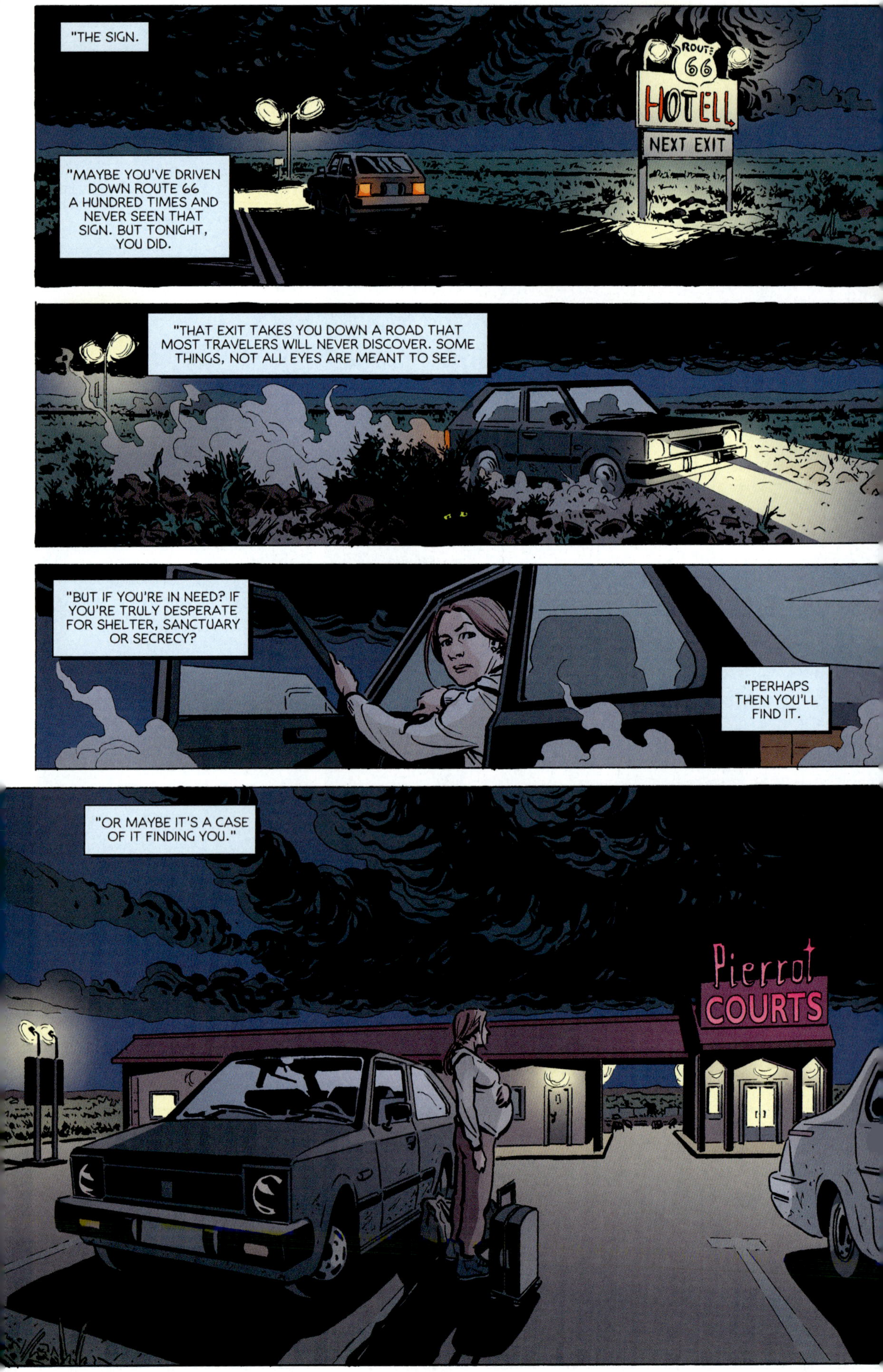
"THE SIGN.
ROUTE 66
HOTELL
NEXT EXIT
"MAYBE YOU'VE DRIVEN DOWN ROUTE 66 A HUNDRED TIMES AND NEVER SEEN THAT SIGN. BUT TONIGHT, YOU DID.
"THAT EXIT TAKES YOU DOWN A ROAD THAT MOST TRAVELERS WILL NEVER DISCOVER. SOME THINGS, NOT ALL EYES ARE MEANT TO SEE.
"BUT IF YOU'RE IN NEED? IF YOU'RE TRULY DESPERATE FOR SHELTER, SANCTUARY OR SECRECY?
"PERHAPS THEN YOU'LL FIND IT.
"OR MAYBE IT'S A CASE OF IT FINDING YOU."
Pierrot
COURTS

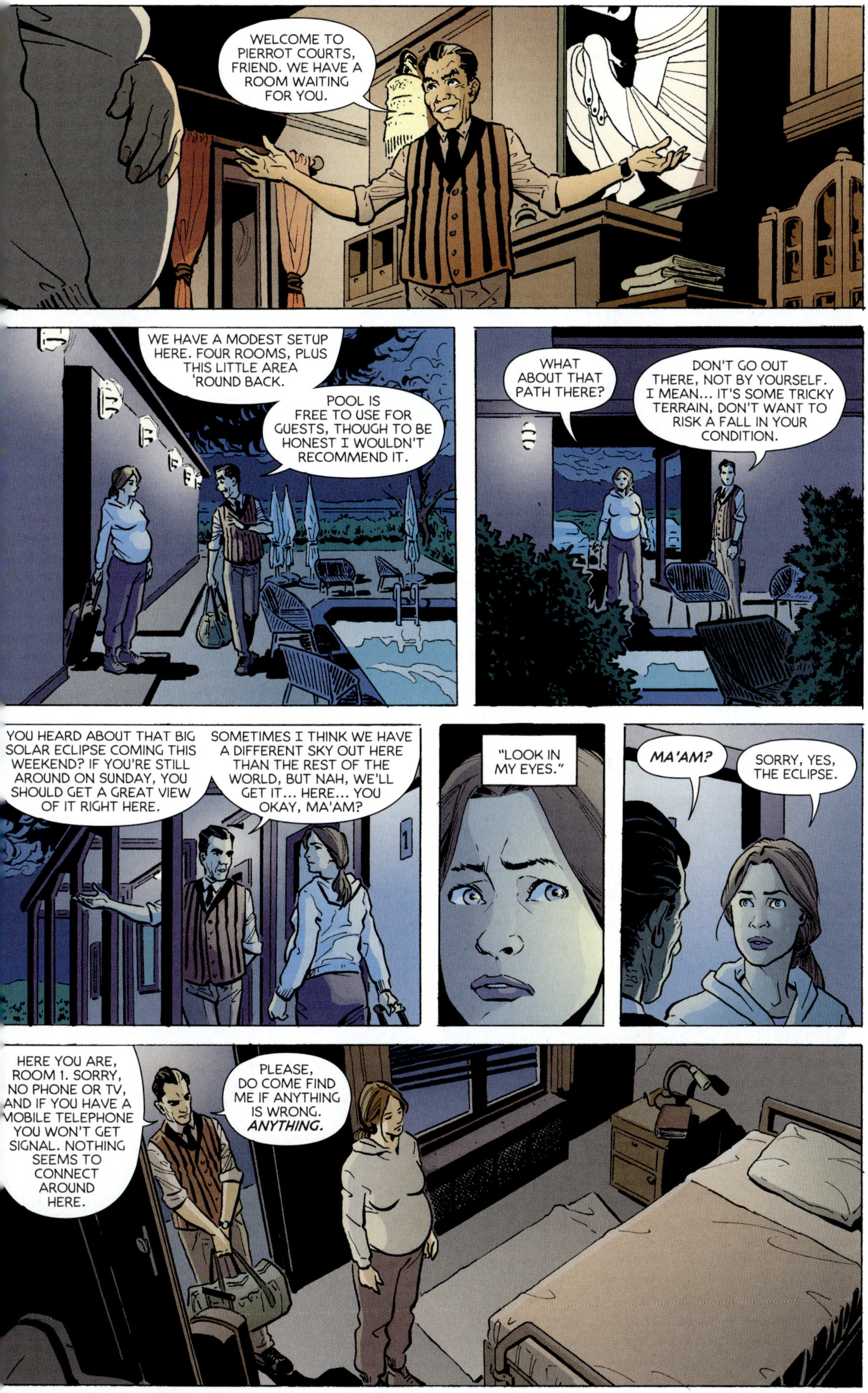
WELCOME TO PIERROT COURTS, FRIEND. WE HAVE A ROOM WAITING FOR YOU.
WE HAVE A MODEST SETUP HERE. FOUR ROOMS, PLUS THIS LITTLE AREA 'ROUND BACK.
POOL IS FREE TO USE FOR GUESTS, THOUGH TO BE HONEST I WOULDN'T RECOMMEND IT.
WHAT ABOUT THAT PATH THERE?
DON'T GO OUT THERE, NOT BY YOURSELF. I MEAN... IT'S SOME TRICKY TERRAIN, DON'T WANT TO RISK A FALL IN YOUR CONDITION.
YOU HEARD ABOUT THAT BIG SOLAR ECLIPSE COMING THIS WEEKEND? IF YOU'RE STILL AROUND ON SUNDAY, YOU SHOULD GET A GREAT VIEW OF IT RIGHT HERE.
SOMETIMES I THINK WE HAVE A DIFFERENT SKY OUT HERE THAN THE REST OF THE WORLD, BUT NAH, WE'LL GET IT... HERE... YOU OKAY, MA'AM?
1
"LOOK IN MY EYES."
MA'AM?
SORRY, YES, THE ECLIPSE.
HERE YOU ARE, ROOM 1. SORRY, NO PHONE OR TV, AND IF YOU HAVE A MOBILE TELEPHONE YOU WON'T GET SIGNAL. NOTHING SEEMS TO CONNECT AROUND HERE.
PLEASE, DO COME FIND ME IF ANYTHING IS WRONG. ***ANYTHING.***

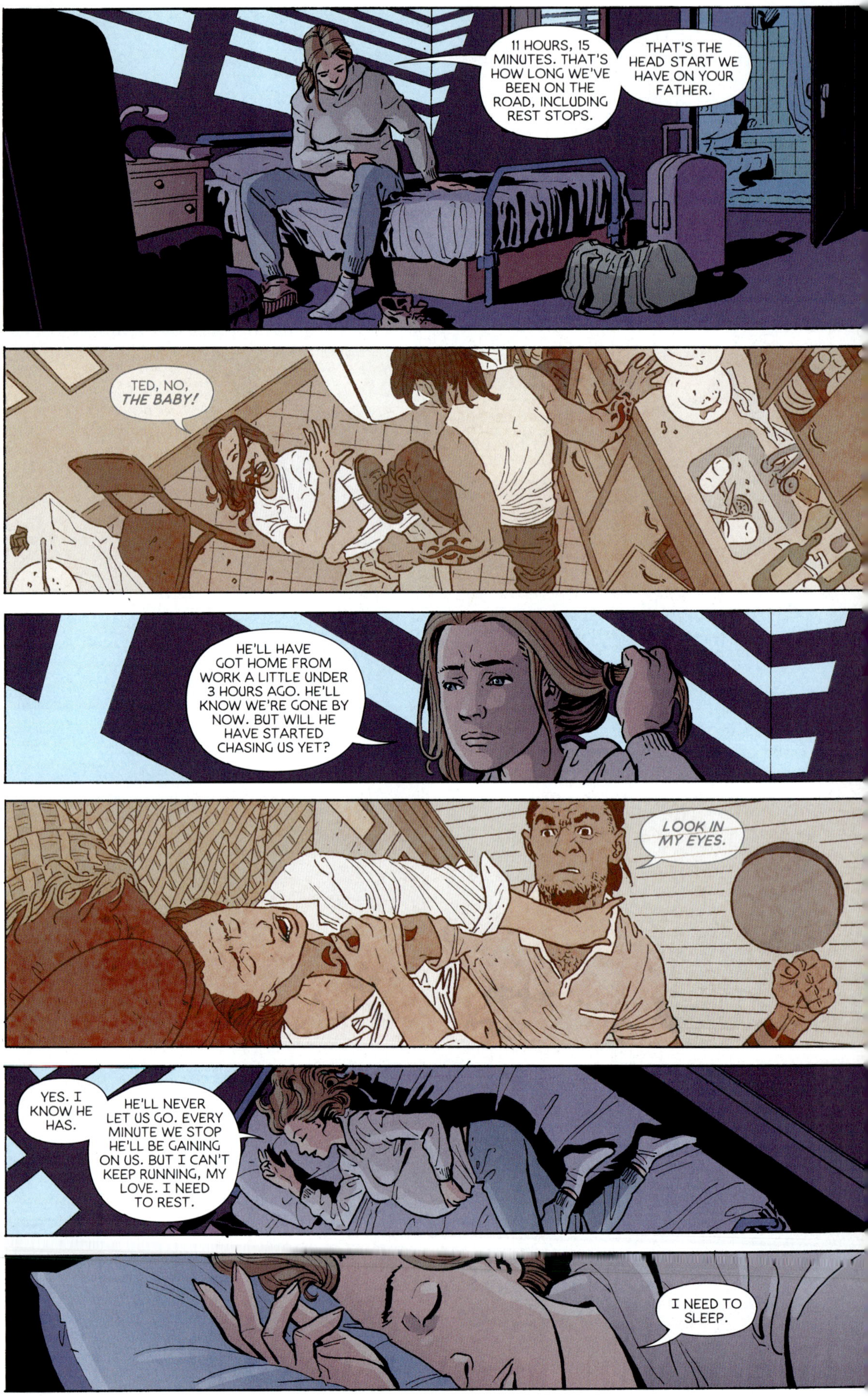
11 HOURS, 15 MINUTES. THAT'S HOW LONG WE'VE BEEN ON THE ROAD, INCLUDING REST STOPS.
THAT'S THE HEAD START WE HAVE ON YOUR FATHER.
TED, NO, *THE BABY!*
HE'LL HAVE GOT HOME FROM WORK A LITTLE UNDER 3 HOURS AGO. HE'LL KNOW WE'RE GONE BY NOW. BUT WILL HE HAVE STARTED CHASING US YET?
LOOK IN MY EYES.
YES. I KNOW HE HAS.
HE'LL NEVER LET US GO. EVERY MINUTE WE STOP HE'LL BE GAINING ON US. BUT I CAN'T KEEP RUNNING, MY LOVE. I NEED TO REST.
I NEED TO SLEEP.

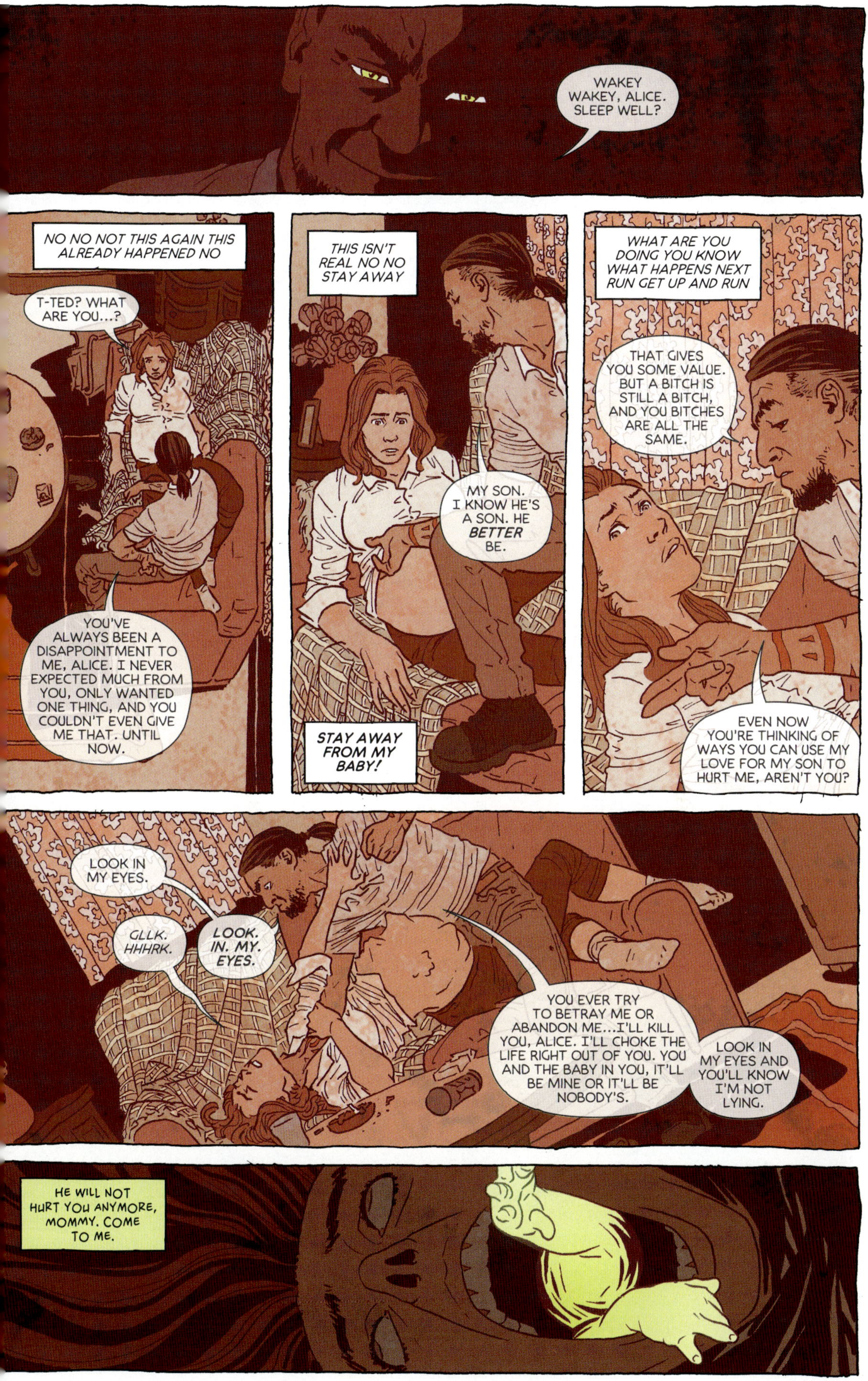

WAKEY WAKEY, ALICE. SLEEP WELL?
NO NO NOT THIS AGAIN THIS ALREADY HAPPENED NO
T-TED? WHAT ARE YOU...?
YOU'VE ALWAYS BEEN A DISAPPOINTMENT TO ME, ALICE. I NEVER EXPECTED MUCH FROM YOU, ONLY WANTED ONE THING, AND YOU COULDN'T EVEN GIVE ME THAT. UNTIL NOW.
THIS ISN'T REAL NO NO STAY AWAY
MY SON. I KNOW HE'S A SON. HE *BETTER* BE.
STAY AWAY FROM MY BABY!
WHAT ARE YOU DOING YOU KNOW WHAT HAPPENS NEXT RUN GET UP AND RUN
THAT GIVES YOU SOME VALUE. BUT A BITCH IS STILL A BITCH, AND YOU BITCHES ARE ALL THE SAME.
EVEN NOW YOU'RE THINKING OF WAYS YOU CAN USE MY LOVE FOR MY SON TO HURT ME, AREN'T YOU?
LOOK IN MY EYES.
GLLK. HHHRK.
LOOK. IN. MY. EYES.
YOU EVER TRY TO BETRAY ME OR ABANDON ME...I'LL KILL YOU, ALICE. I'LL CHOKE THE LIFE RIGHT OUT OF YOU. YOU AND THE BABY IN YOU, IT'LL BE MINE OR IT'LL BE NOBODY'S.
LOOK IN MY EYES AND YOU'LL KNOW I'M NOT LYING.
HE WILL NOT HURT YOU ANYMORE, MOMMY. COME TO ME.

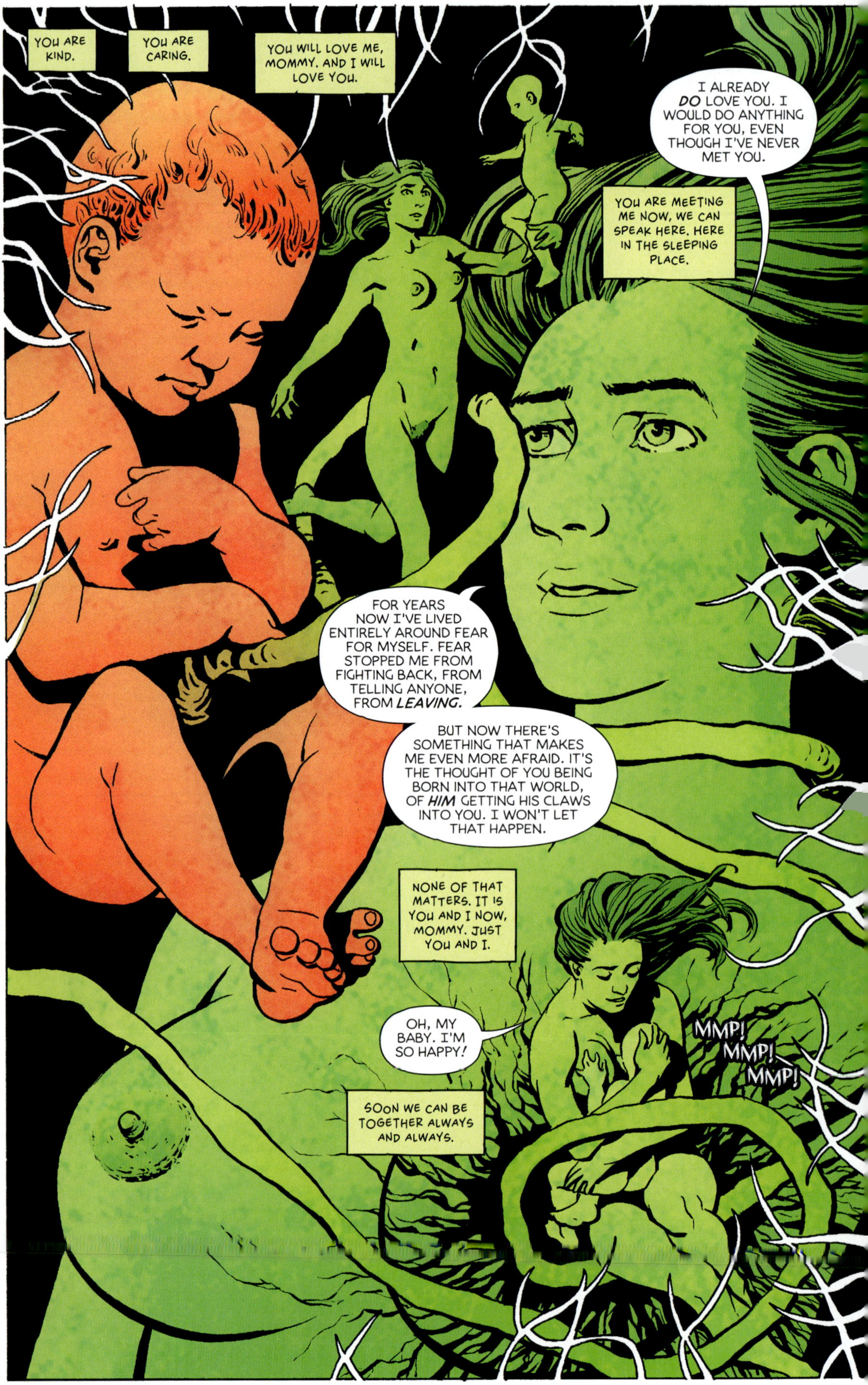
YOU ARE KIND.
YOU ARE CARING.
YOU WILL LOVE ME, MOMMY. AND I WILL LOVE YOU.
I ALREADY *DO* LOVE YOU. I WOULD DO ANYTHING FOR YOU, EVEN THOUGH I'VE NEVER MET YOU.
YOU ARE MEETING ME NOW. WE CAN SPEAK HERE. HERE IN THE SLEEPING PLACE.
FOR YEARS NOW I'VE LIVED ENTIRELY AROUND FEAR FOR MYSELF. FEAR STOPPED ME FROM FIGHTING BACK, FROM TELLING ANYONE, FROM *LEAVING.*
BUT NOW THERE'S SOMETHING THAT MAKES ME EVEN MORE AFRAID. IT'S THE THOUGHT OF YOU BEING BORN INTO THAT WORLD, OF *HIM* GETTING HIS CLAWS INTO YOU. I WON'T LET THAT HAPPEN.
NONE OF THAT MATTERS. IT IS YOU AND I NOW, MOMMY. JUST YOU AND I.
OH, MY BABY. I'M SO HAPPY!
MMP! MMP! MMP!
SOON WE CAN BE TOGETHER ALWAYS AND ALWAYS.

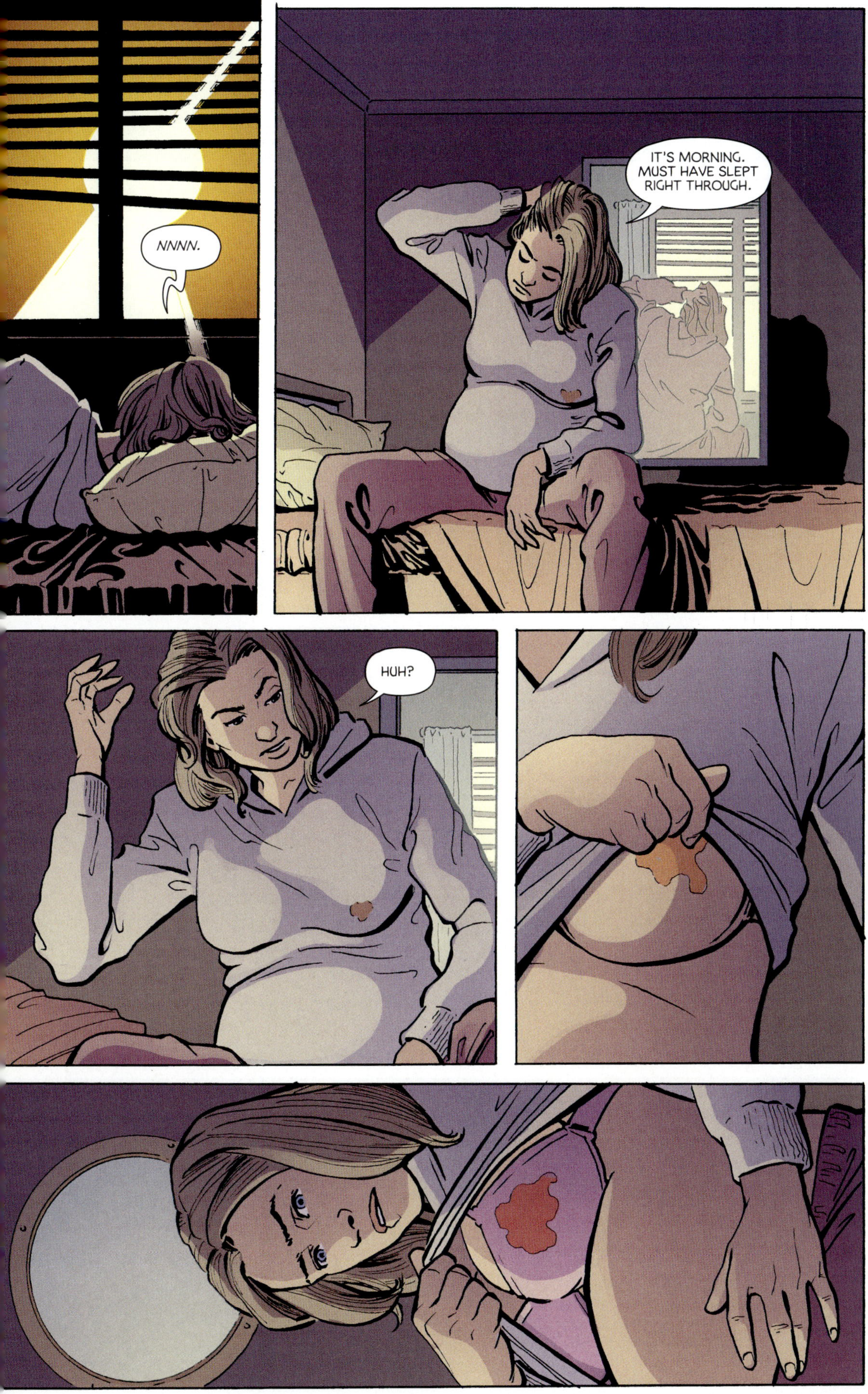
NNNN.
IT'S MORNING. MUST HAVE SLEPT RIGHT THROUGH.
HUH?

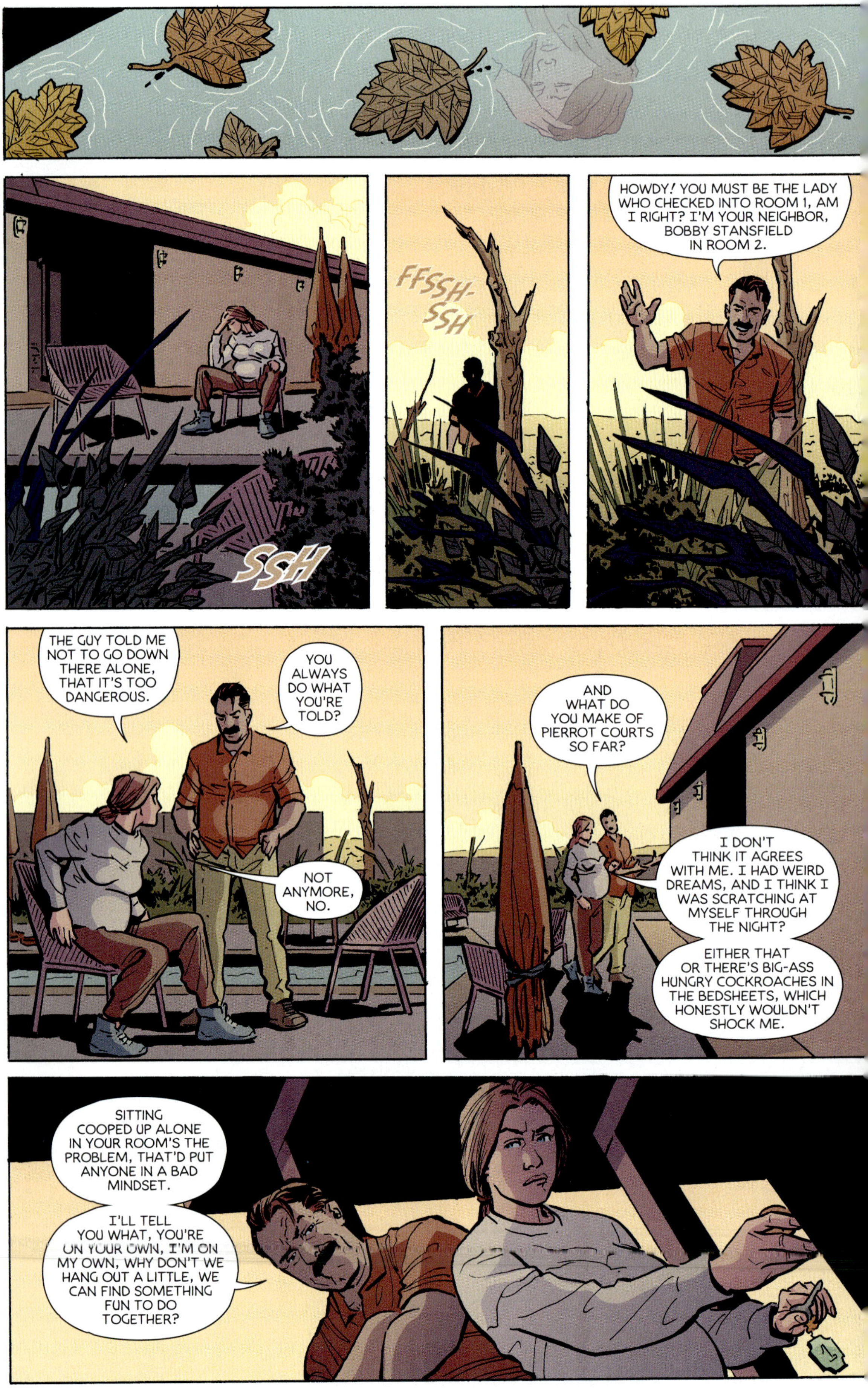
SSH
FFSSH-SSH
HOWDY! YOU MUST BE THE LADY WHO CHECKED INTO ROOM 1, AM I RIGHT? I'M YOUR NEIGHBOR, BOBBY STANSFIELD IN ROOM 2.
THE GUY TOLD ME NOT TO GO DOWN THERE ALONE, THAT IT'S TOO DANGEROUS.
YOU ALWAYS DO WHAT YOU'RE TOLD?
NOT ANYMORE, NO.
AND WHAT DO YOU MAKE OF PIERROT COURTS SO FAR?
I DON'T THINK IT AGREES WITH ME. I HAD WEIRD DREAMS, AND I THINK I WAS SCRATCHING AT MYSELF THROUGH THE NIGHT?
EITHER THAT OR THERE'S BIG-ASS HUNGRY COCKROACHES IN THE BEDSHEETS, WHICH HONESTLY WOULDN'T SHOCK ME.
SITTING COOPED UP ALONE IN YOUR ROOM'S THE PROBLEM, THAT'D PUT ANYONE IN A BAD MINDSET.
I'LL TELL YOU WHAT, YOU'RE ON YOUR OWN, I'M ON MY OWN, WHY DON'T WE HANG OUT A LITTLE, WE CAN FIND SOMETHING FUN TO DO TOGETHER?

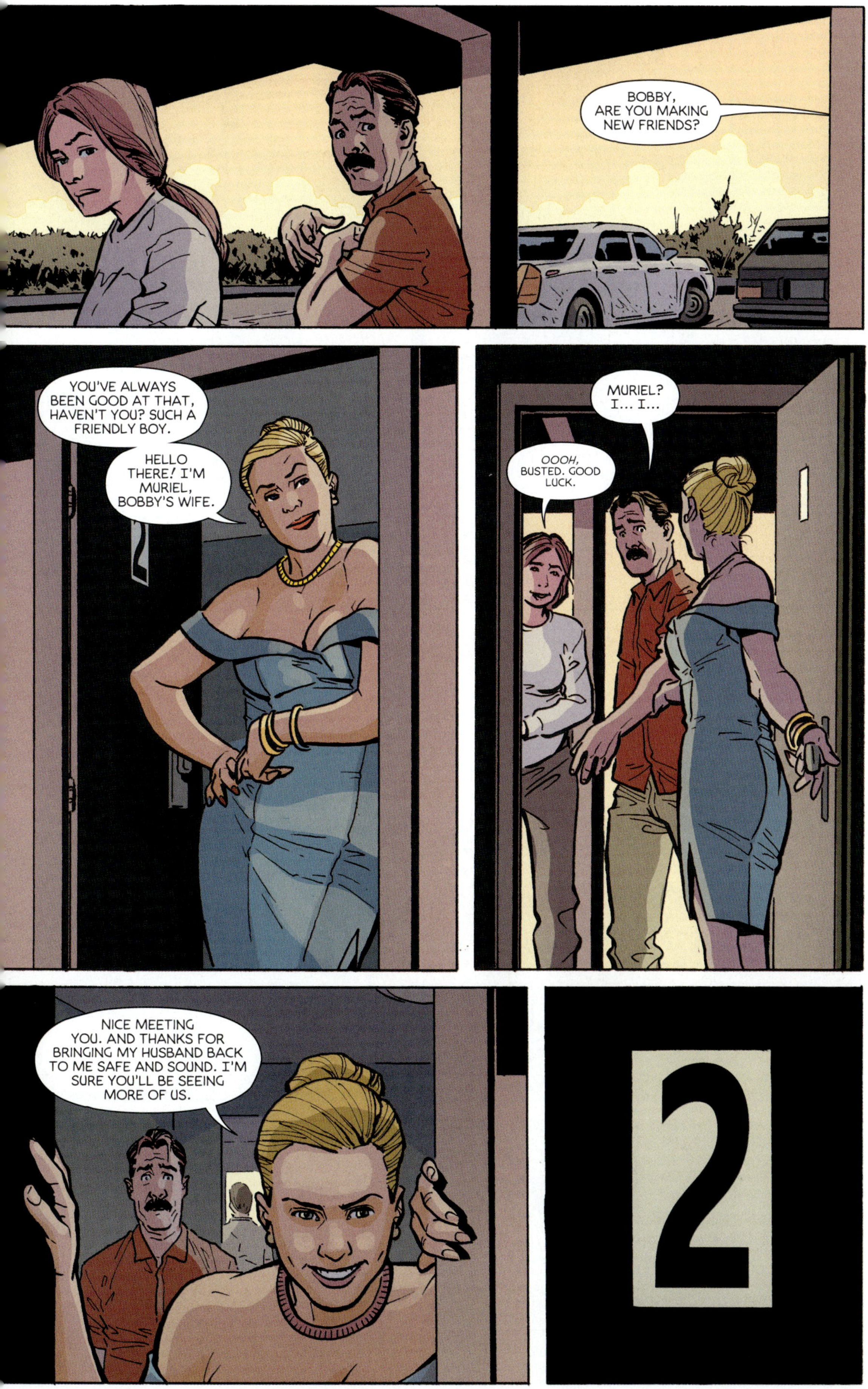
BOBBY, ARE YOU MAKING NEW FRIENDS?
YOU'VE ALWAYS BEEN GOOD AT THAT, HAVEN'T YOU? SUCH A FRIENDLY BOY.
HELLO THERE! I'M MURIEL, BOBBY'S WIFE.
MURIEL? I... I...
OOOH, BUSTED. GOOD LUCK.
NICE MEETING YOU. AND THANKS FOR BRINGING MY HUSBAND BACK TO ME SAFE AND SOUND. I'M SURE YOU'LL BE SEEING MORE OF US.
2

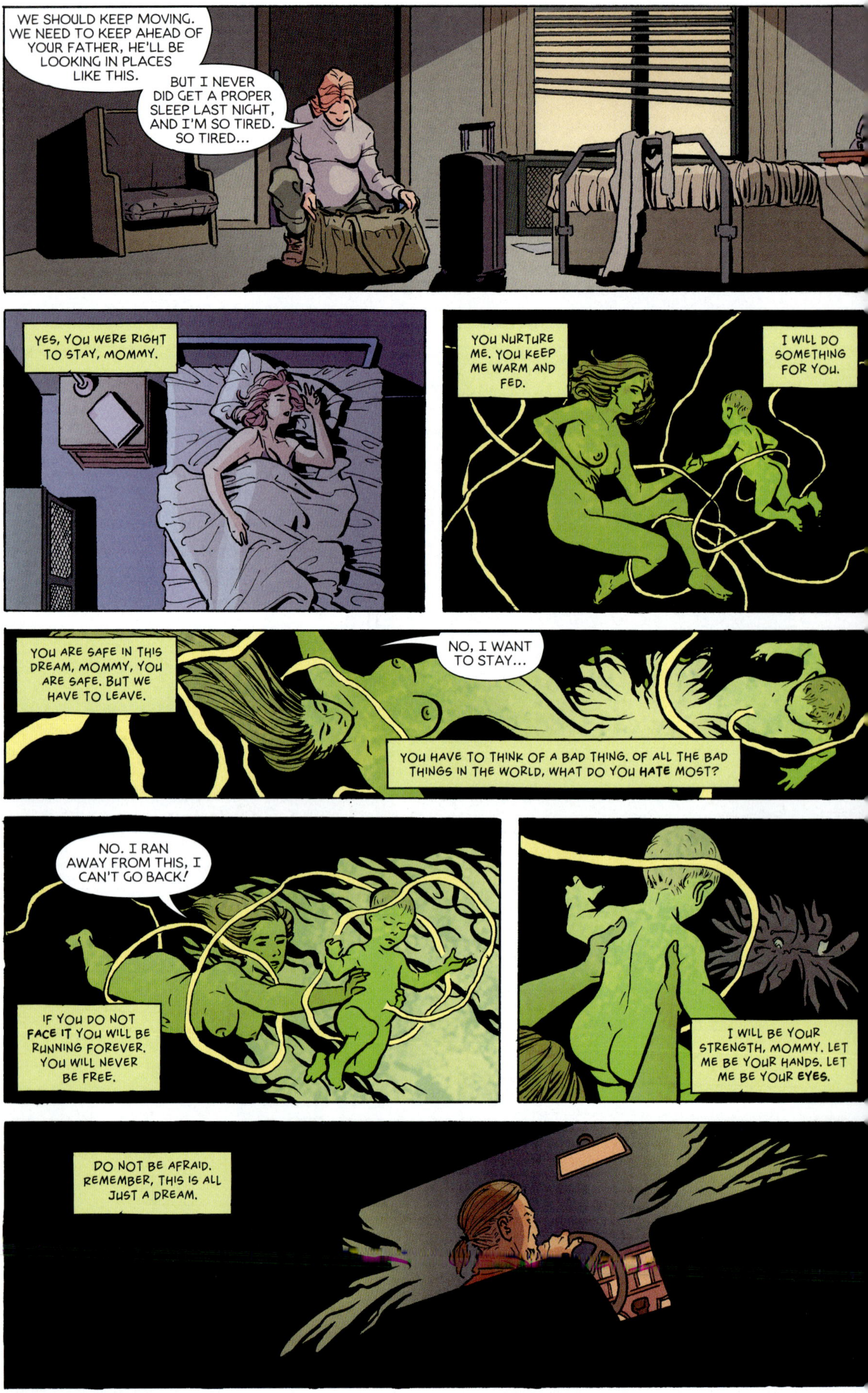
WE SHOULD KEEP MOVING. WE NEED TO KEEP AHEAD OF YOUR FATHER, HE'LL BE LOOKING IN PLACES LIKE THIS.
BUT I NEVER DID GET A PROPER SLEEP LAST NIGHT, AND I'M SO TIRED. SO TIRED...
YES, YOU WERE RIGHT TO STAY, MOMMY.
YOU NURTURE ME. YOU KEEP ME WARM AND FED.
I WILL DO SOMETHING FOR YOU.
YOU ARE SAFE IN THIS DREAM, MOMMY. YOU ARE SAFE. BUT WE HAVE TO LEAVE.
NO, I WANT TO STAY...
YOU HAVE TO THINK OF A BAD THING. OF ALL THE BAD THINGS IN THE WORLD, WHAT DO YOU **HATE** MOST?
NO. I RAN AWAY FROM THIS, I CAN'T GO BACK!
IF YOU DO NOT **FACE IT** YOU WILL BE RUNNING FOREVER. YOU WILL NEVER BE FREE.
I WILL BE YOUR STRENGTH, MOMMY. LET ME BE YOUR HANDS. LET ME BE YOUR **EYES**.
DO NOT BE AFRAID. REMEMBER, THIS IS ALL JUST A DREAM.

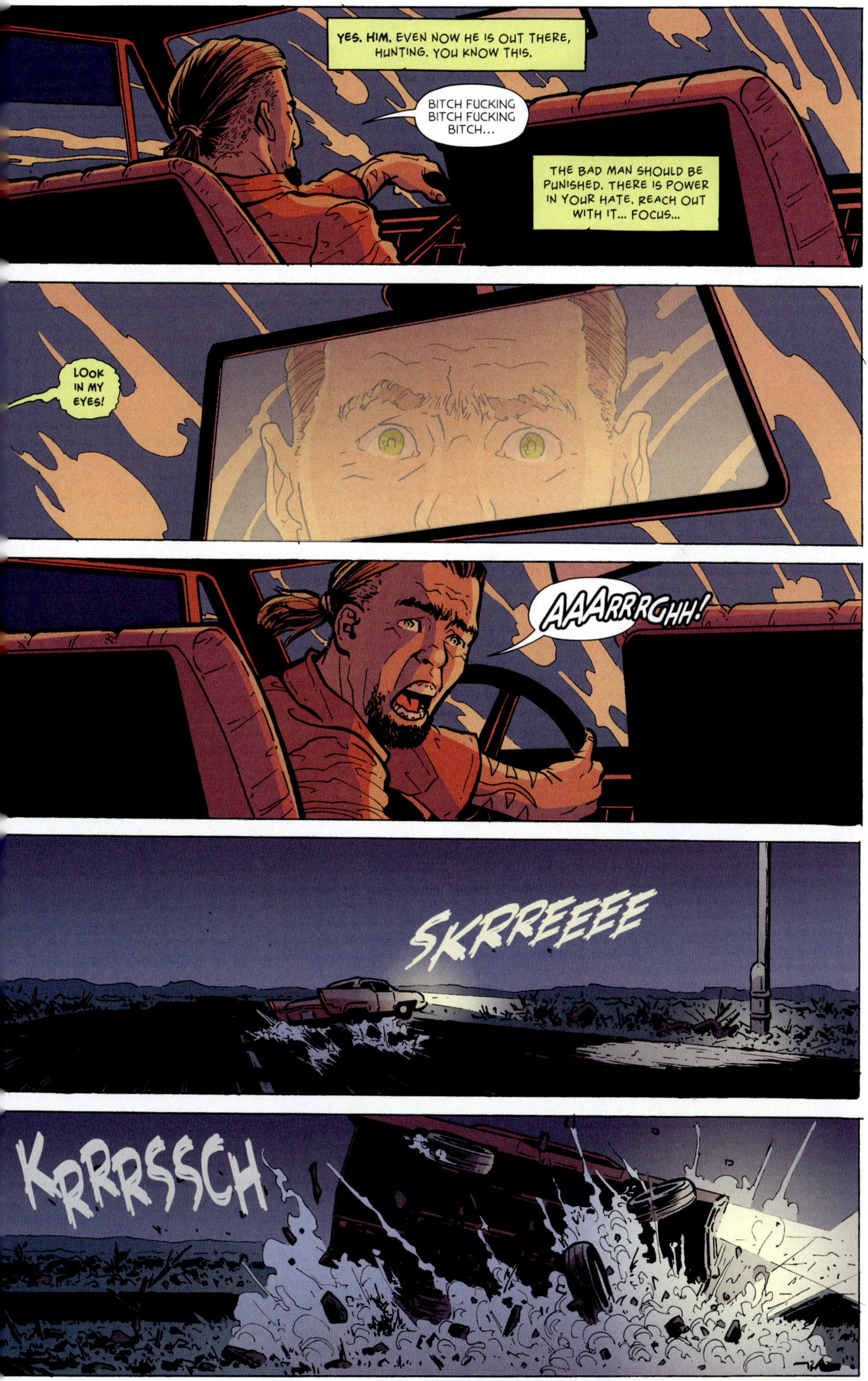
YES. HIM. EVEN NOW HE IS OUT THERE, HUNTING. YOU KNOW THIS.
BITCH FUCKING BITCH FUCKING BITCH...
THE BAD MAN SHOULD BE PUNISHED. THERE IS POWER IN YOUR HATE. REACH OUT WITH IT... FOCUS...
LOOK IN MY EYES!
AAARRRGHH!
SKRREEEE
KRRRSSCH

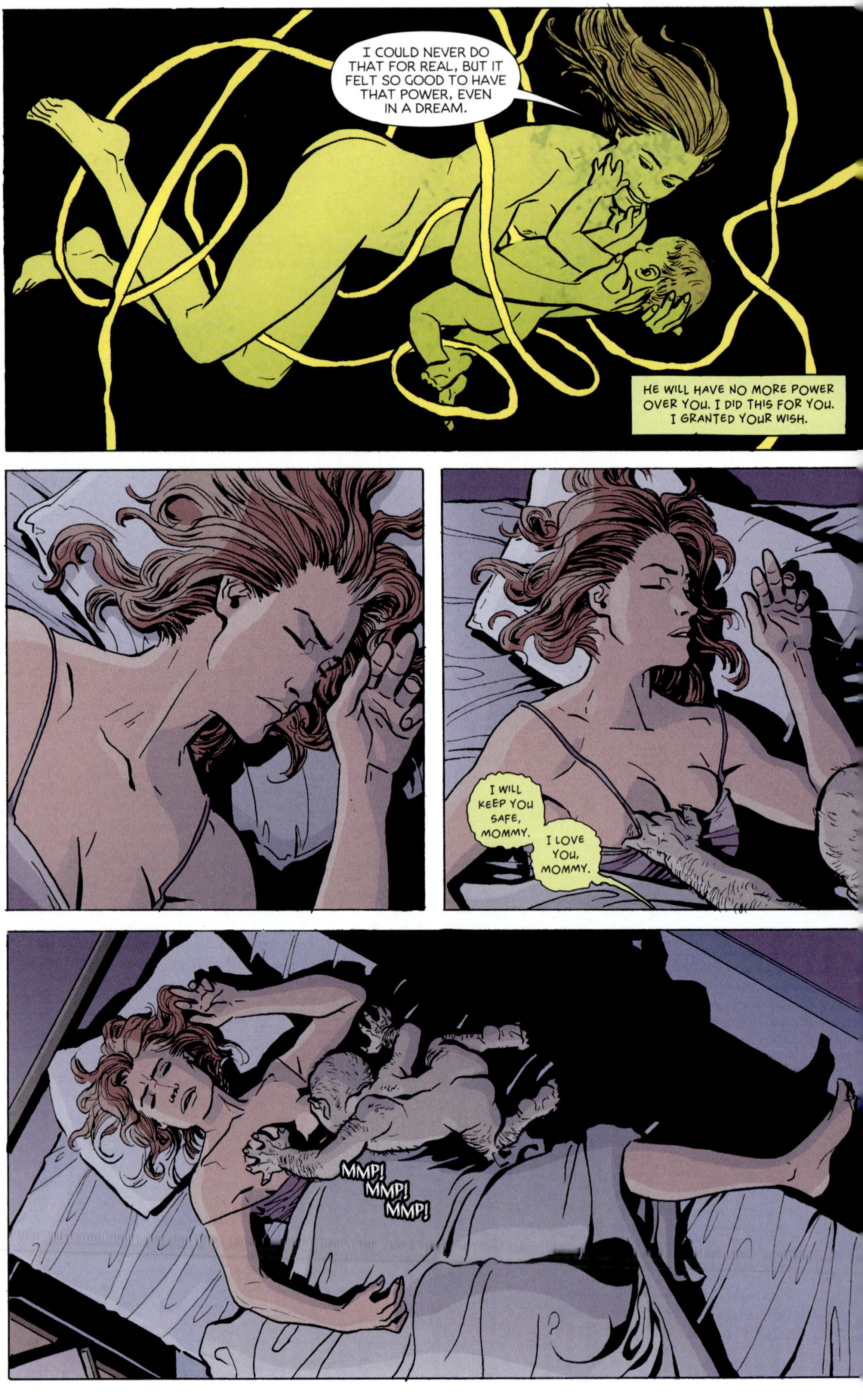
I COULD NEVER DO THAT FOR REAL, BUT IT FELT SO GOOD TO HAVE THAT POWER, EVEN IN A DREAM.
HE WILL HAVE NO MORE POWER OVER YOU. I DID THIS FOR YOU. I GRANTED YOUR WISH.
I WILL KEEP YOU SAFE, MOMMY.
I LOVE YOU, MOMMY.
MMP! MMP! MMP!

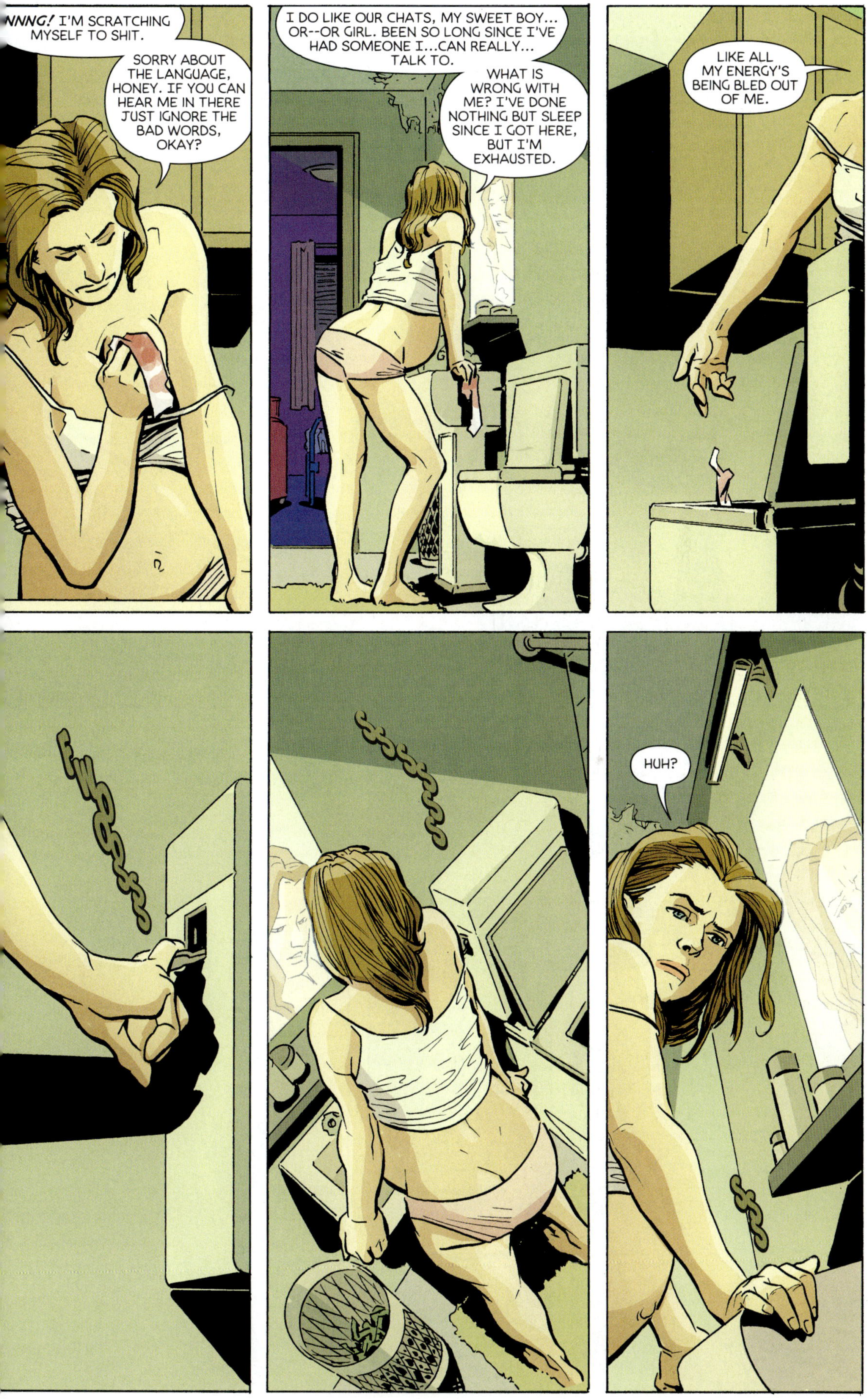

NNNG! I'M SCRATCHING MYSELF TO SHIT.
SORRY ABOUT THE LANGUAGE, HONEY. IF YOU CAN HEAR ME IN THERE JUST IGNORE THE BAD WORDS, OKAY?
I DO LIKE OUR CHATS, MY SWEET BOY... OR--OR GIRL. BEEN SO LONG SINCE I'VE HAD SOMEONE I...CAN REALLY... TALK TO.
WHAT IS WRONG WITH ME? I'VE DONE NOTHING BUT SLEEP SINCE I GOT HERE, BUT I'M EXHAUSTED.
LIKE ALL MY ENERGY'S BEING BLED OUT OF ME.
FWOOSSS
SSSSSSS
HUH?
SSS

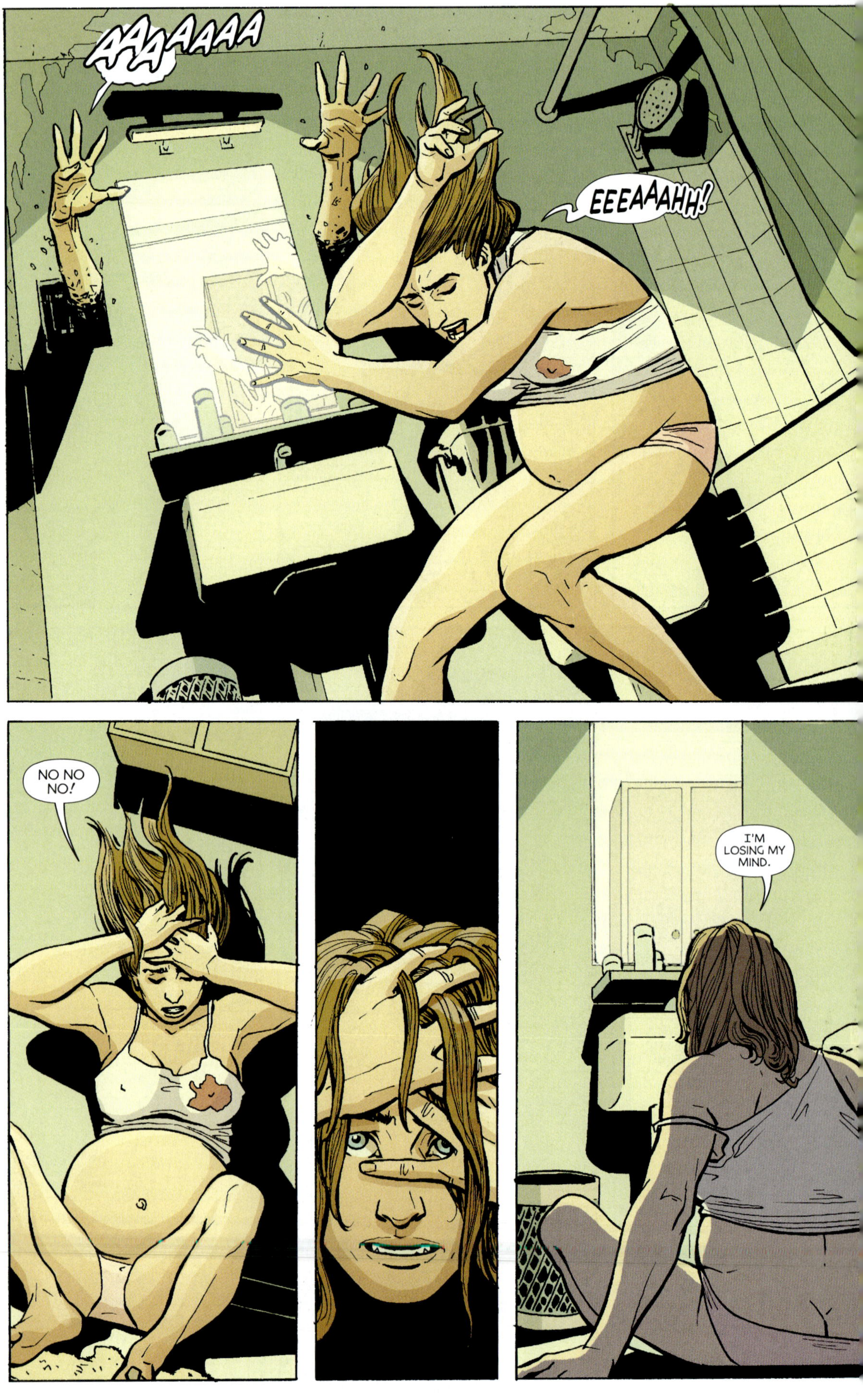
AAAAAAA
EEEAAAHH!
NO NO NO!
I'M LOSING MY MIND.

THERE'S SOMETHING WRONG ABOUT ALL THIS. THERE'S NO RATIONAL REASON FOR US TO STILL BE HERE.
WE NEED TO BE ON THE MOVE AGAIN. WE NEED TO GET OUT OF THIS MOTEL!
JUST GO ALREADY! WHY CAN'T I MAKE MYSELF GET UP AND LEAVE?
THERE'S SOMETHING I'M MISSING HERE...
SOMETHING... JUST OUT...OF REACH...
CAN'T... THINK...SO... TIRED...

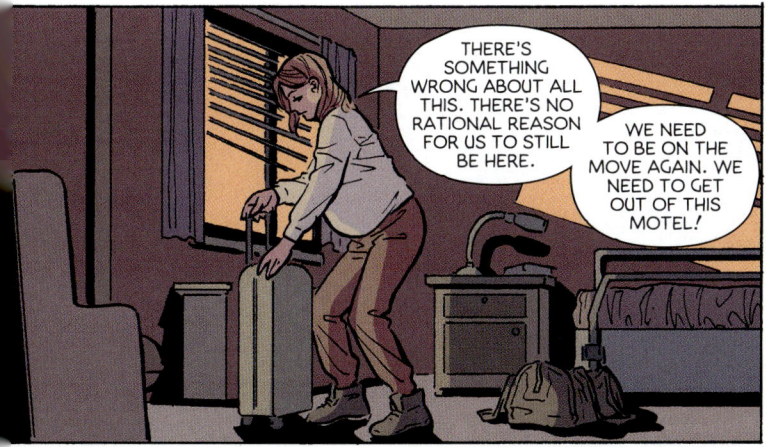

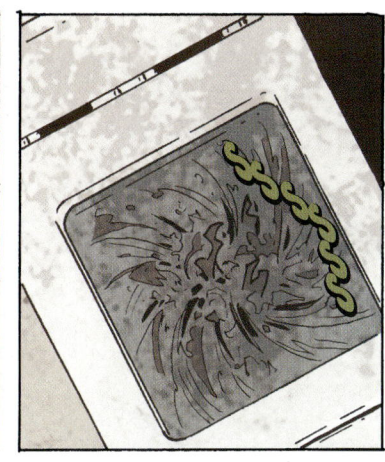

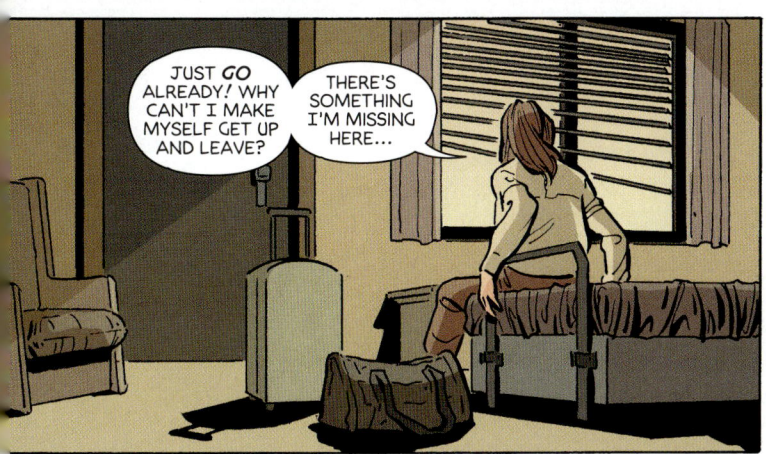

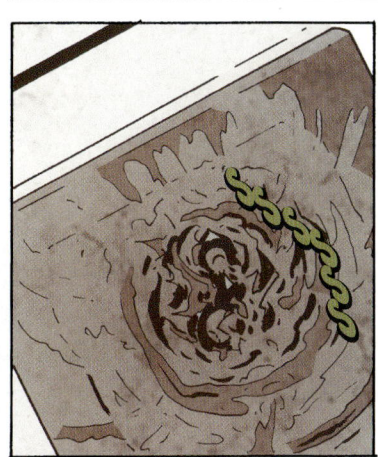

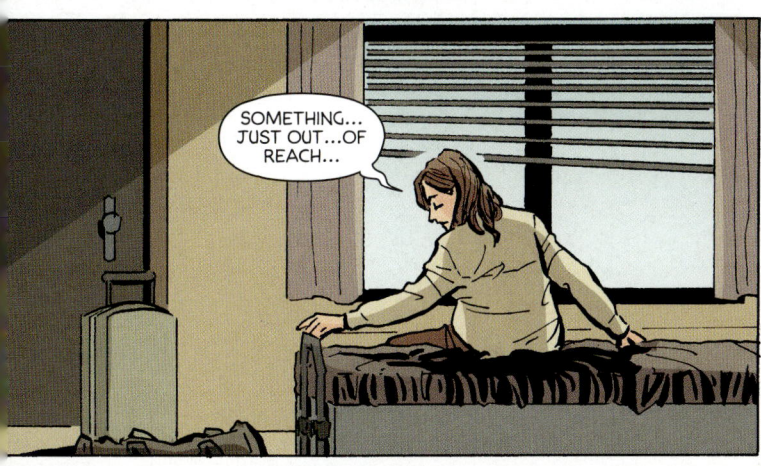

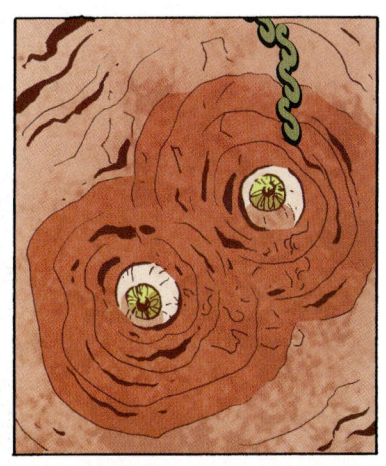

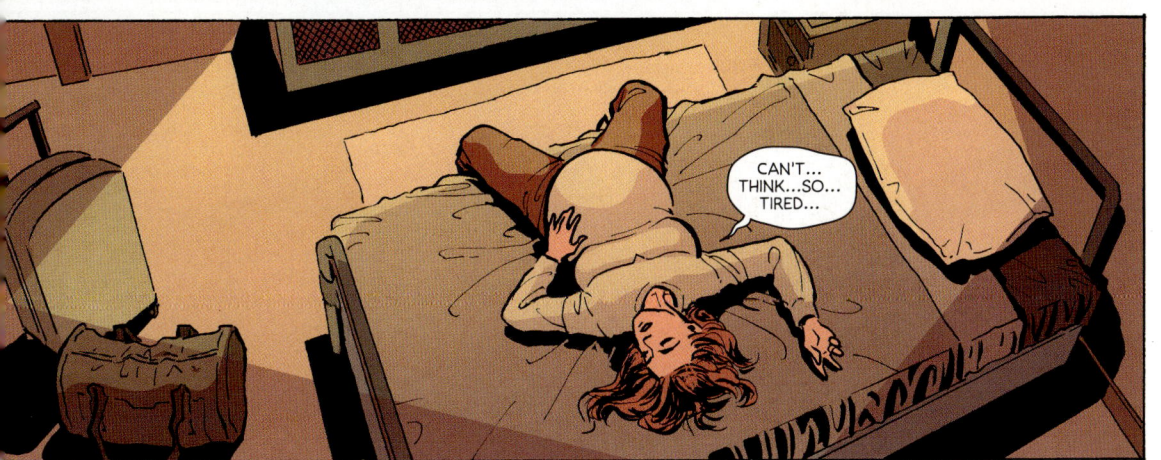

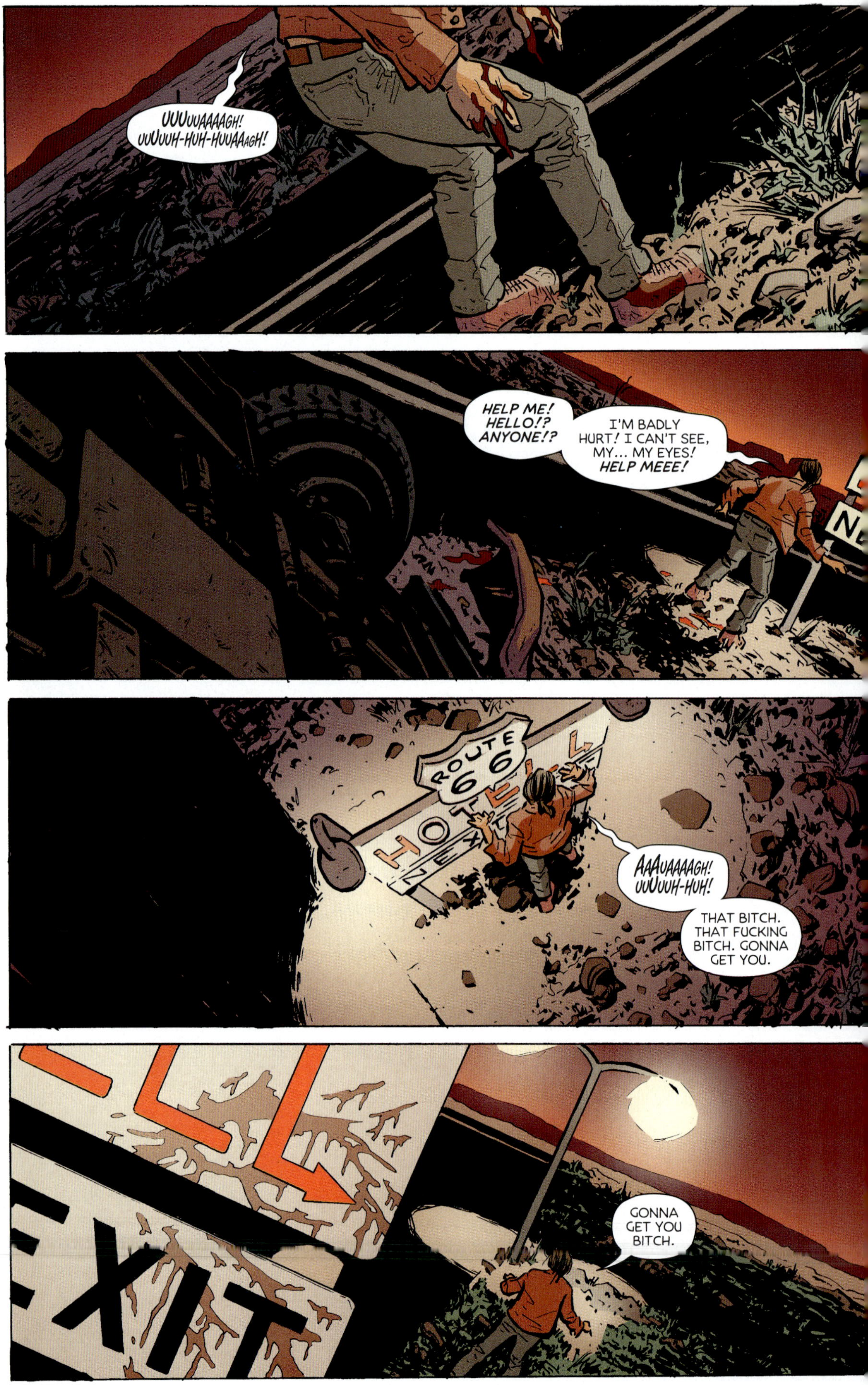
UUUuuAAAAGH! uuUuuH-HUH-HUUAAAGH!
HELP ME! HELLO!? ANYONE!?
I'M BADLY HURT! I CAN'T SEE, MY... MY EYES! HELP MEEE!
ROUTE 66
AAAuAAAAGH! uuUuuH-HUH!
THAT BITCH. THAT FUCKING BITCH. GONNA GET YOU.
EXIT
GONNA GET YOU BITCH.

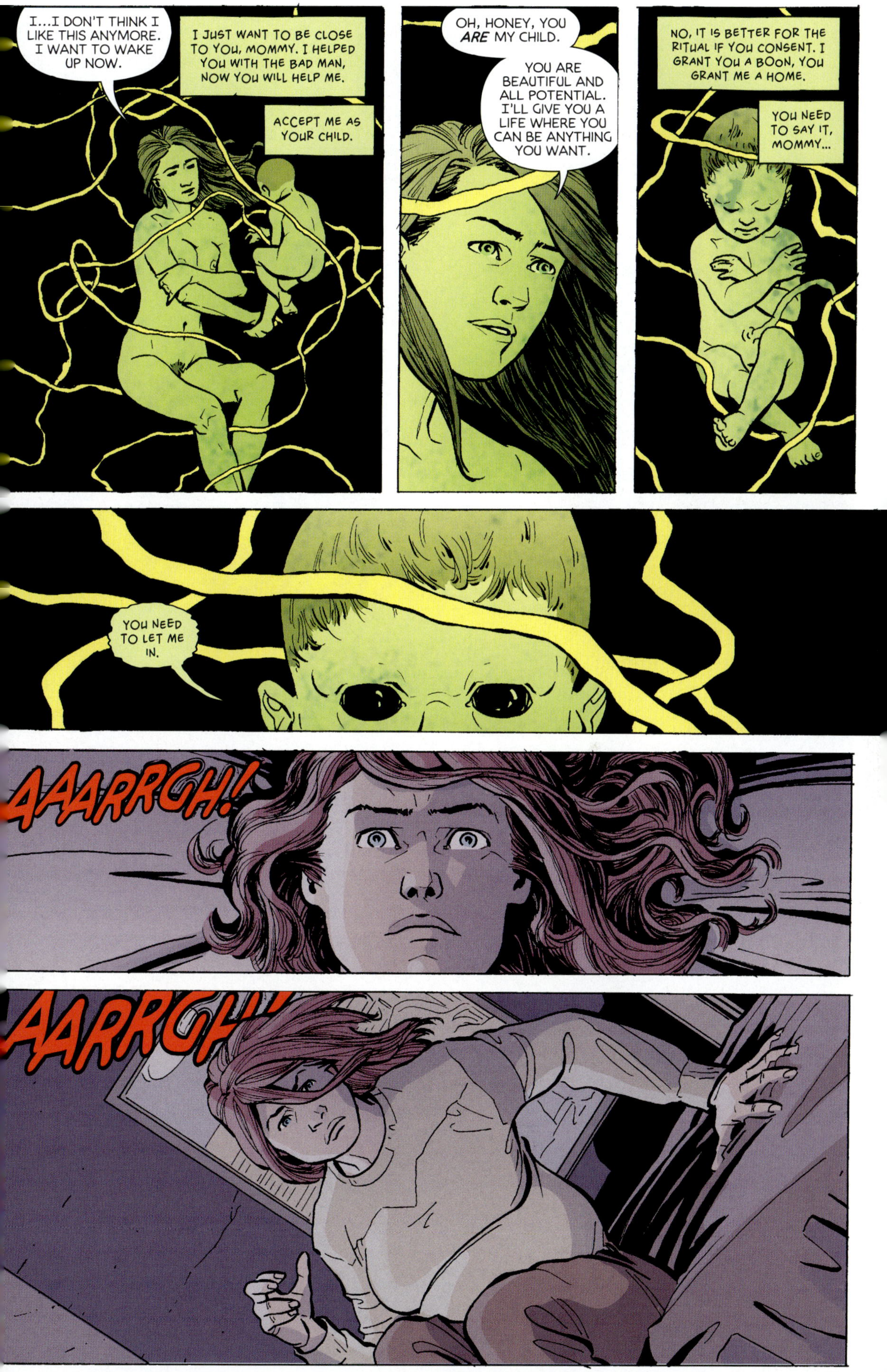
I...I DON'T THINK I LIKE THIS ANYMORE. I WANT TO WAKE UP NOW.
I JUST WANT TO BE CLOSE TO YOU, MOMMY. I HELPED YOU WITH THE BAD MAN, NOW YOU WILL HELP ME.
ACCEPT ME AS YOUR CHILD.
OH, HONEY, YOU *ARE* MY CHILD.
YOU ARE BEAUTIFUL AND ALL POTENTIAL. I'LL GIVE YOU A LIFE WHERE YOU CAN BE ANYTHING YOU WANT.
NO, IT IS BETTER FOR THE RITUAL IF YOU CONSENT. I GRANT YOU A BOON, YOU GRANT ME A HOME.
YOU NEED TO SAY IT, MOMMY...
YOU NEED TO LET ME IN.
AAARRGH!
AARRGH!

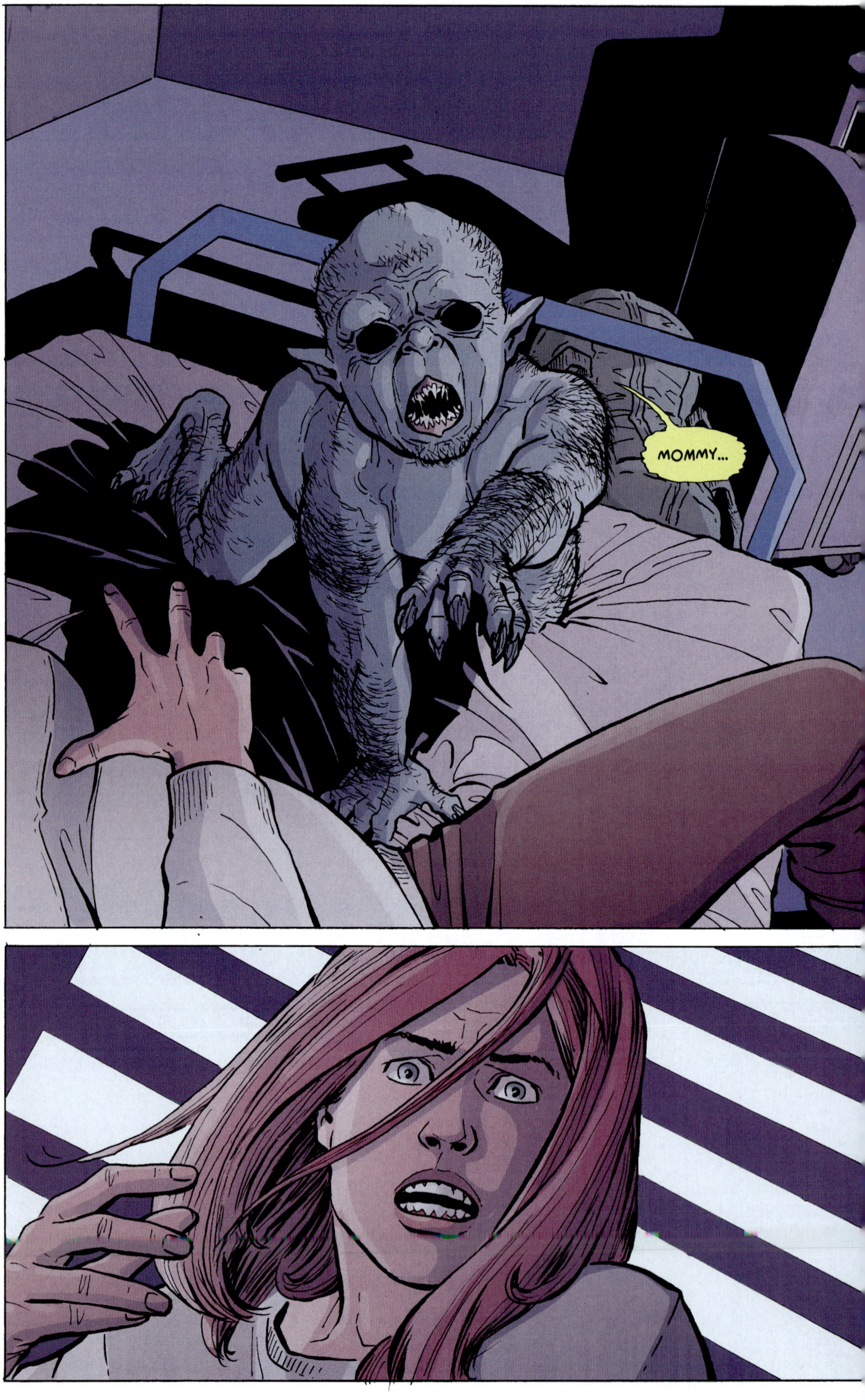
MOMMY...

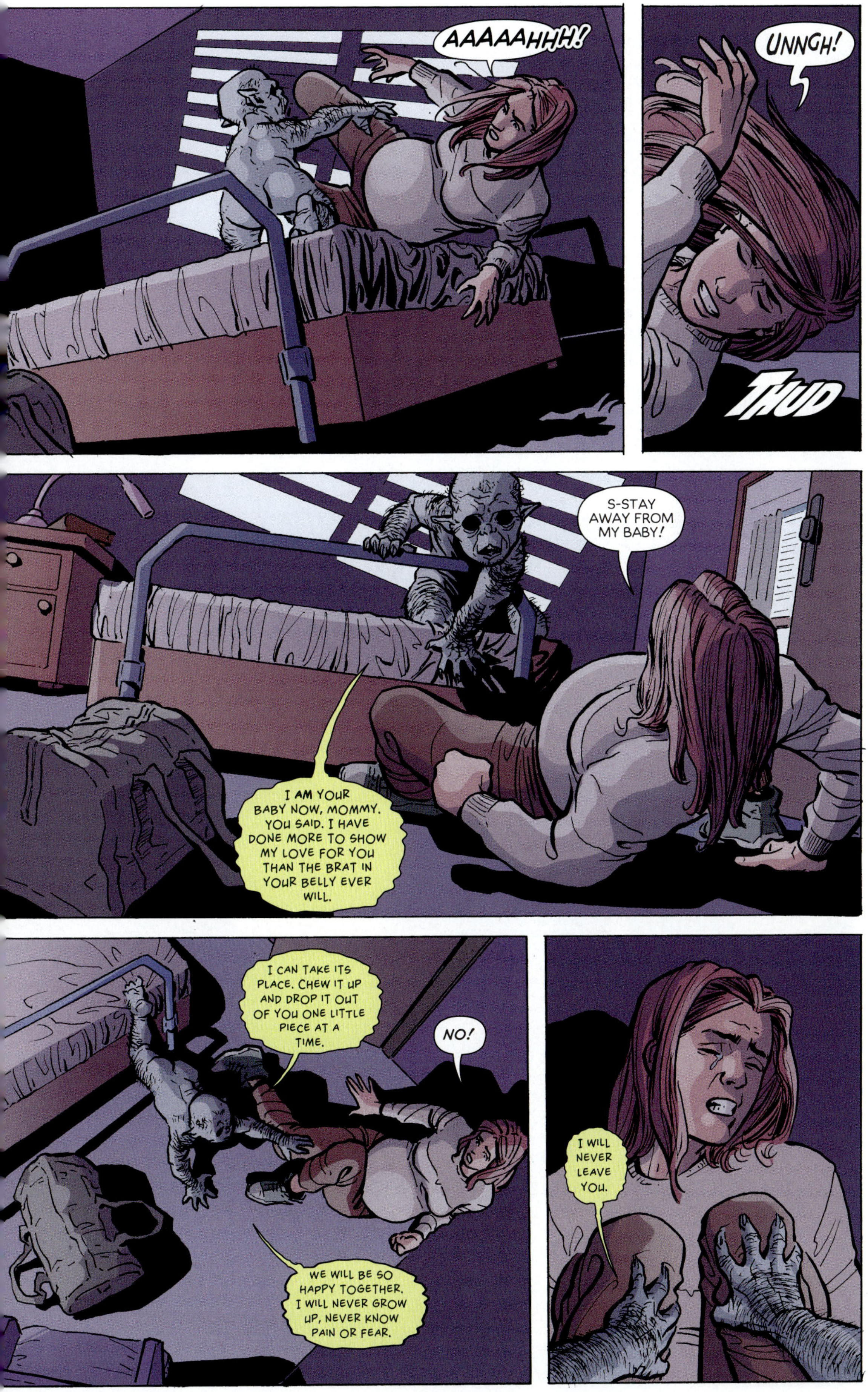
AAAAAHHH!
UNNGH!
THUD
S-STAY AWAY FROM MY BABY!
I AM YOUR BABY NOW, MOMMY. YOU SAID. I HAVE DONE MORE TO SHOW MY LOVE FOR YOU THAN THE BRAT IN YOUR BELLY EVER WILL.
I CAN TAKE ITS PLACE. CHEW IT UP AND DROP IT OUT OF YOU ONE LITTLE PIECE AT A TIME.
NO!
WE WILL BE SO HAPPY TOGETHER. I WILL NEVER GROW UP, NEVER KNOW PAIN OR FEAR.
I WILL NEVER LEAVE YOU.

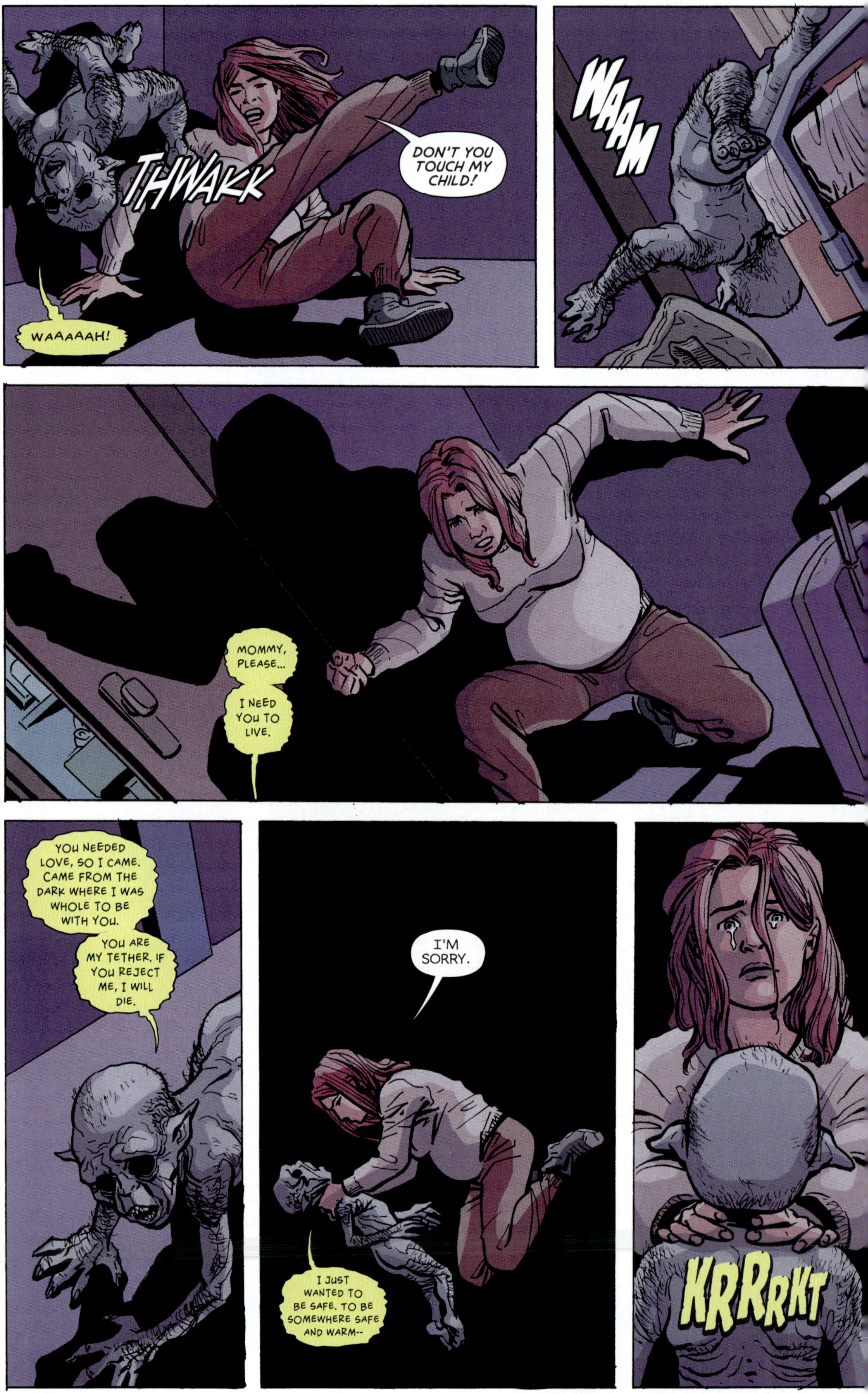
THWAKK
DON'T YOU TOUCH MY CHILD!
WAAAAAH!
WAAM
MOMMY, PLEASE...
I NEED YOU TO LIVE.
YOU NEEDED LOVE, SO I CAME. CAME FROM THE DARK WHERE I WAS WHOLE TO BE WITH YOU.
YOU ARE MY TETHER. IF YOU REJECT ME, I WILL DIE.
I'M SORRY.
I JUST WANTED TO BE SAFE. TO BE SOMEWHERE SAFE AND WARM--
KRRRKT

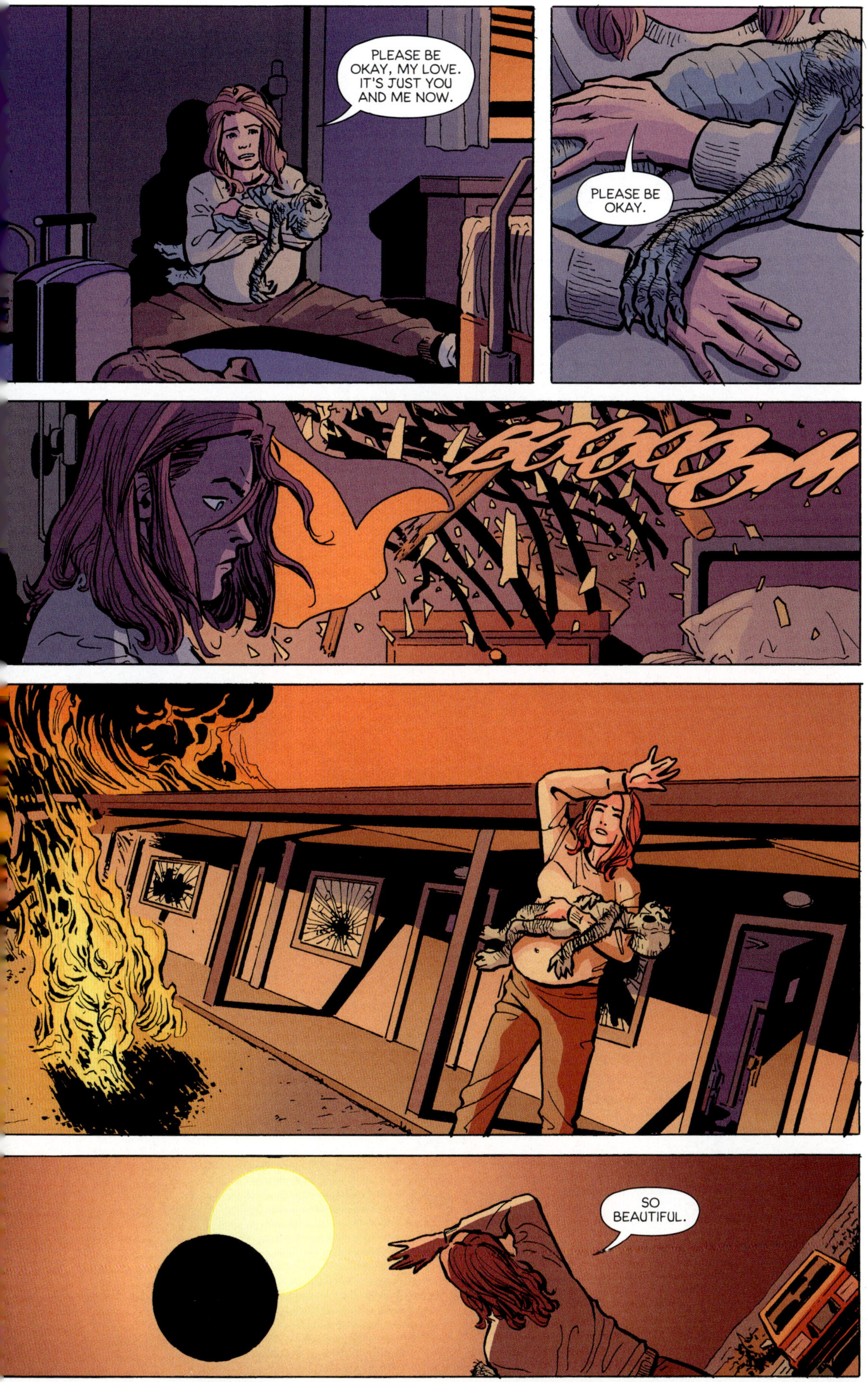
PLEASE BE OKAY, MY LOVE. IT'S JUST YOU AND ME NOW.
PLEASE BE OKAY.
SO BEAUTIFUL.

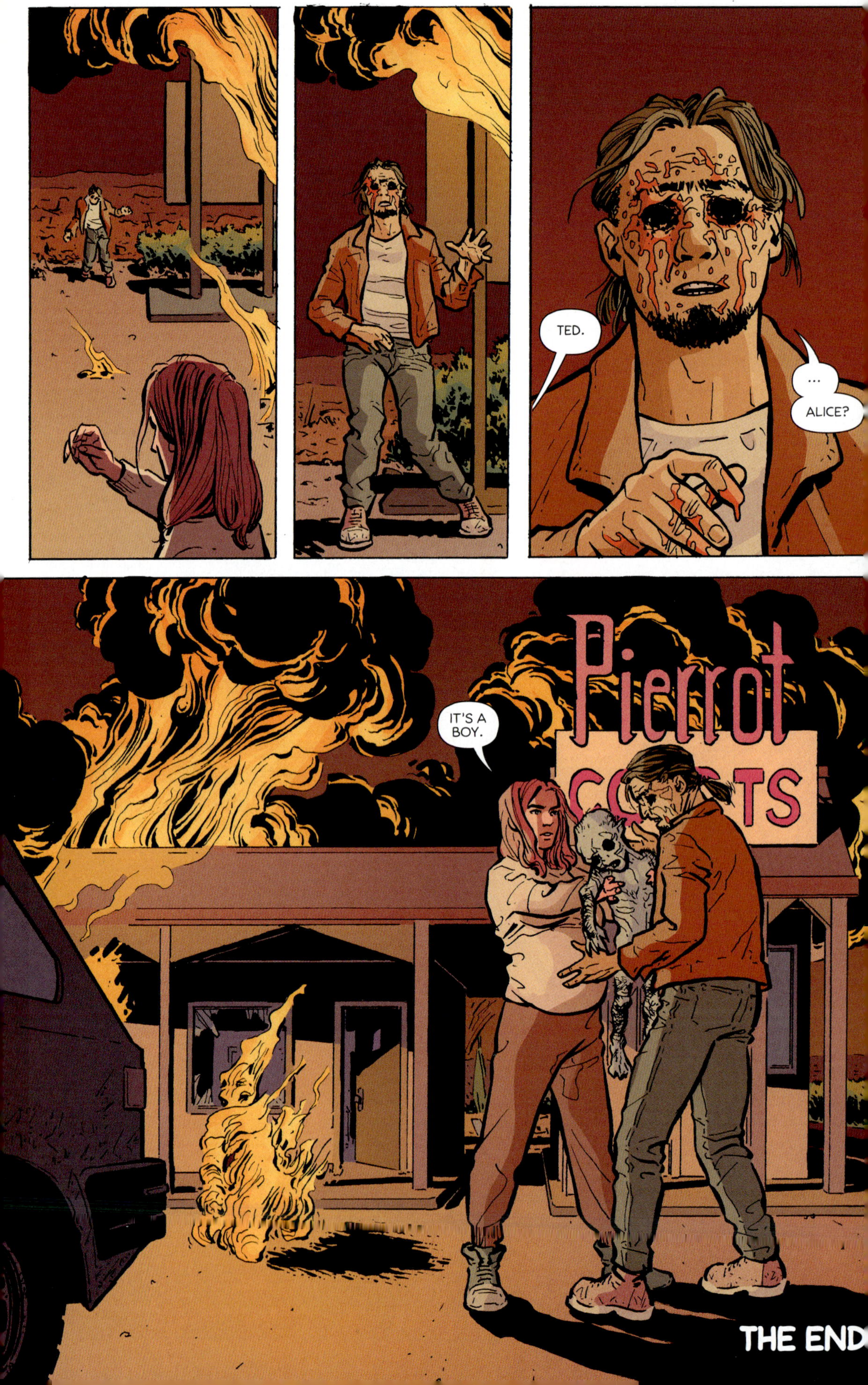
TED.
...
ALICE?
IT'S A BOY.
Pierrot
THE END

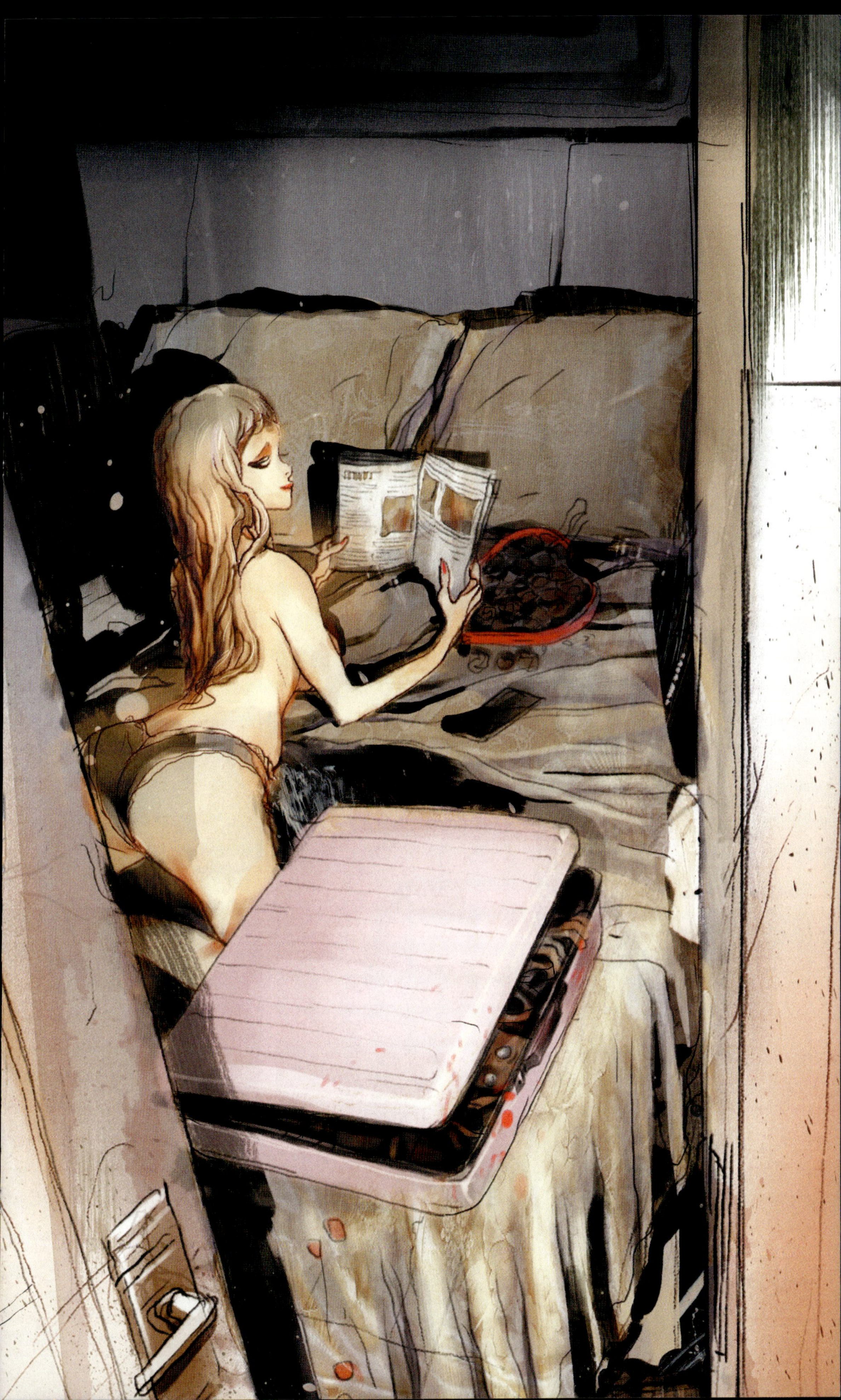

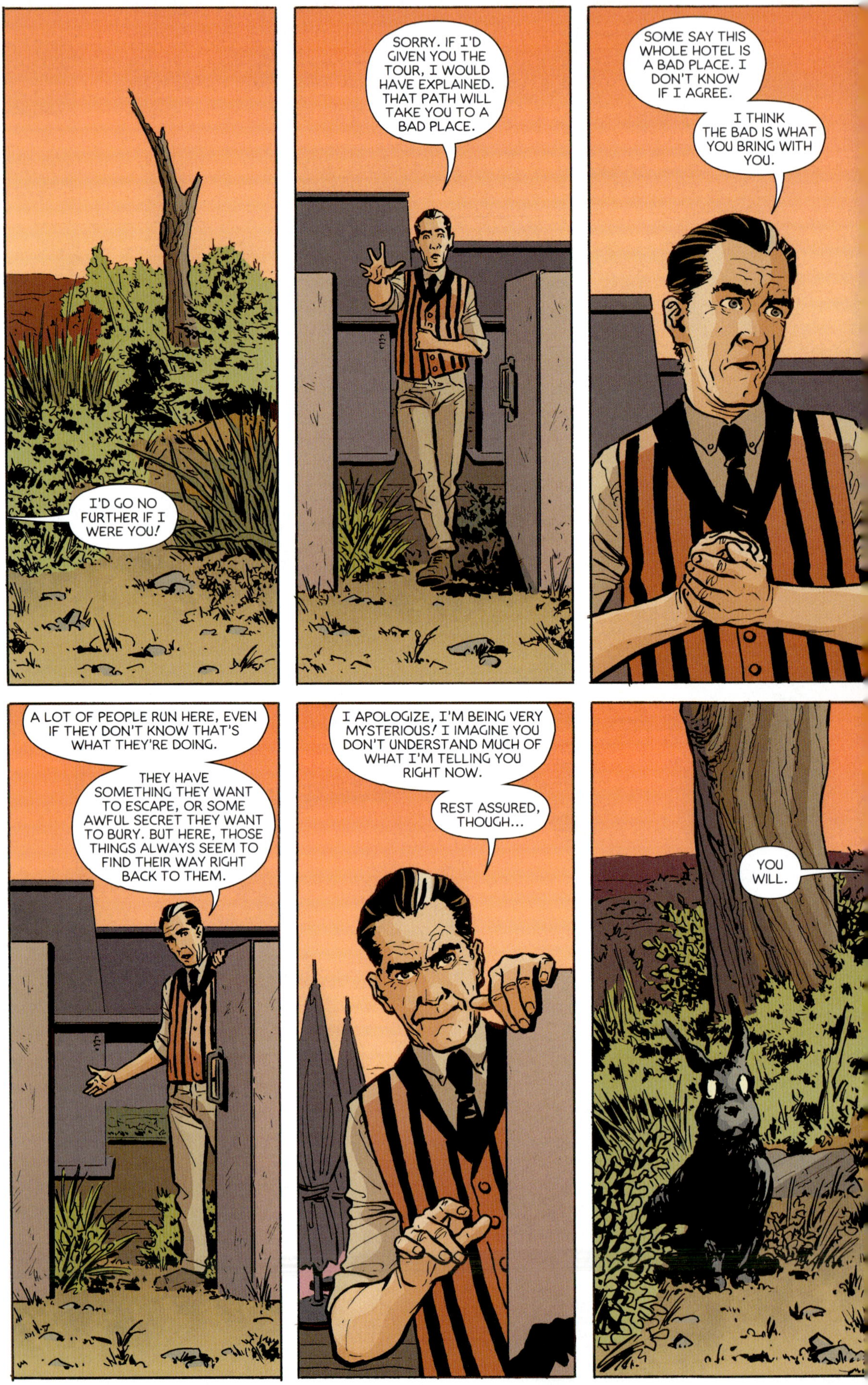
I'D GO NO FURTHER IF I WERE YOU!
SORRY. IF I'D GIVEN YOU THE TOUR, I WOULD HAVE EXPLAINED. THAT PATH WILL TAKE YOU TO A BAD PLACE.
SOME SAY THIS WHOLE HOTEL IS A BAD PLACE. I DON'T KNOW IF I AGREE.
I THINK THE BAD IS WHAT YOU BRING WITH YOU.
A LOT OF PEOPLE RUN HERE, EVEN IF THEY DON'T KNOW THAT'S WHAT THEY'RE DOING.
THEY HAVE SOMETHING THEY WANT TO ESCAPE, OR SOME AWFUL SECRET THEY WANT TO BURY. BUT HERE, THOSE THINGS ALWAYS SEEM TO FIND THEIR WAY RIGHT BACK TO THEM.
I APOLOGIZE, I'M BEING VERY MYSTERIOUS! I IMAGINE YOU DON'T UNDERSTAND MUCH OF WHAT I'M TELLING YOU RIGHT NOW.
REST ASSURED, THOUGH...
YOU WILL.

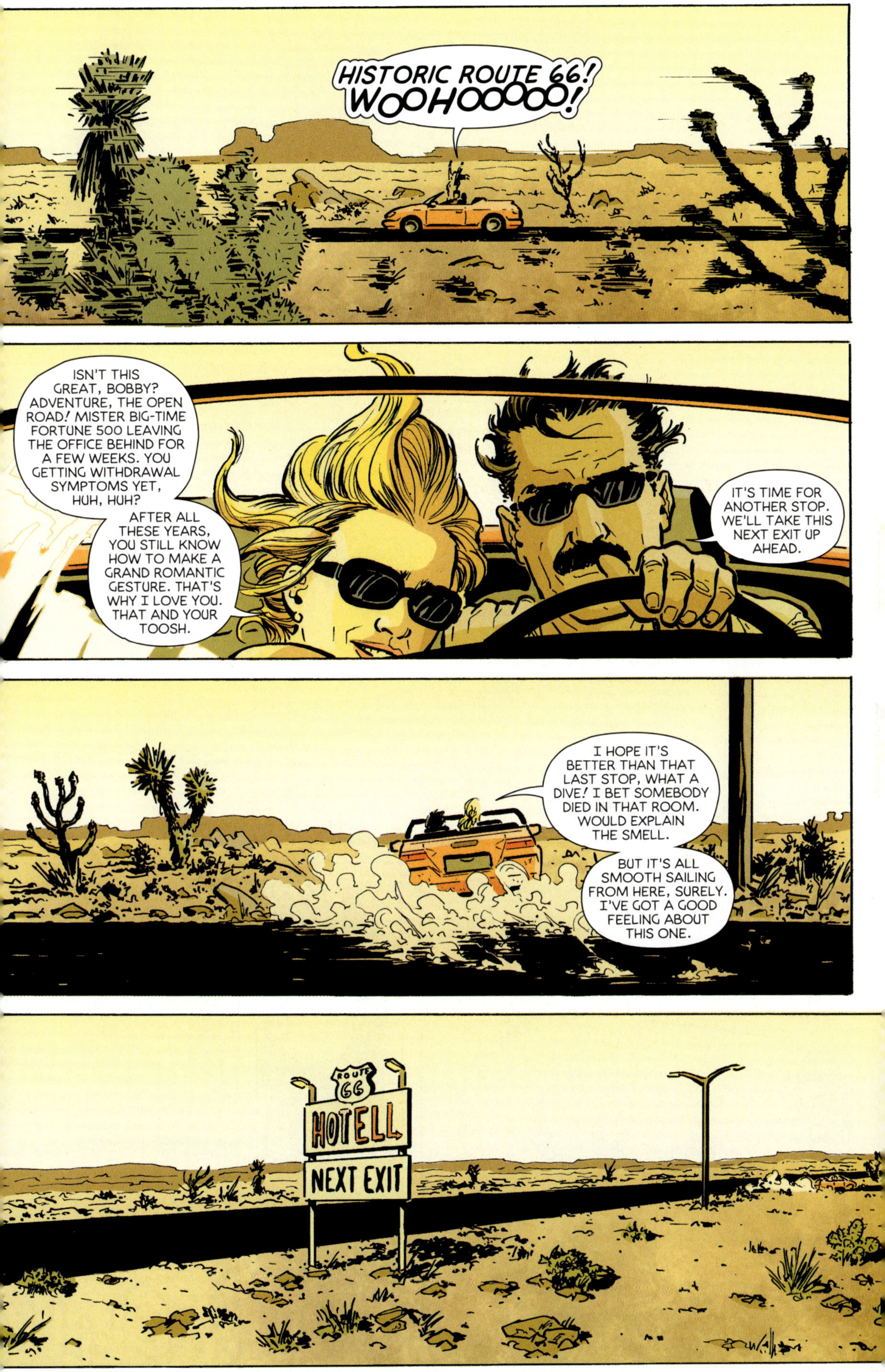
HISTORIC ROUTE 66! WOOHOOOOOO!
ISN'T THIS GREAT, BOBBY? ADVENTURE, THE OPEN ROAD! MISTER BIG-TIME FORTUNE 500 LEAVING THE OFFICE BEHIND FOR A FEW WEEKS. YOU GETTING WITHDRAWAL SYMPTOMS YET, HUH, HUH?
AFTER ALL THESE YEARS, YOU STILL KNOW HOW TO MAKE A GRAND ROMANTIC GESTURE. THAT'S WHY I LOVE YOU. THAT AND YOUR TOOSH.
IT'S TIME FOR ANOTHER STOP. WE'LL TAKE THIS NEXT EXIT UP AHEAD.
I HOPE IT'S BETTER THAN THAT LAST STOP, WHAT A DIVE! I BET SOMEBODY DIED IN THAT ROOM. WOULD EXPLAIN THE SMELL.
BUT IT'S ALL SMOOTH SAILING FROM HERE, SURELY. I'VE GOT A GOOD FEELING ABOUT THIS ONE.
ROUTE 66
HOTELL
NEXT EXIT

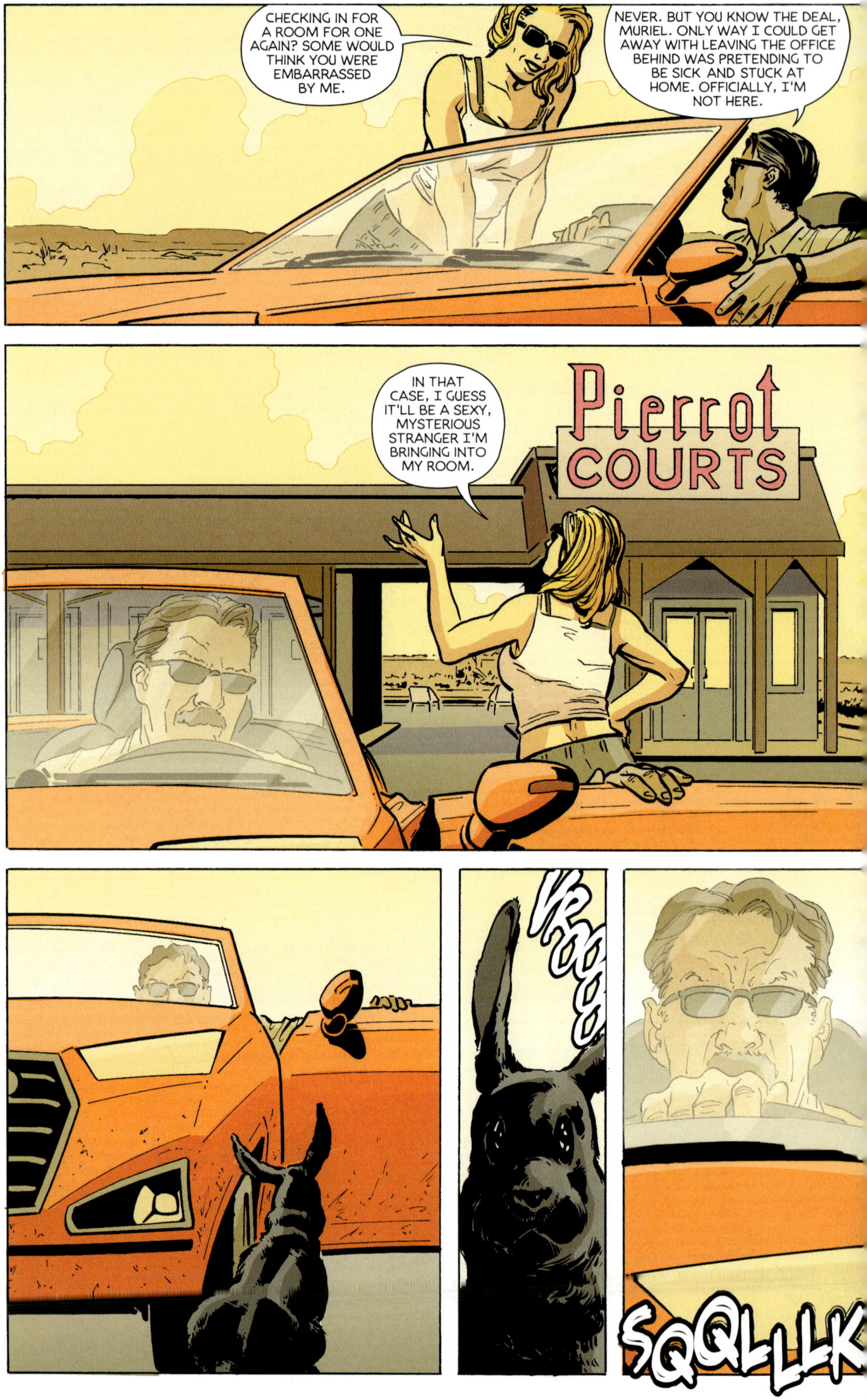
CHECKING IN FOR A ROOM FOR ONE AGAIN? SOME WOULD THINK YOU WERE EMBARRASSED BY ME.
NEVER. BUT YOU KNOW THE DEAL, MURIEL. ONLY WAY I COULD GET AWAY WITH LEAVING THE OFFICE BEHIND WAS PRETENDING TO BE SICK AND STUCK AT HOME. OFFICIALLY, I'M NOT HERE.
IN THAT CASE, I GUESS IT'LL BE A SEXY, MYSTERIOUS STRANGER I'M BRINGING INTO MY ROOM.
Pierrot COURTS
VROOOO
SQQLLLK

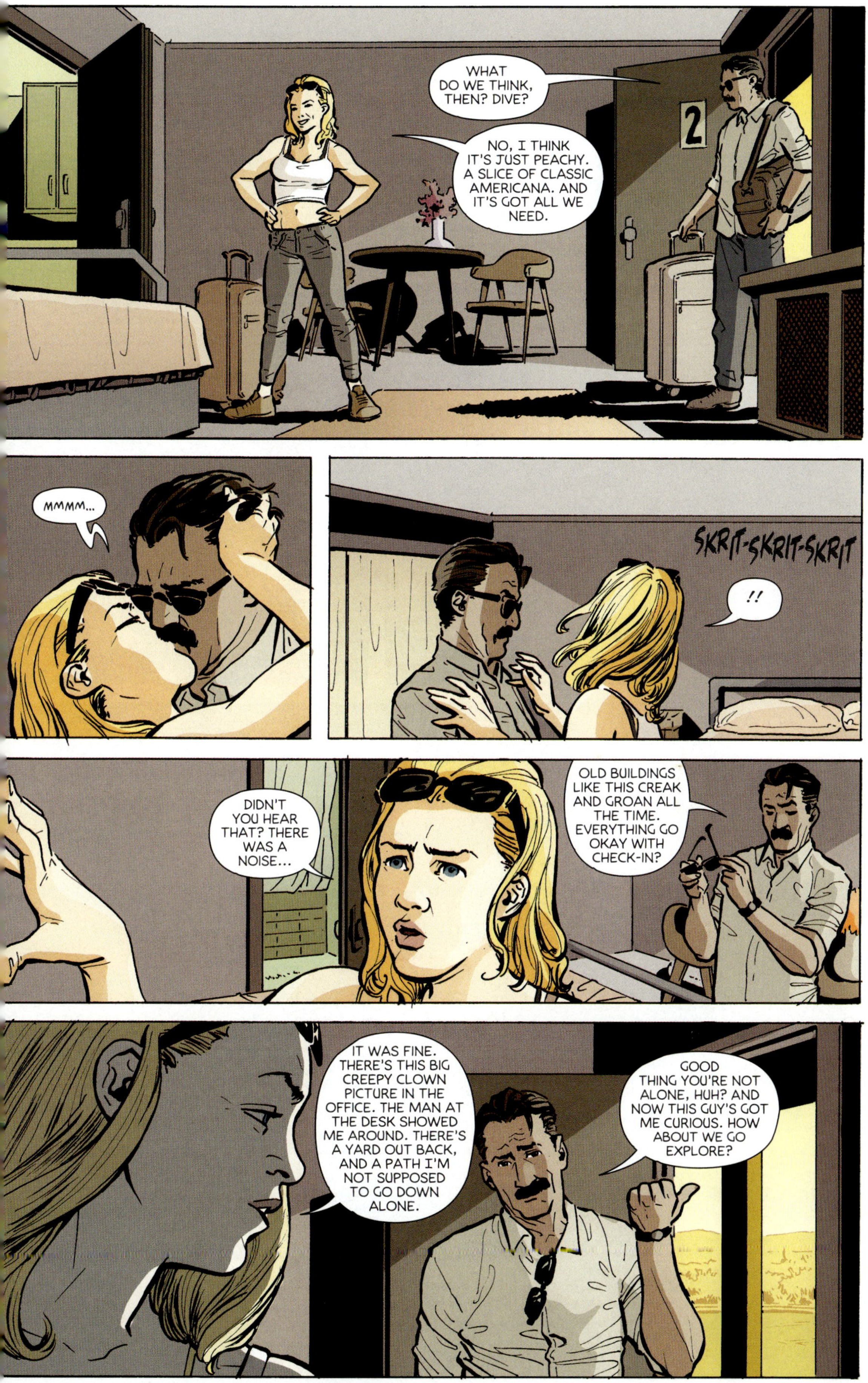
WHAT DO WE THINK, THEN? DIVE?
NO, I THINK IT'S JUST PEACHY. A SLICE OF CLASSIC AMERICANA. AND IT'S GOT ALL WE NEED.
2
MMMM...
SKRIT-SKRIT-SKRIT
!!
DIDN'T YOU HEAR THAT? THERE WAS A NOISE...
OLD BUILDINGS LIKE THIS CREAK AND GROAN ALL THE TIME. EVERYTHING GO OKAY WITH CHECK-IN?
IT WAS FINE. THERE'S THIS BIG CREEPY CLOWN PICTURE IN THE OFFICE. THE MAN AT THE DESK SHOWED ME AROUND. THERE'S A YARD OUT BACK, AND A PATH I'M NOT SUPPOSED TO GO DOWN ALONE.
GOOD THING YOU'RE NOT ALONE, HUH? AND NOW THIS GUY'S GOT ME CURIOUS. HOW ABOUT WE GO EXPLORE?

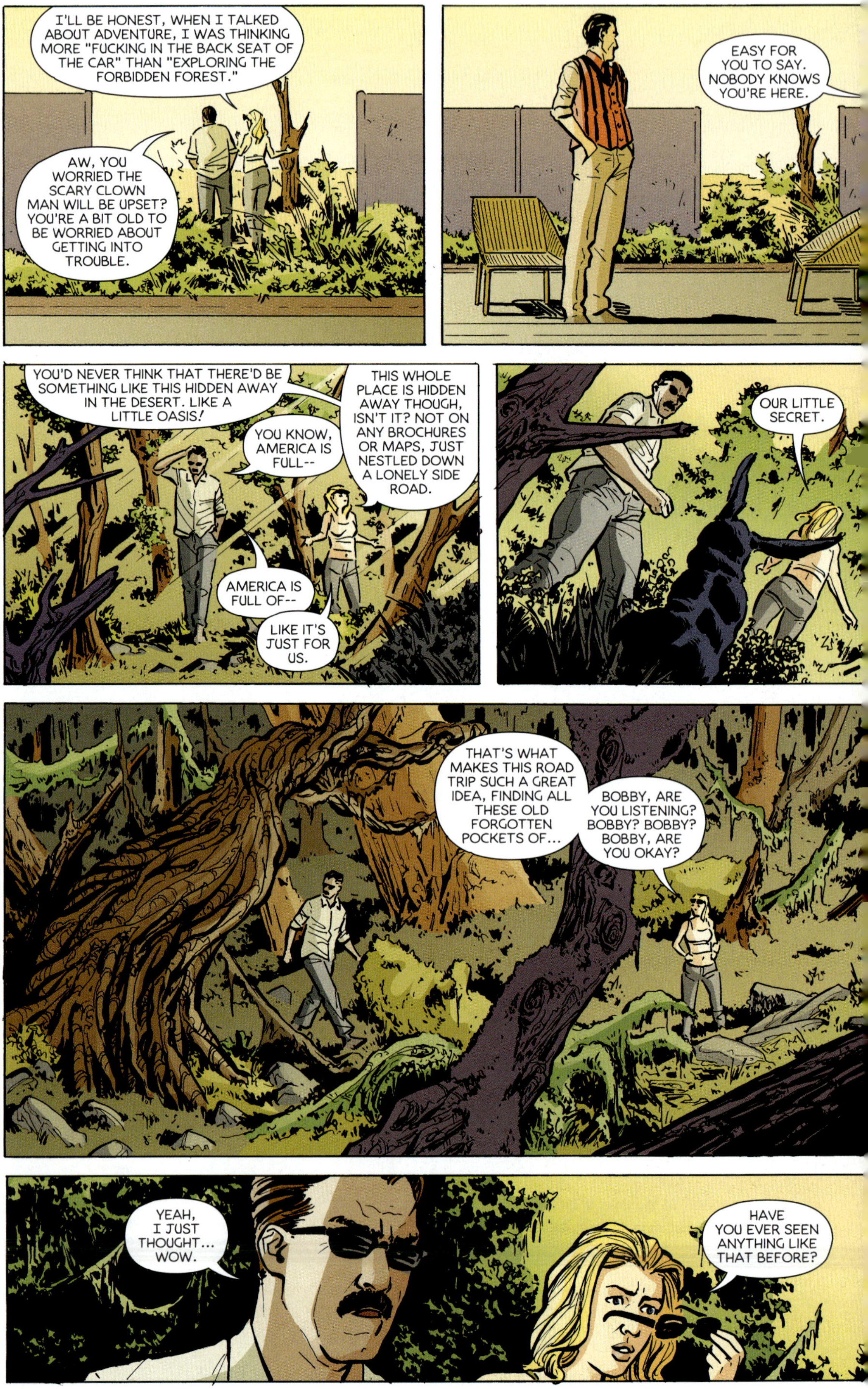
I'LL BE HONEST, WHEN I TALKED ABOUT ADVENTURE, I WAS THINKING MORE "FUCKING IN THE BACK SEAT OF THE CAR" THAN "EXPLORING THE FORBIDDEN FOREST."
AW, YOU WORRIED THE SCARY CLOWN MAN WILL BE UPSET? YOU'RE A BIT OLD TO BE WORRIED ABOUT GETTING INTO TROUBLE.
EASY FOR YOU TO SAY. NOBODY KNOWS YOU'RE HERE.
YOU'D NEVER THINK THAT THERE'D BE SOMETHING LIKE THIS HIDDEN AWAY IN THE DESERT. LIKE A LITTLE OASIS!
THIS WHOLE PLACE IS HIDDEN AWAY THOUGH, ISN'T IT? NOT ON ANY BROCHURES OR MAPS, JUST NESTLED DOWN A LONELY SIDE ROAD.
YOU KNOW, AMERICA IS FULL--
AMERICA IS FULL OF--
LIKE IT'S JUST FOR US.
OUR LITTLE SECRET.
THAT'S WHAT MAKES THIS ROAD TRIP SUCH A GREAT IDEA, FINDING ALL THESE OLD FORGOTTEN POCKETS OF...
BOBBY, ARE YOU LISTENING? BOBBY? BOBBY? BOBBY, ARE YOU OKAY?
YEAH, I JUST THOUGHT... WOW.
HAVE YOU EVER SEEN ANYTHING LIKE THAT BEFORE?

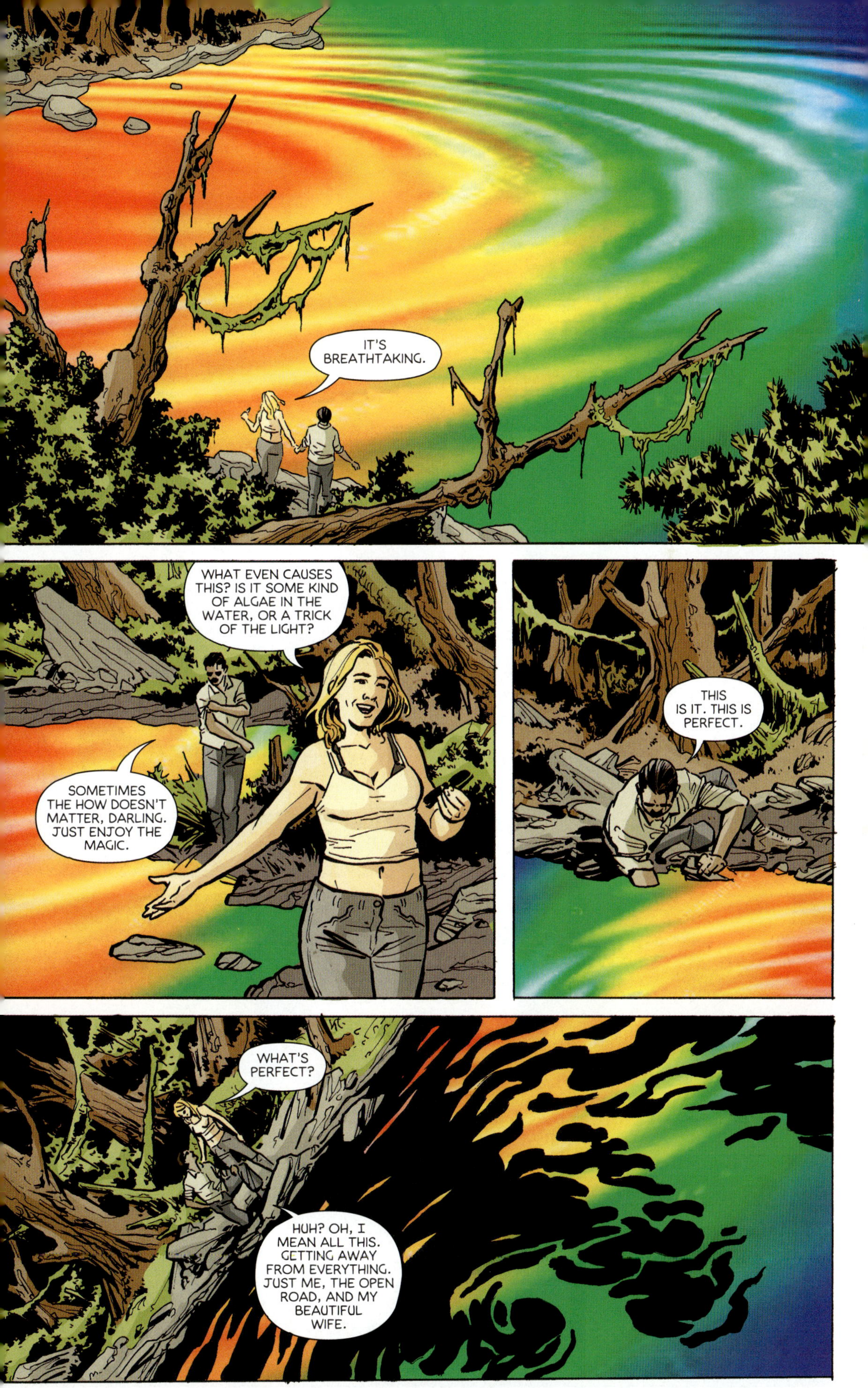
IT'S BREATHTAKING.
WHAT EVEN CAUSES THIS? IS IT SOME KIND OF ALGAE IN THE WATER, OR A TRICK OF THE LIGHT?
SOMETIMES THE HOW DOESN'T MATTER, DARLING. JUST ENJOY THE MAGIC.
THIS IS IT. THIS IS PERFECT.
WHAT'S PERFECT?
HUH? OH, I MEAN ALL THIS. GETTING AWAY FROM EVERYTHING. JUST ME, THE OPEN ROAD, AND MY BEAUTIFUL WIFE.

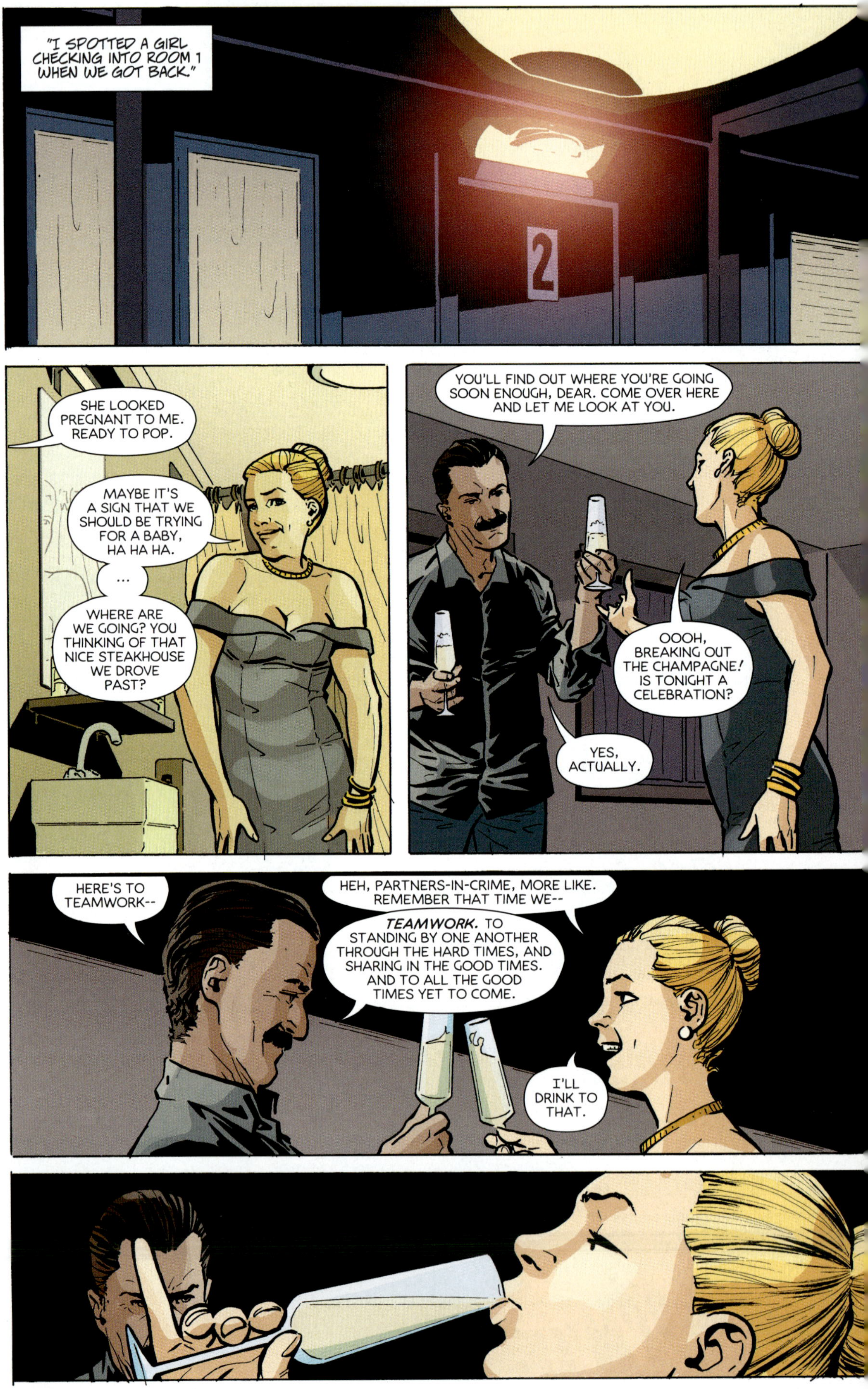
"I SPOTTED A GIRL CHECKING INTO ROOM 1 WHEN WE GOT BACK."
2
SHE LOOKED PREGNANT TO ME. READY TO POP.
MAYBE IT'S A SIGN THAT WE SHOULD BE TRYING FOR A BABY, HA HA HA.
...
WHERE ARE WE GOING? YOU THINKING OF THAT NICE STEAKHOUSE WE DROVE PAST?
YOU'LL FIND OUT WHERE YOU'RE GOING SOON ENOUGH, DEAR. COME OVER HERE AND LET ME LOOK AT YOU.
OOOH, BREAKING OUT THE CHAMPAGNE! IS TONIGHT A CELEBRATION?
YES, ACTUALLY.
HERE'S TO TEAMWORK--
HEH, PARTNERS-IN-CRIME, MORE LIKE. REMEMBER THAT TIME WE--
TEAMWORK. TO STANDING BY ONE ANOTHER THROUGH THE HARD TIMES, AND SHARING IN THE GOOD TIMES. AND TO ALL THE GOOD TIMES YET TO COME.
I'LL DRINK TO THAT.

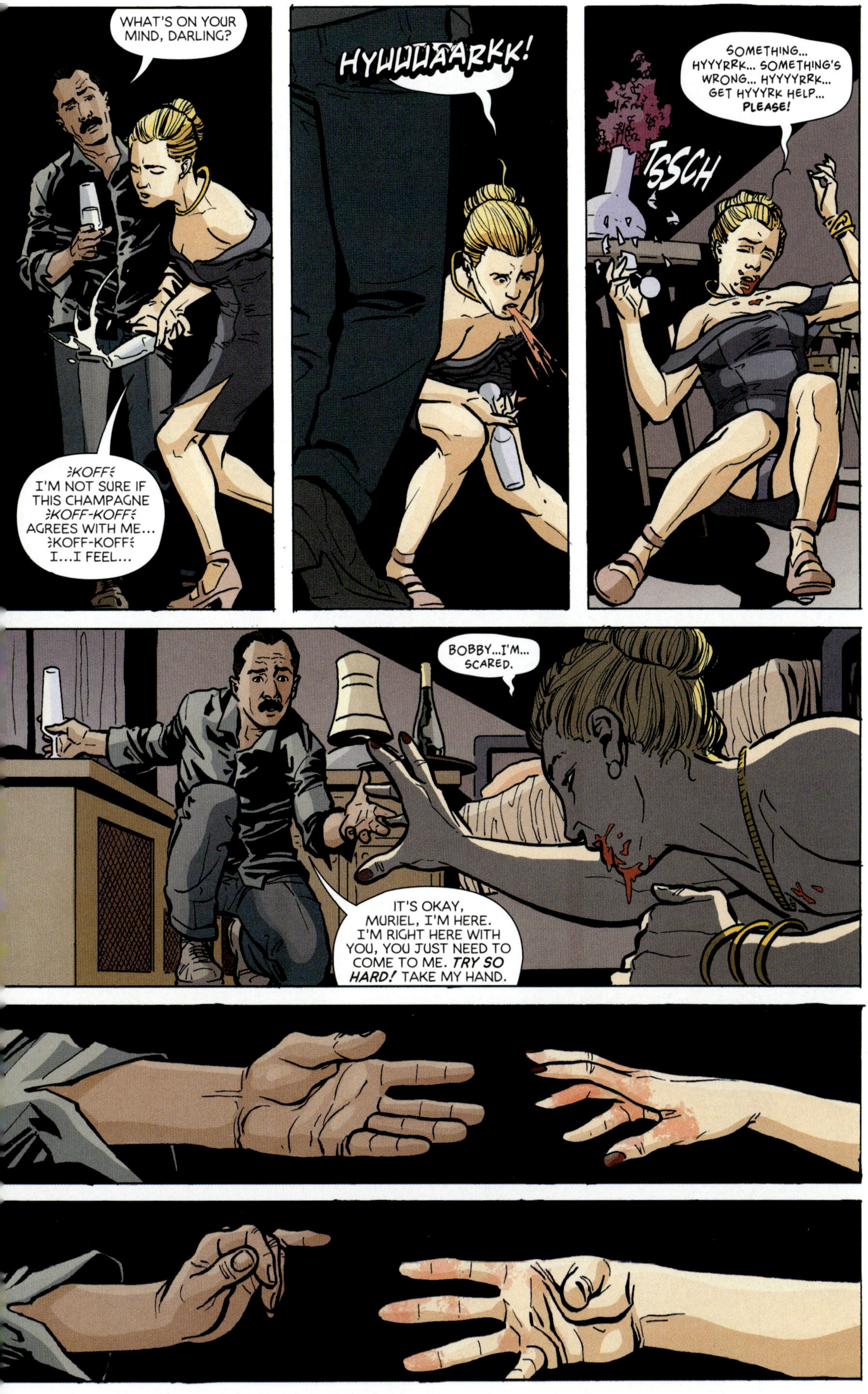

WHAT'S ON YOUR MIND, DARLING?
KOFF I'M NOT SURE IF THIS CHAMPAGNE KOFF-KOFF AGREES WITH ME... KOFF-KOFF I...I FEEL...
HYUUUAARKK!
SOMETHING... HYYYRRK... SOMETHING'S WRONG... HYYYYRRK... GET HYYYRK HELP... PLEASE!
TSSCH
BOBBY...I'M... SCARED.
IT'S OKAY, MURIEL, I'M HERE. I'M RIGHT HERE WITH YOU, YOU JUST NEED TO COME TO ME. TRY SO HARD! TAKE MY HAND.

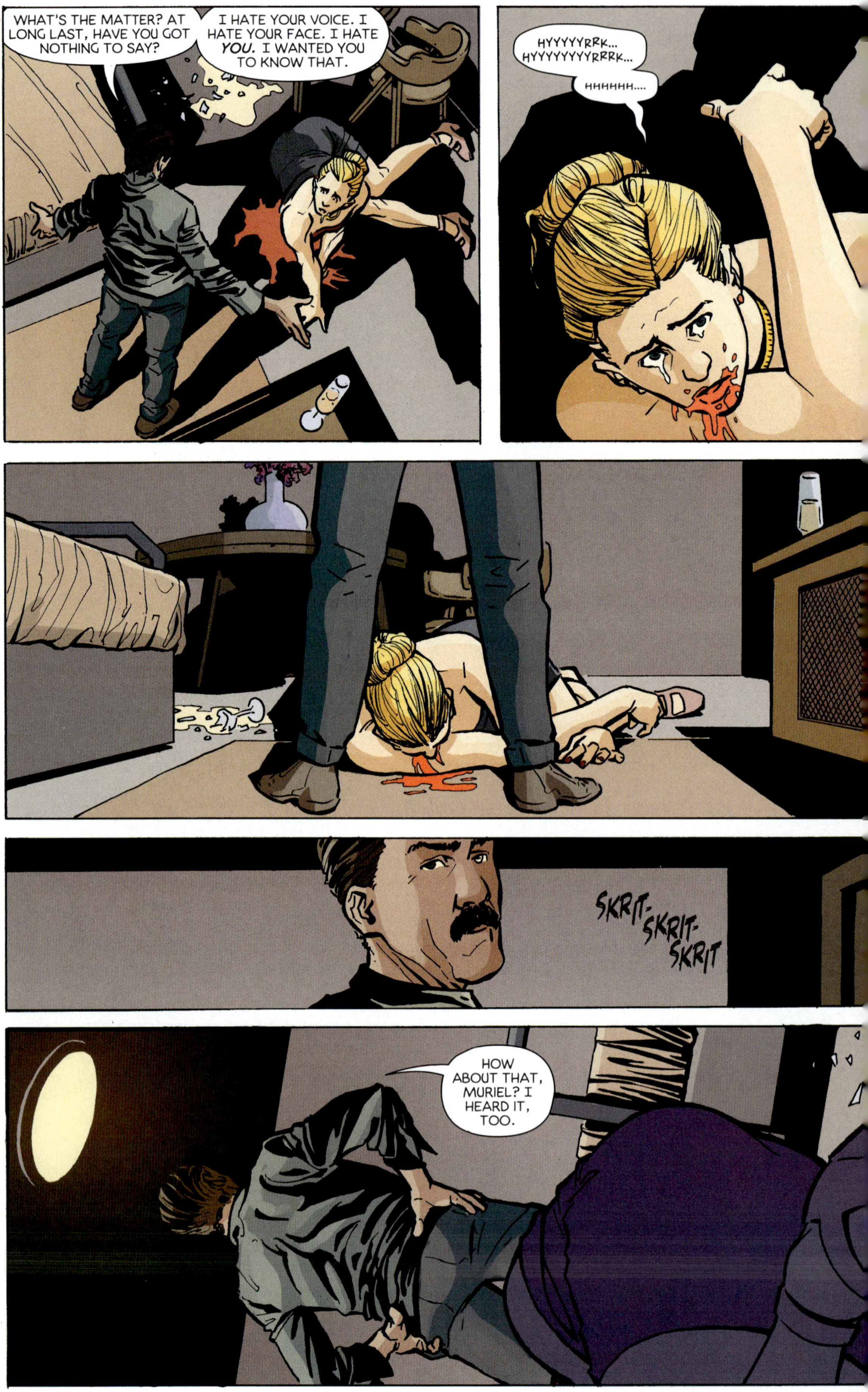
WHAT'S THE MATTER? AT LONG LAST, HAVE YOU GOT NOTHING TO SAY?
I HATE YOUR VOICE. I HATE YOUR FACE. I HATE *YOU.* I WANTED YOU TO KNOW THAT.
HYYYYYRRK... HYYYYYYYYRRRK...
HHHHHH....
SKRIT-SKRIT-SKRIT
HOW ABOUT THAT, MURIEL? I HEARD IT, TOO.

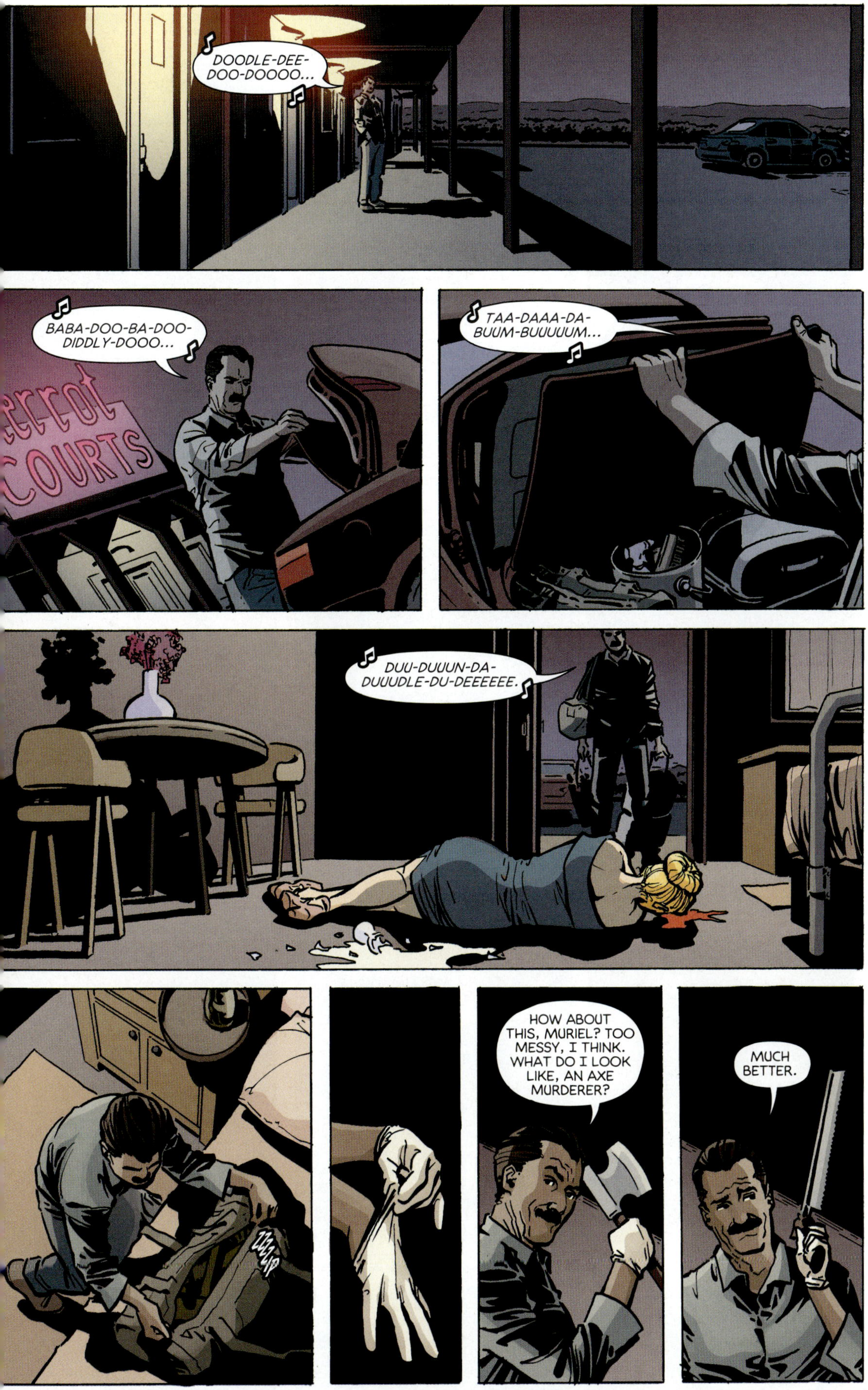
DOODLE-DEE-DOO-DOOOO...
BABA-DOO-BA-DOO-DIDDLY-DOOO...
COURTS
TAA-DAAA-DA BUUM-BUUUUUM...
DUU-DUUUN-DA-DUUUDLE-DU-DEEEEEE.
ZZZZIP
HOW ABOUT THIS, MURIEL? TOO MESSY, I THINK. WHAT DO I LOOK LIKE, AN AXE MURDERER?
MUCH BETTER.

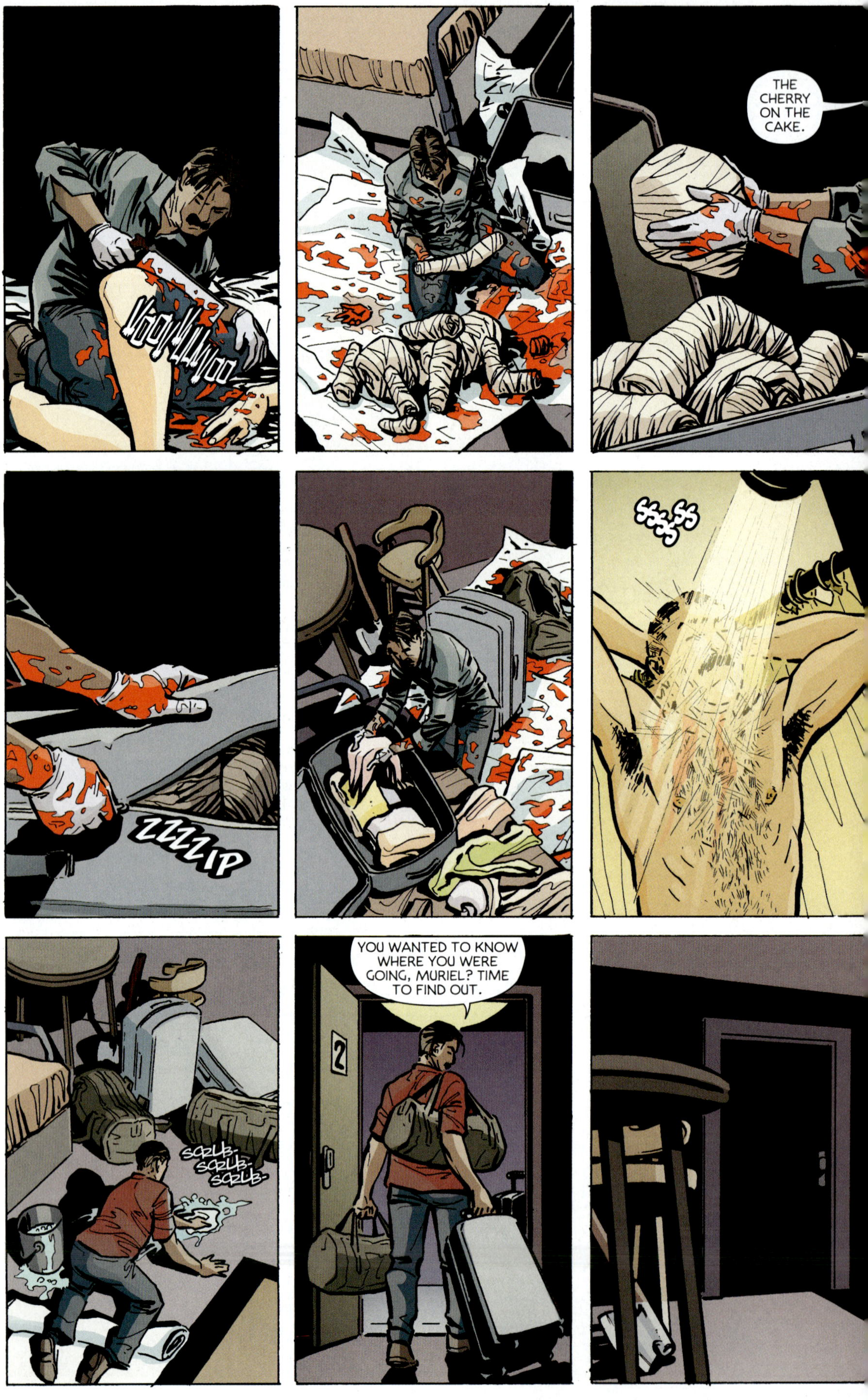

THE CHERRY ON THE CAKE.
ZZZZIP
SCRUB-SCRUB-SCRUB-
YOU WANTED TO KNOW WHERE YOU WERE GOING, MURIEL? TIME TO FIND OUT.

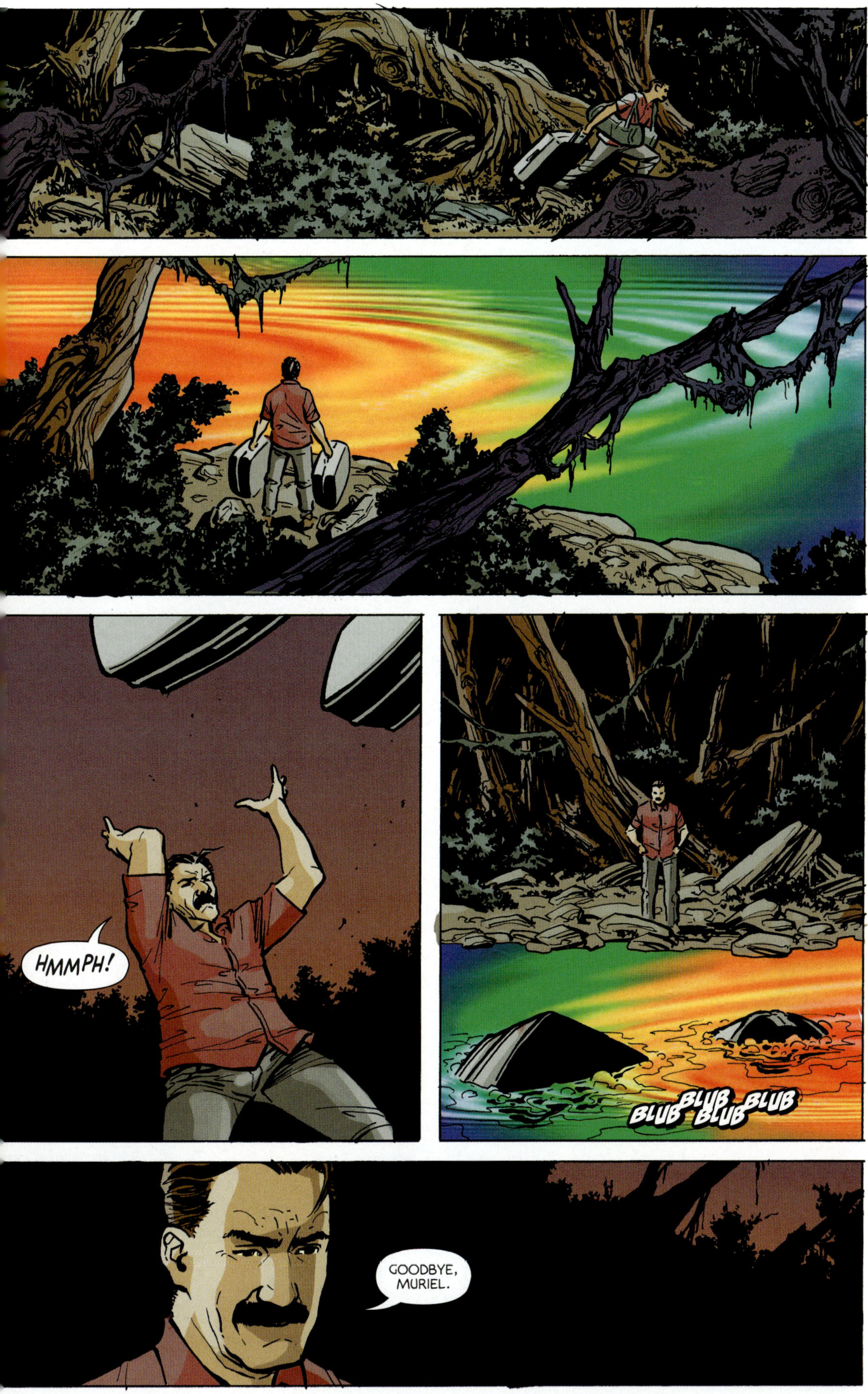
HMMPH!
BLUB BLUB BLUB BLUB BLUB
GOODBYE, MURIEL.

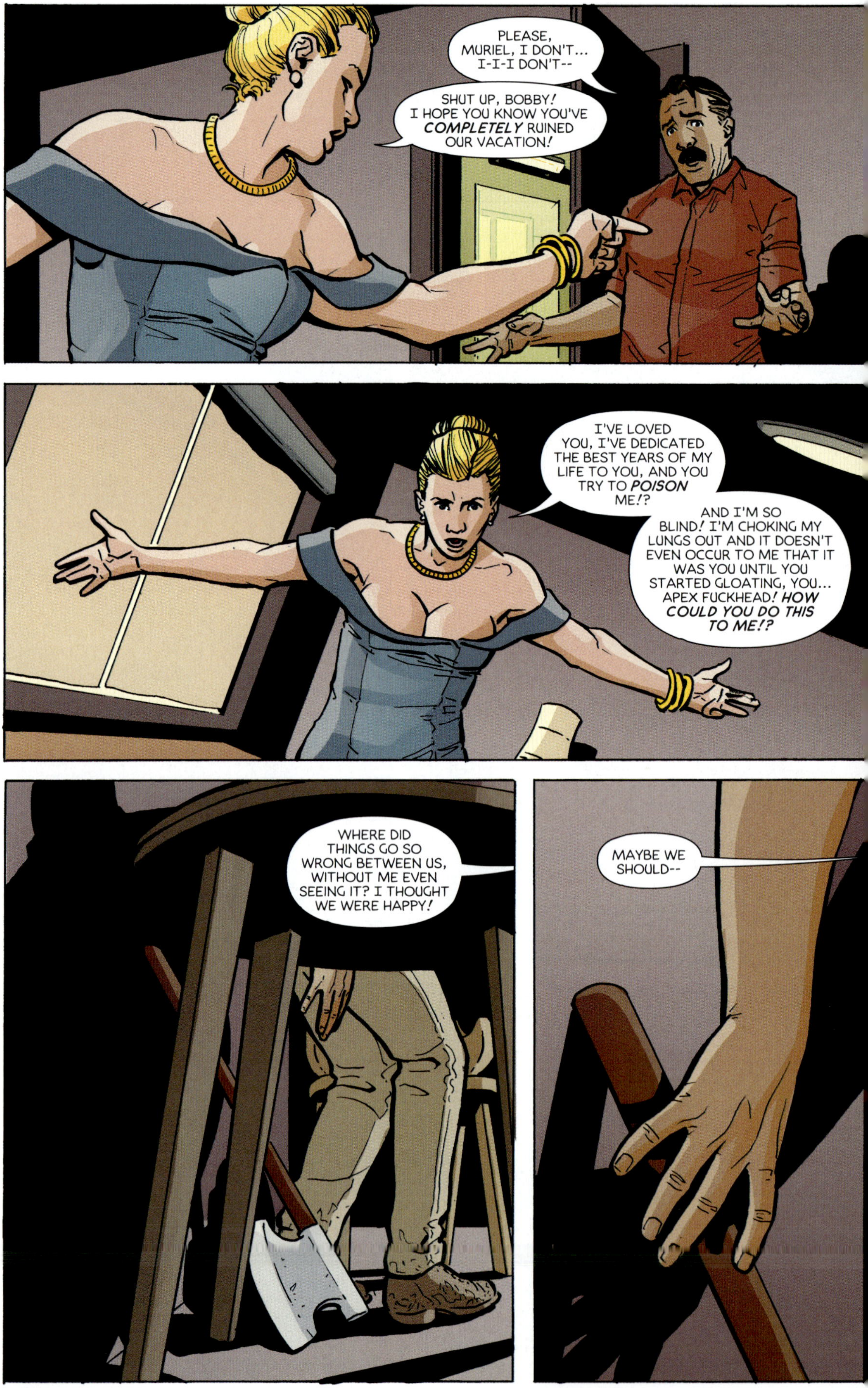
PLEASE, MURIEL, I DON'T... I-I-I DON'T--
SHUT UP, BOBBY! I HOPE YOU KNOW YOU'VE COMPLETELY RUINED OUR VACATION!
I'VE LOVED YOU, I'VE DEDICATED THE BEST YEARS OF MY LIFE TO YOU, AND YOU TRY TO POISON ME!?
AND I'M SO BLIND! I'M CHOKING MY LUNGS OUT AND IT DOESN'T EVEN OCCUR TO ME THAT IT WAS YOU UNTIL YOU STARTED GLOATING, YOU... APEX FUCKHEAD! HOW COULD YOU DO THIS TO ME!?
WHERE DID THINGS GO SO WRONG BETWEEN US, WITHOUT ME EVEN SEEING IT? I THOUGHT WE WERE HAPPY!
MAYBE WE SHOULD--

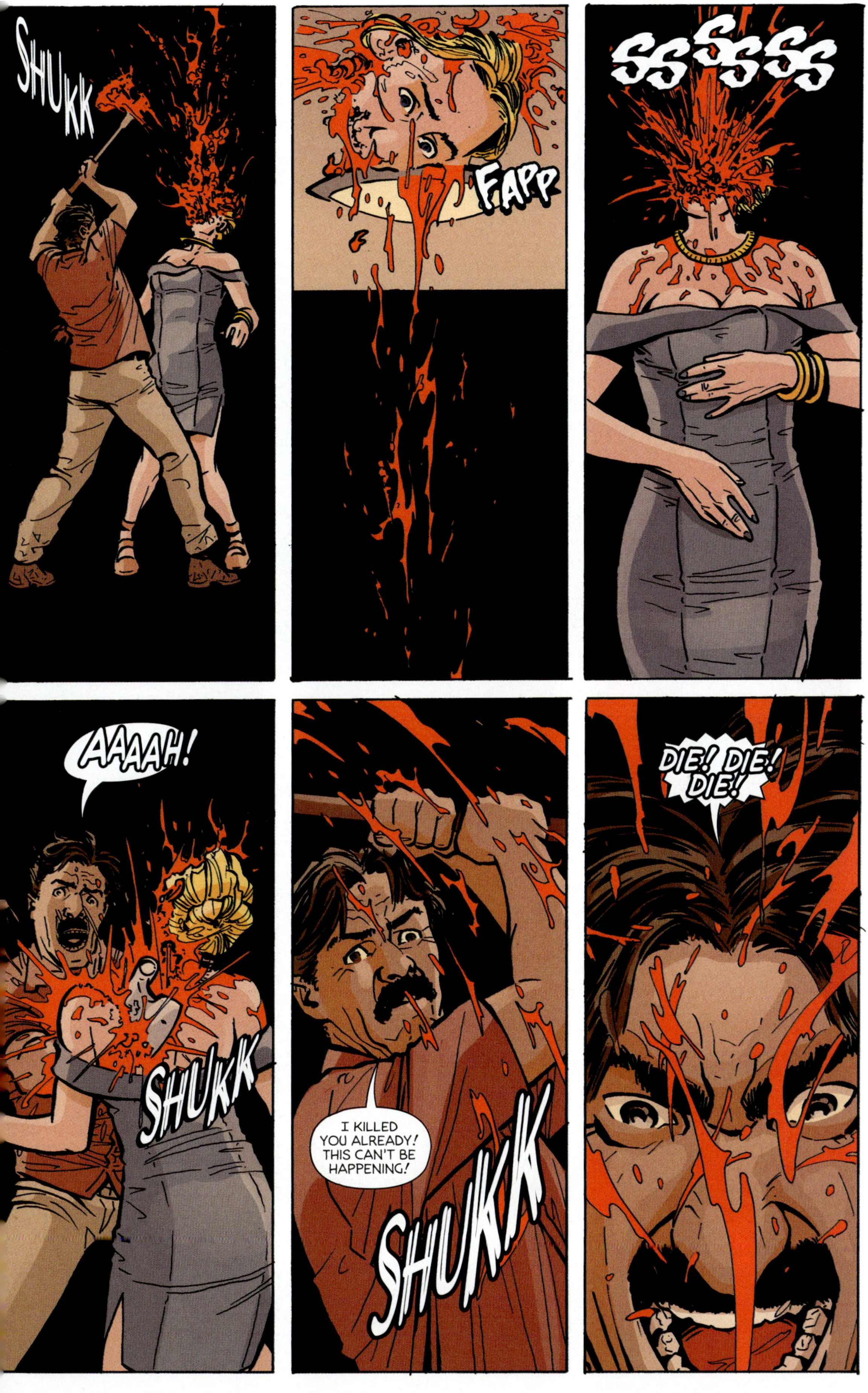
SHUKK
FAPP
SSSSSS
AAAAH!
SHUKK
I KILLED YOU ALREADY! THIS CAN'T BE HAPPENING!
SHUKK
DIE! DIE! DIE!

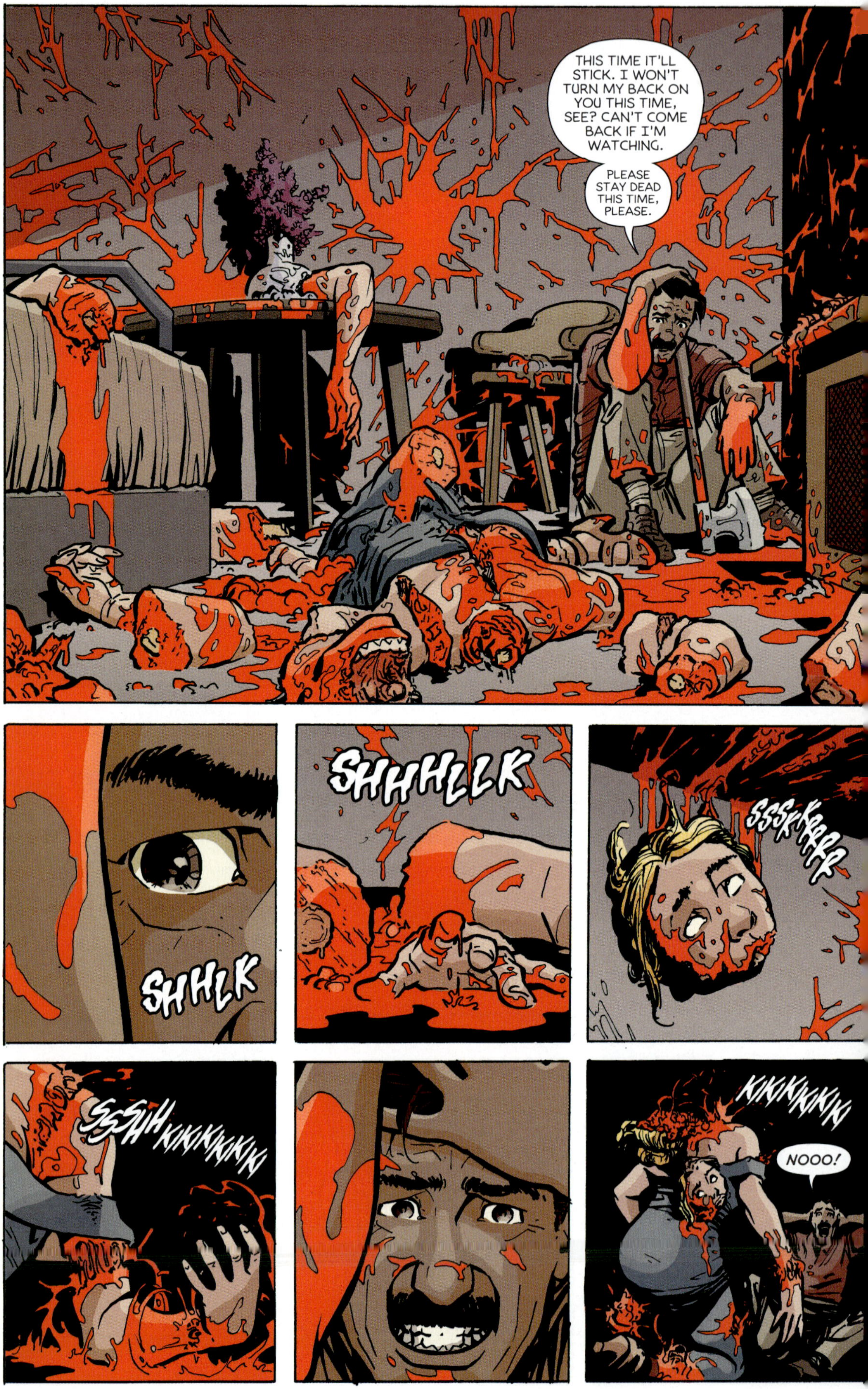
THIS TIME IT'LL STICK. I WON'T TURN MY BACK ON YOU THIS TIME, SEE? CAN'T COME BACK IF I'M WATCHING.
PLEASE STAY DEAD THIS TIME, PLEASE.
SHHLK
SHHHLLK
SSSKRRRR
SSSHKIKIKIKIKIKI
KIKIKIKIKIKI
NOOO!

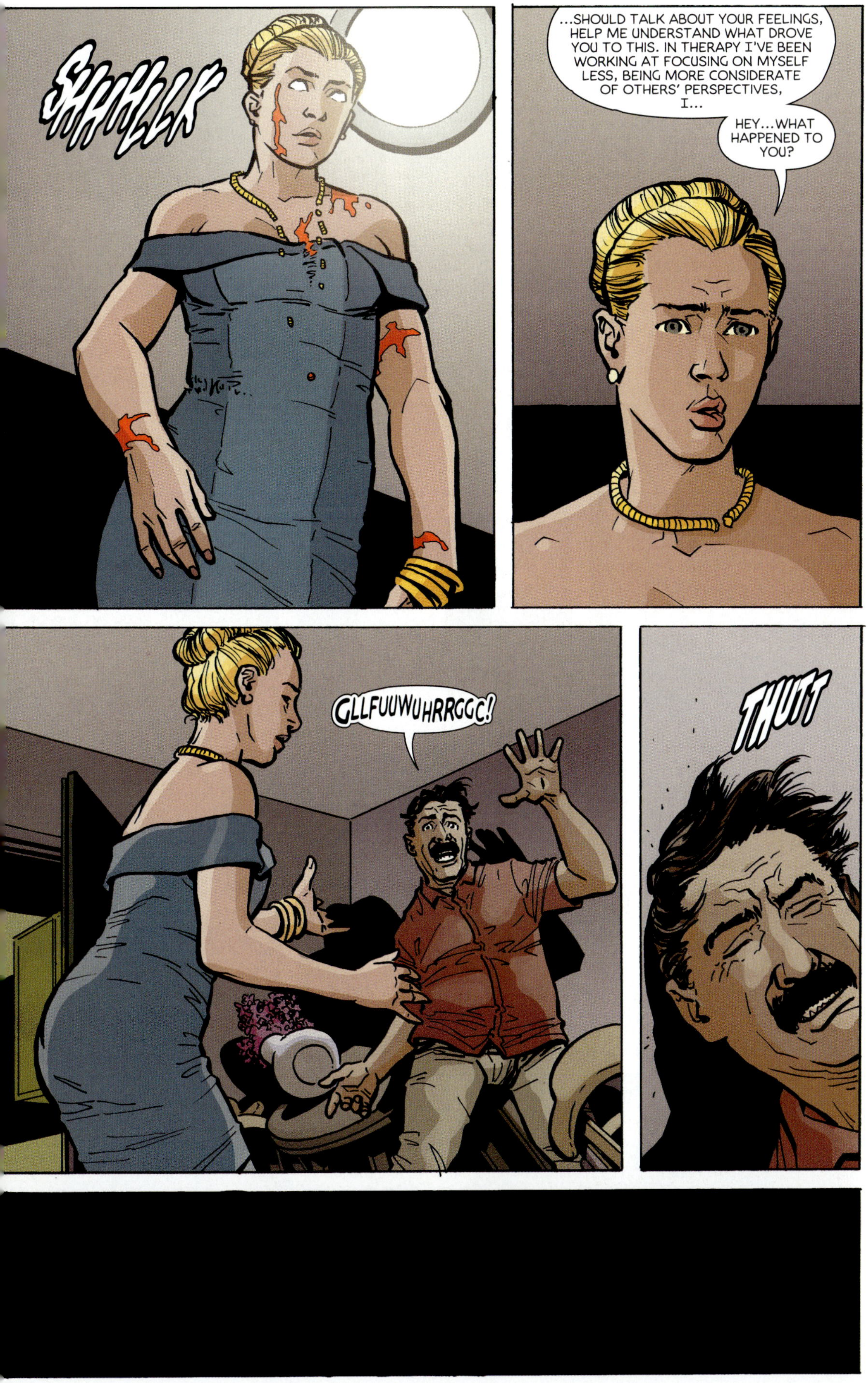
SHHHLLK
...SHOULD TALK ABOUT YOUR FEELINGS, HELP ME UNDERSTAND WHAT DROVE YOU TO THIS. IN THERAPY I'VE BEEN WORKING AT FOCUSING ON MYSELF LESS, BEING MORE CONSIDERATE OF OTHERS' PERSPECTIVES, I...
HEY...WHAT HAPPENED TO YOU?
GLLFUUWUHRRGGC!
THUTT

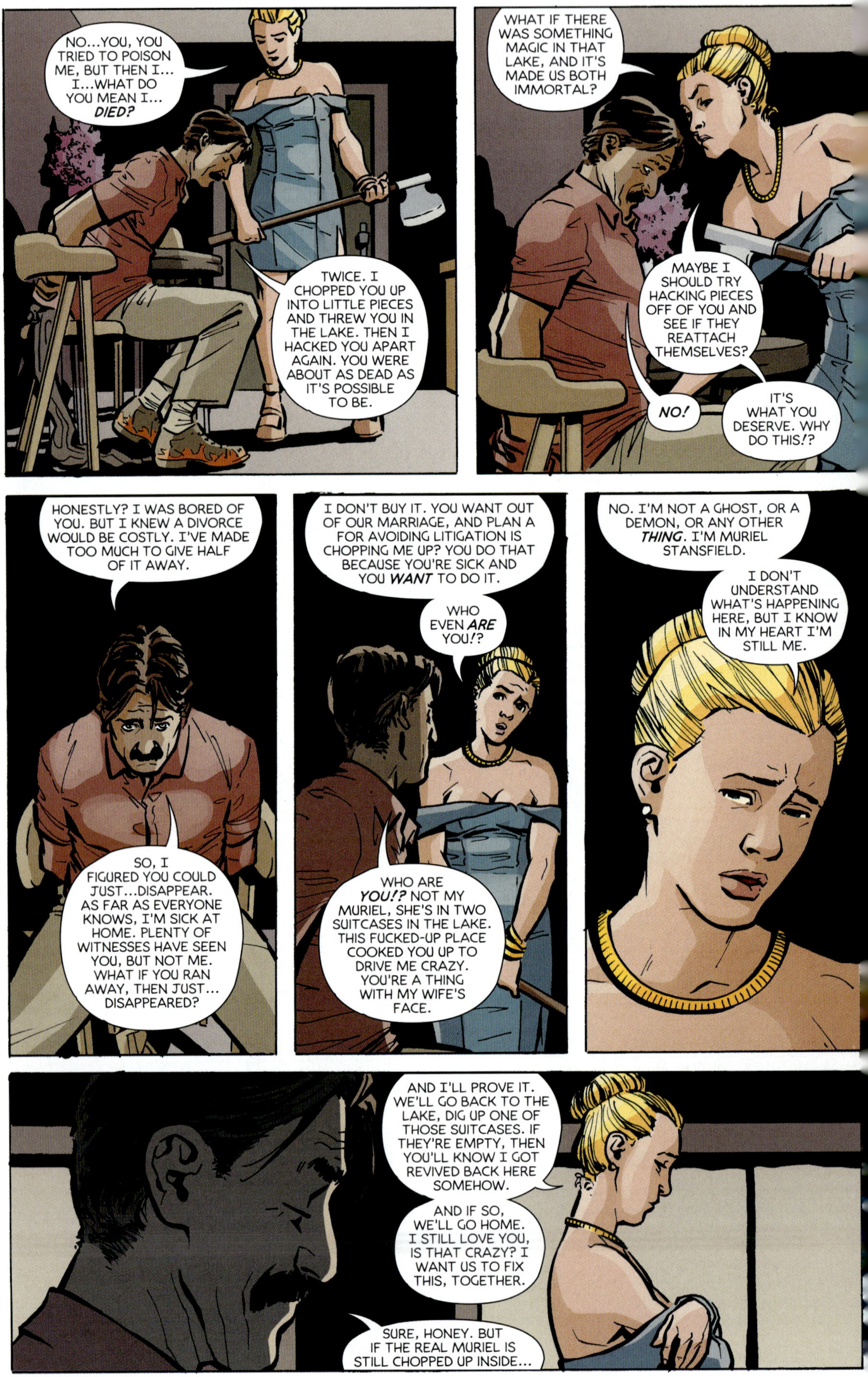
NO...YOU, YOU TRIED TO POISON ME, BUT THEN I... I...WHAT DO YOU MEAN I... DIED?
TWICE. I CHOPPED YOU UP INTO LITTLE PIECES AND THREW YOU IN THE LAKE. THEN I HACKED YOU APART AGAIN. YOU WERE ABOUT AS DEAD AS IT'S POSSIBLE TO BE.
WHAT IF THERE WAS SOMETHING MAGIC IN THAT LAKE, AND IT'S MADE US BOTH IMMORTAL?
MAYBE I SHOULD TRY HACKING PIECES OFF OF YOU AND SEE IF THEY REATTACH THEMSELVES?
NO!
IT'S WHAT YOU DESERVE. WHY DO THIS!?
HONESTLY? I WAS BORED OF YOU. BUT I KNEW A DIVORCE WOULD BE COSTLY. I'VE MADE TOO MUCH TO GIVE HALF OF IT AWAY.
SO, I FIGURED YOU COULD JUST...DISAPPEAR. AS FAR AS EVERYONE KNOWS, I'M SICK AT HOME. PLENTY OF WITNESSES HAVE SEEN YOU, BUT NOT ME. WHAT IF YOU RAN AWAY, THEN JUST... DISAPPEARED?
I DON'T BUY IT. YOU WANT OUT OF OUR MARRIAGE, AND PLAN A FOR AVOIDING LITIGATION IS CHOPPING ME UP? YOU DO THAT BECAUSE YOU'RE SICK AND YOU WANT TO DO IT.
WHO EVEN ARE YOU!?
WHO ARE YOU!? NOT MY MURIEL, SHE'S IN TWO SUITCASES IN THE LAKE. THIS FUCKED-UP PLACE COOKED YOU UP TO DRIVE ME CRAZY. YOU'RE A THING WITH MY WIFE'S FACE.
NO. I'M NOT A GHOST, OR A DEMON, OR ANY OTHER THING. I'M MURIEL STANSFIELD.
I DON'T UNDERSTAND WHAT'S HAPPENING HERE, BUT I KNOW IN MY HEART I'M STILL ME.
AND I'LL PROVE IT. WE'LL GO BACK TO THE LAKE, DIG UP ONE OF THOSE SUITCASES. IF THEY'RE EMPTY, THEN YOU'LL KNOW I GOT REVIVED BACK HERE SOMEHOW.
AND IF SO, WE'LL GO HOME. I STILL LOVE YOU, IS THAT CRAZY? I WANT US TO FIX THIS, TOGETHER.
SURE, HONEY. BUT IF THE REAL MURIEL IS STILL CHOPPED UP INSIDE...

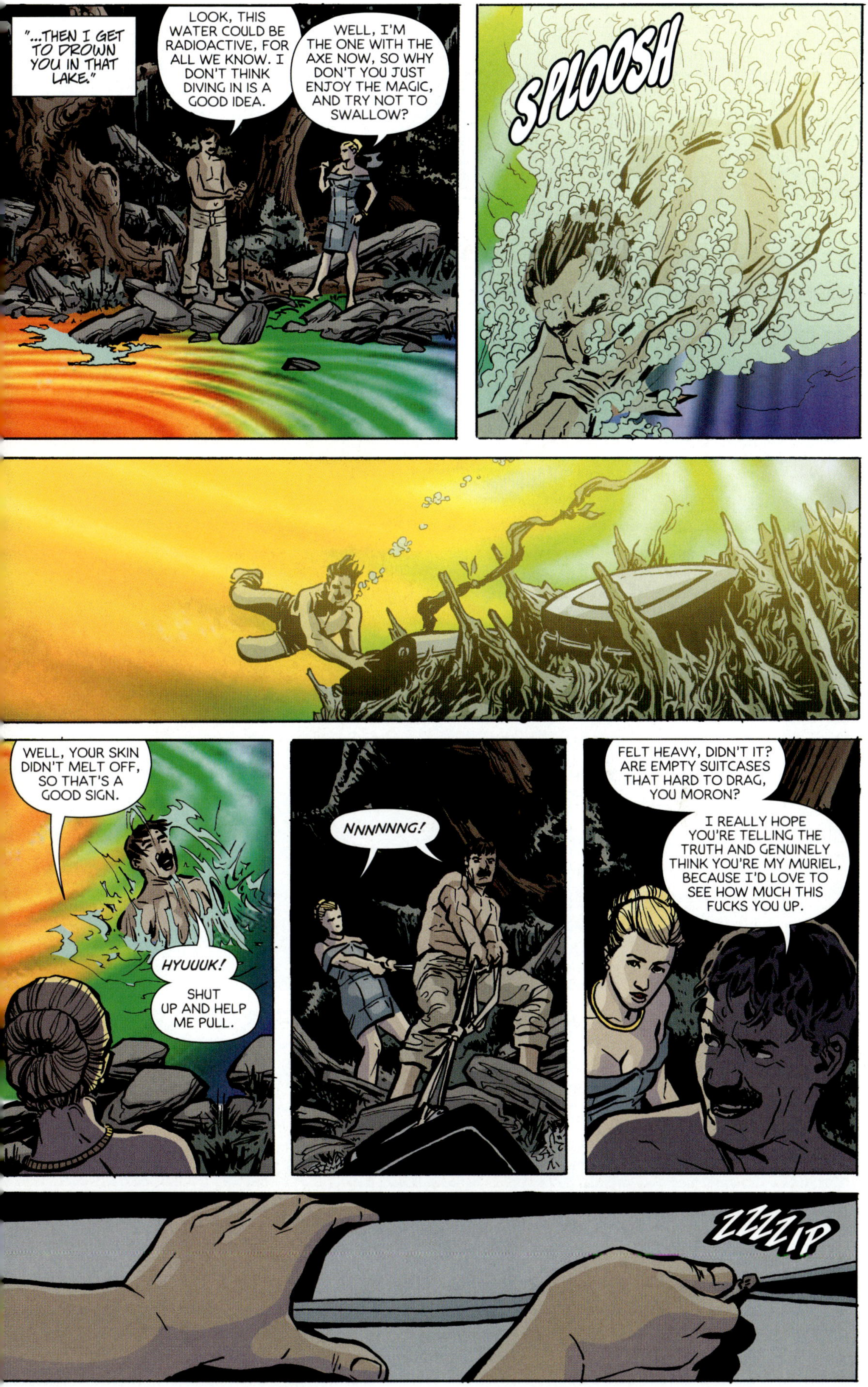
"...THEN I GET TO DROWN YOU IN THAT LAKE."
LOOK, THIS WATER COULD BE RADIOACTIVE, FOR ALL WE KNOW. I DON'T THINK DIVING IN IS A GOOD IDEA.
WELL, I'M THE ONE WITH THE AXE NOW, SO WHY DON'T YOU JUST ENJOY THE MAGIC, AND TRY NOT TO SWALLOW?
SPLOOSH
WELL, YOUR SKIN DIDN'T MELT OFF, SO THAT'S A GOOD SIGN.
HYUUUK!
SHUT UP AND HELP ME PULL.
NNNNNNG!
FELT HEAVY, DIDN'T IT? ARE EMPTY SUITCASES THAT HARD TO DRAG, YOU MORON?
I REALLY HOPE YOU'RE TELLING THE TRUTH AND GENUINELY THINK YOU'RE MY MURIEL, BECAUSE I'D LOVE TO SEE HOW MUCH THIS FUCKS YOU UP.
ZZZZIP

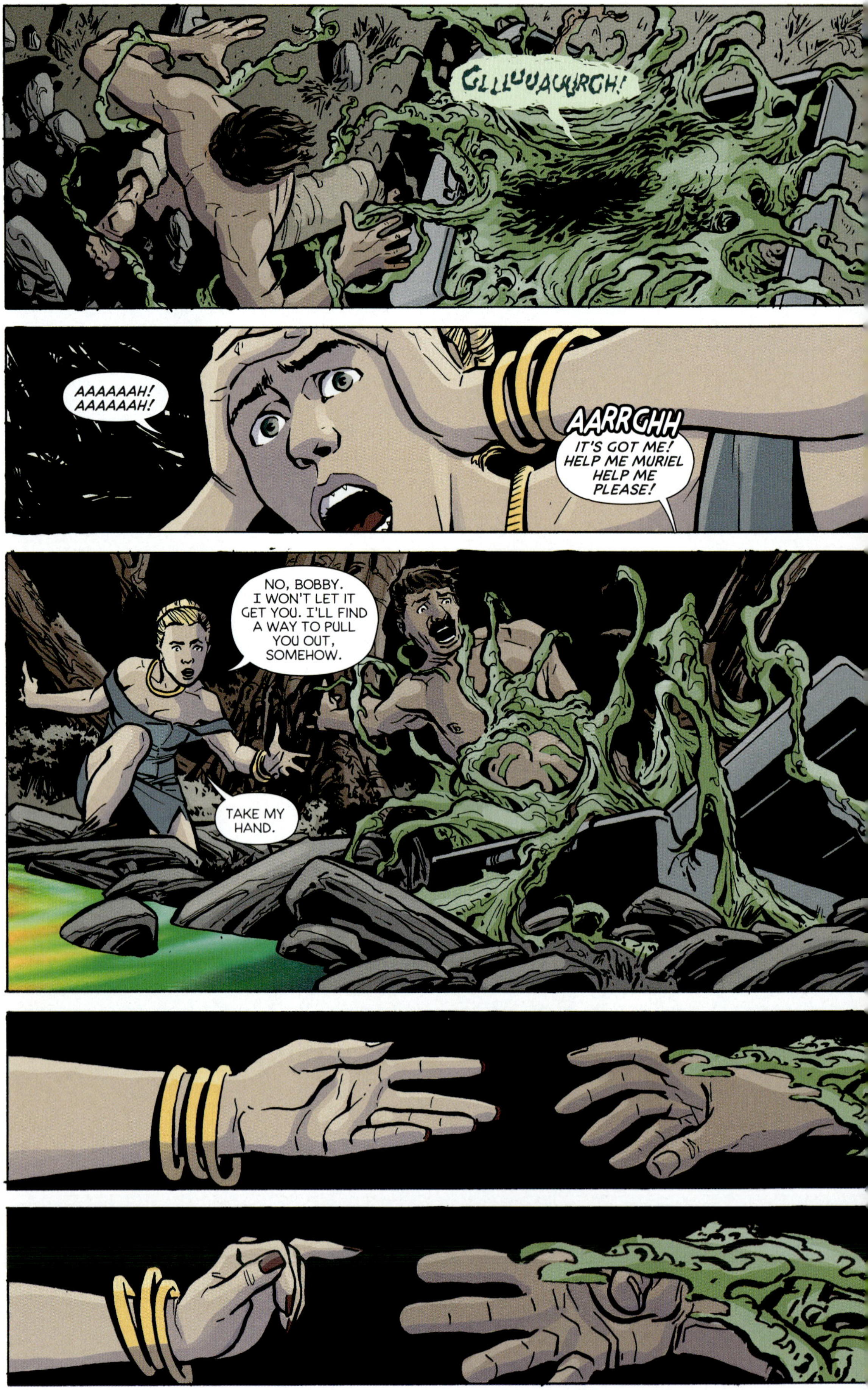
GLLUUUAUURGH!
AAAAAAH! AAAAAAH!
AARRGHH
IT'S GOT ME! HELP ME MURIEL HELP ME PLEASE!
NO, BOBBY. I WON'T LET IT GET YOU. I'LL FIND A WAY TO PULL YOU OUT, SOMEHOW.
TAKE MY HAND.

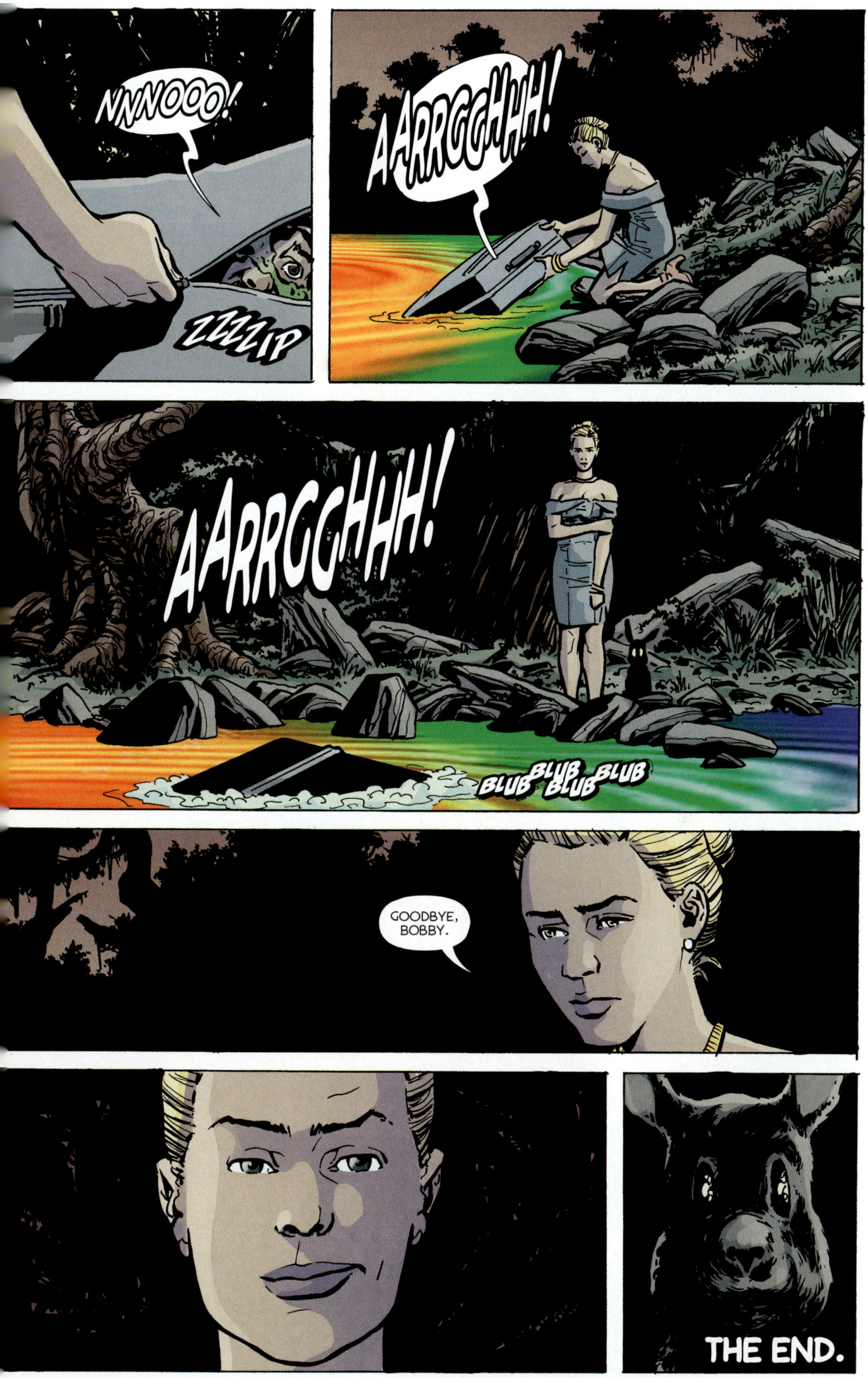
NNNOOO!
ZZZZIP
AARRGGHHH!
AARRGGHHH!
BLUB BLUB BLUB BLUB
GOODBYE, BOBBY.
THE END.

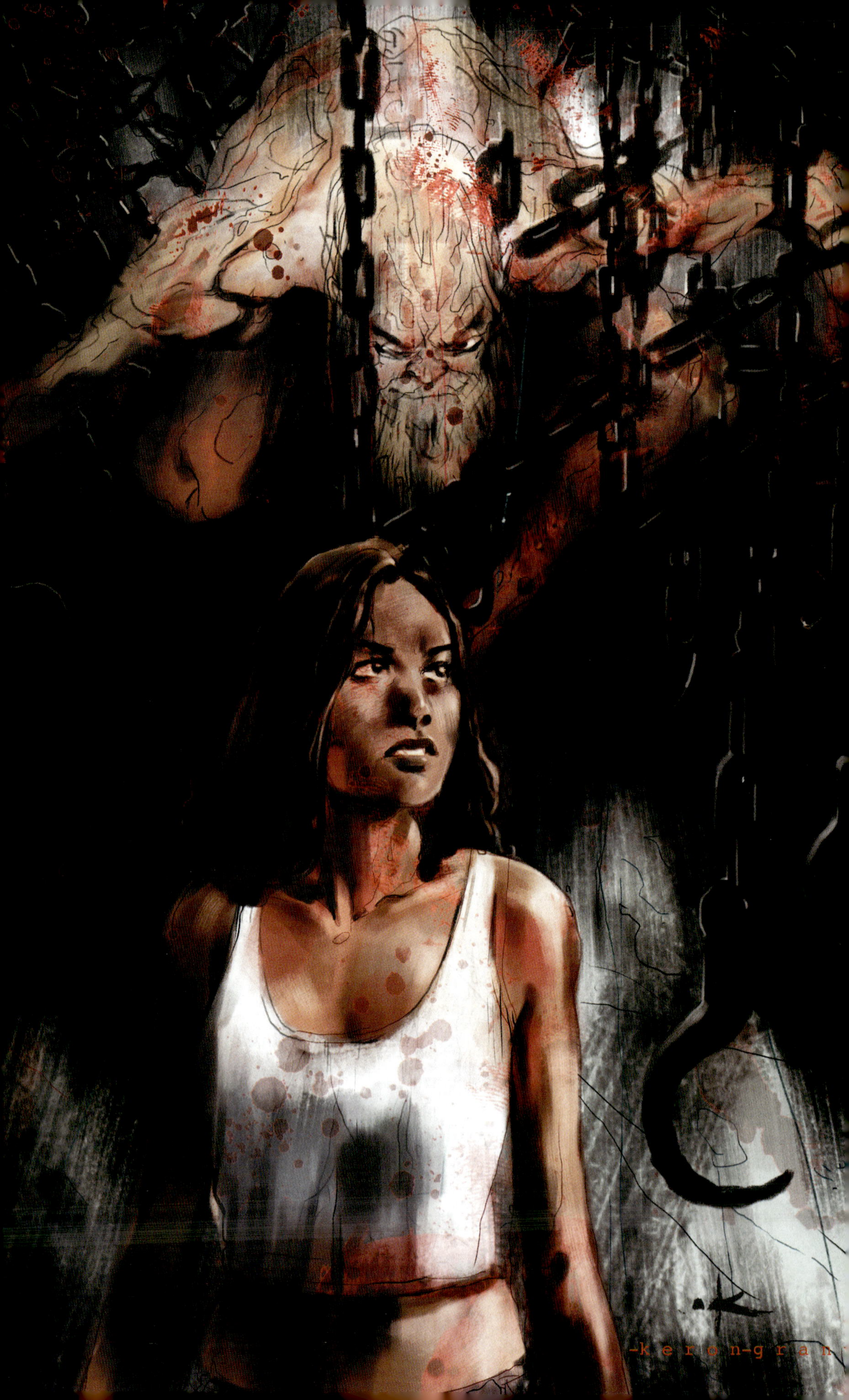
-k e r o n-g r a n

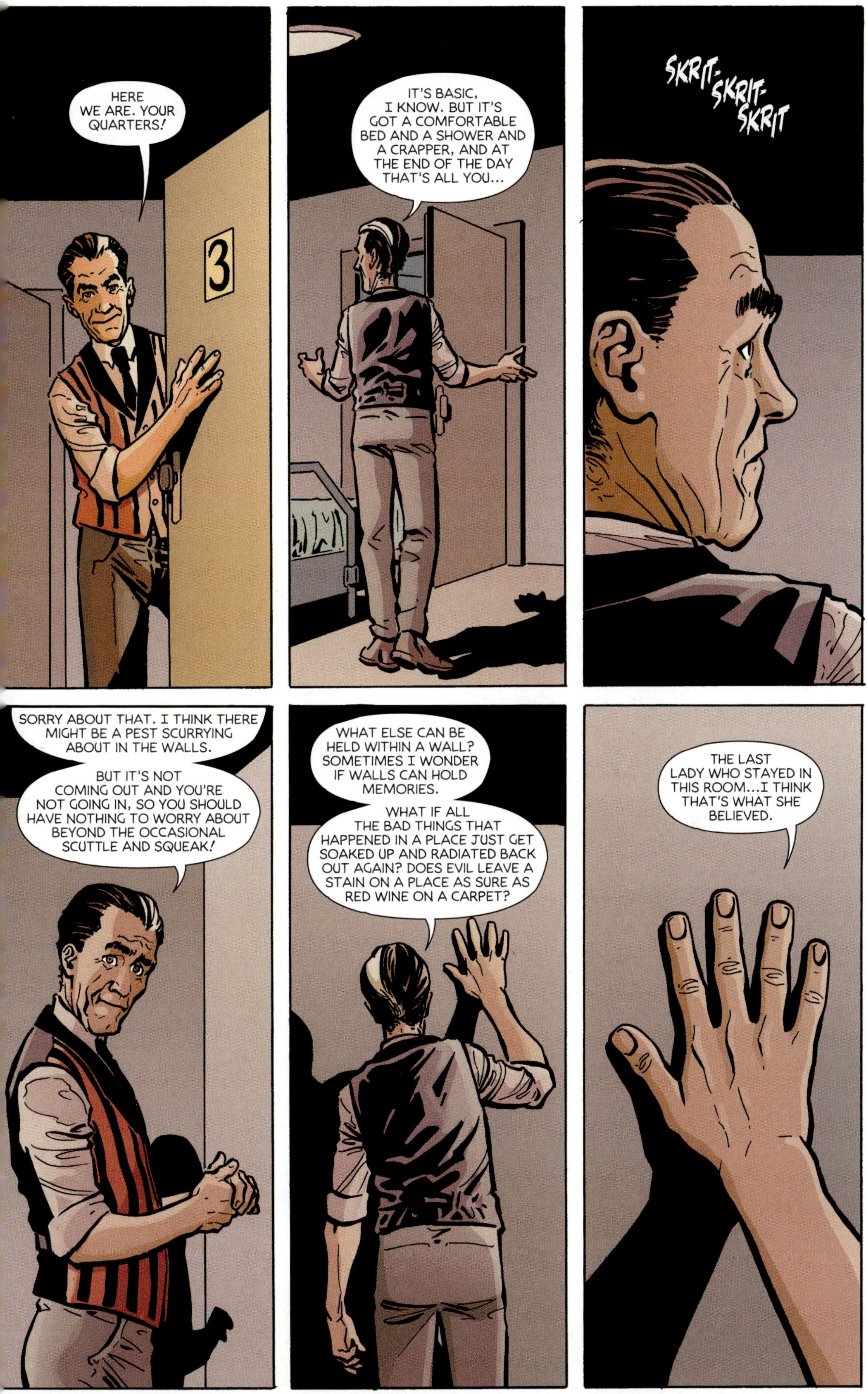
HERE WE ARE. YOUR QUARTERS!
3
IT'S BASIC, I KNOW. BUT IT'S GOT A COMFORTABLE BED AND A SHOWER AND A CRAPPER, AND AT THE END OF THE DAY THAT'S ALL YOU...
SKRIT-SKRIT-SKRIT
SORRY ABOUT THAT. I THINK THERE MIGHT BE A PEST SCURRYING ABOUT IN THE WALLS.
BUT IT'S NOT COMING OUT AND YOU'RE NOT GOING IN, SO YOU SHOULD HAVE NOTHING TO WORRY ABOUT BEYOND THE OCCASIONAL SCUTTLE AND SQUEAK!
WHAT ELSE CAN BE HELD WITHIN A WALL? SOMETIMES I WONDER IF WALLS CAN HOLD MEMORIES.
WHAT IF ALL THE BAD THINGS THAT HAPPENED IN A PLACE JUST GET SOAKED UP AND RADIATED BACK OUT AGAIN? DOES EVIL LEAVE A STAIN ON A PLACE AS SURE AS RED WINE ON A CARPET?
THE LAST LADY WHO STAYED IN THIS ROOM...I THINK THAT'S WHAT SHE BELIEVED.

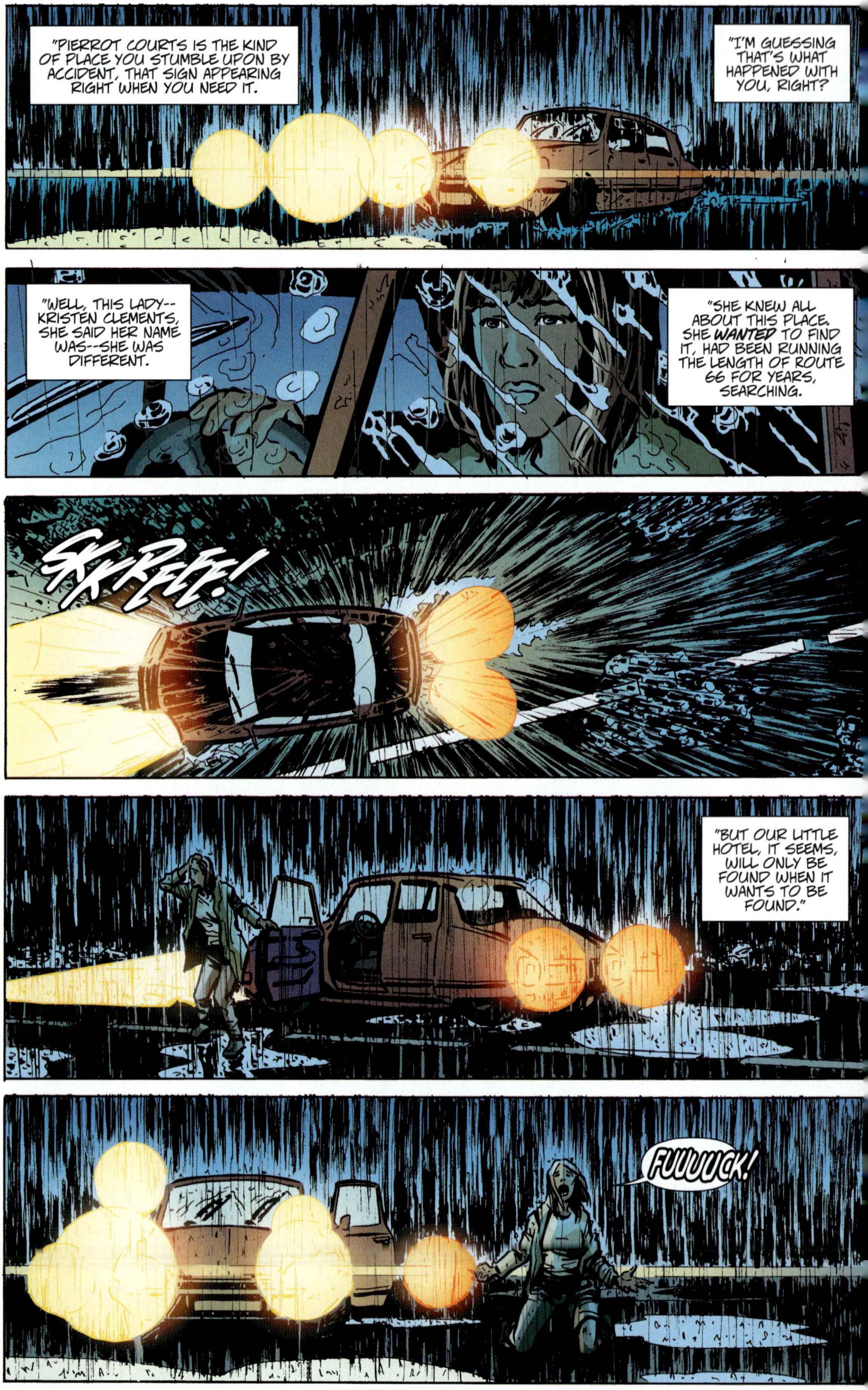
"PIERROT COURTS IS THE KIND OF PLACE YOU STUMBLE UPON BY ACCIDENT, THAT SIGN APPEARING RIGHT WHEN YOU NEED IT.
"I'M GUESSING THAT'S WHAT HAPPENED WITH YOU, RIGHT?
"WELL, THIS LADY--KRISTEN CLEMENTS, SHE SAID HER NAME WAS--SHE WAS DIFFERENT.
"SHE KNEW ALL ABOUT THIS PLACE. SHE **WANTED** TO FIND IT, HAD BEEN RUNNING THE LENGTH OF ROUTE 66 FOR YEARS, SEARCHING.
SKKREEE!
"BUT OUR LITTLE HOTEL, IT SEEMS, WILL ONLY BE FOUND WHEN IT WANTS TO BE FOUND."
FUUUUCK!

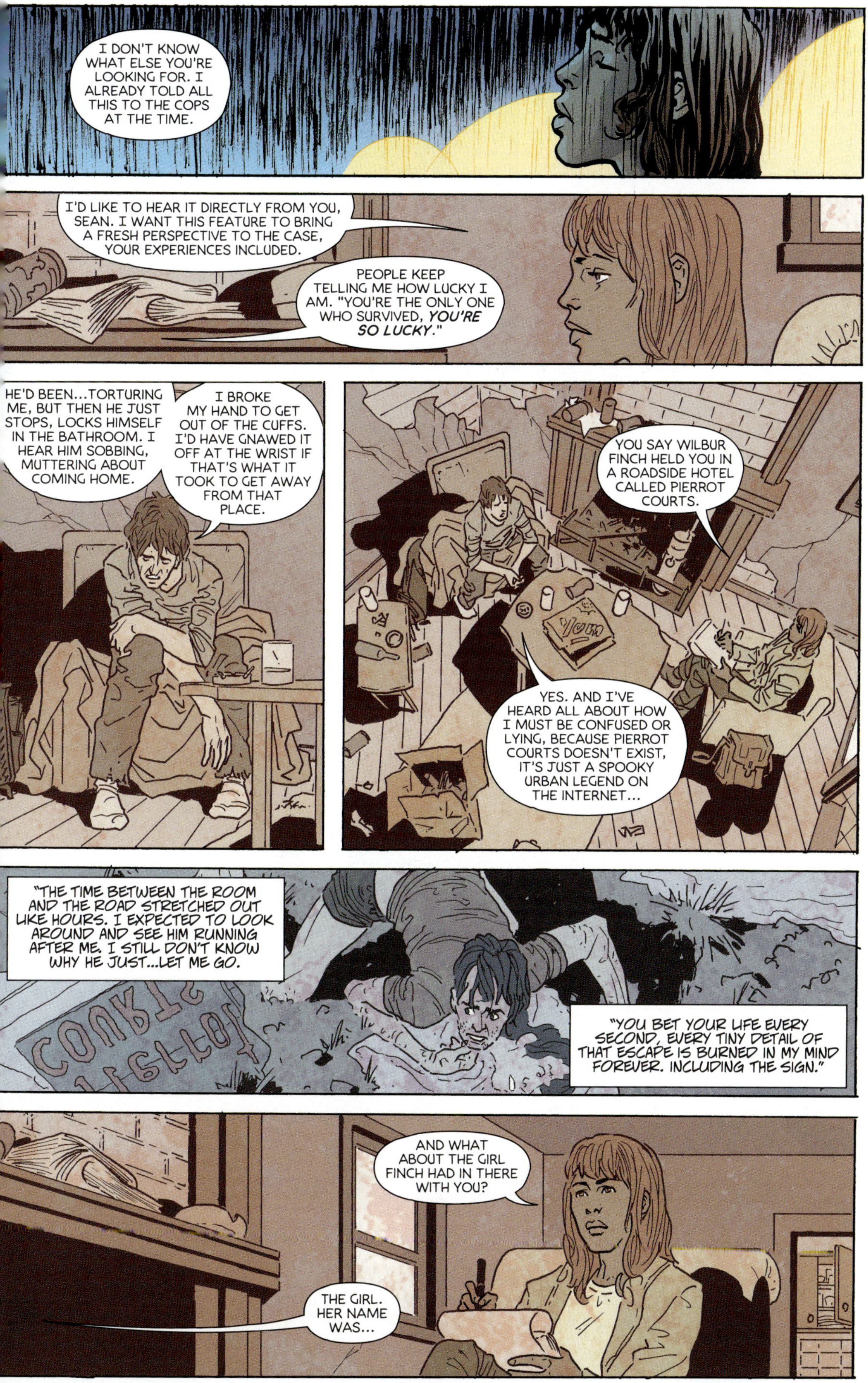
I DON'T KNOW WHAT ELSE YOU'RE LOOKING FOR. I ALREADY TOLD ALL THIS TO THE COPS AT THE TIME.
I'D LIKE TO HEAR IT DIRECTLY FROM YOU, SEAN. I WANT THIS FEATURE TO BRING A FRESH PERSPECTIVE TO THE CASE, YOUR EXPERIENCES INCLUDED.
PEOPLE KEEP TELLING ME HOW LUCKY I AM. "YOU'RE THE ONLY ONE WHO SURVIVED, *YOU'RE SO LUCKY*."
HE'D BEEN...TORTURING ME, BUT THEN HE JUST STOPS, LOCKS HIMSELF IN THE BATHROOM. I HEAR HIM SOBBING, MUTTERING ABOUT COMING HOME.
I BROKE MY HAND TO GET OUT OF THE CUFFS. I'D HAVE GNAWED IT OFF AT THE WRIST IF THAT'S WHAT IT TOOK TO GET AWAY FROM THAT PLACE.
YOU SAY WILBUR FINCH HELD YOU IN A ROADSIDE HOTEL CALLED PIERROT COURTS.
YES. AND I'VE HEARD ALL ABOUT HOW I MUST BE CONFUSED OR LYING, BECAUSE PIERROT COURTS DOESN'T EXIST, IT'S JUST A SPOOKY URBAN LEGEND ON THE INTERNET...
"THE TIME BETWEEN THE ROOM AND THE ROAD STRETCHED OUT LIKE HOURS. I EXPECTED TO LOOK AROUND AND SEE HIM RUNNING AFTER ME. I STILL DON'T KNOW WHY HE JUST...LET ME GO.
"YOU BET YOUR LIFE EVERY SECOND, EVERY TINY DETAIL OF THAT ESCAPE IS BURNED IN MY MIND FOREVER. INCLUDING THE SIGN."
AND WHAT ABOUT THE GIRL FINCH HAD IN THERE WITH YOU?
THE GIRL. HER NAME WAS...

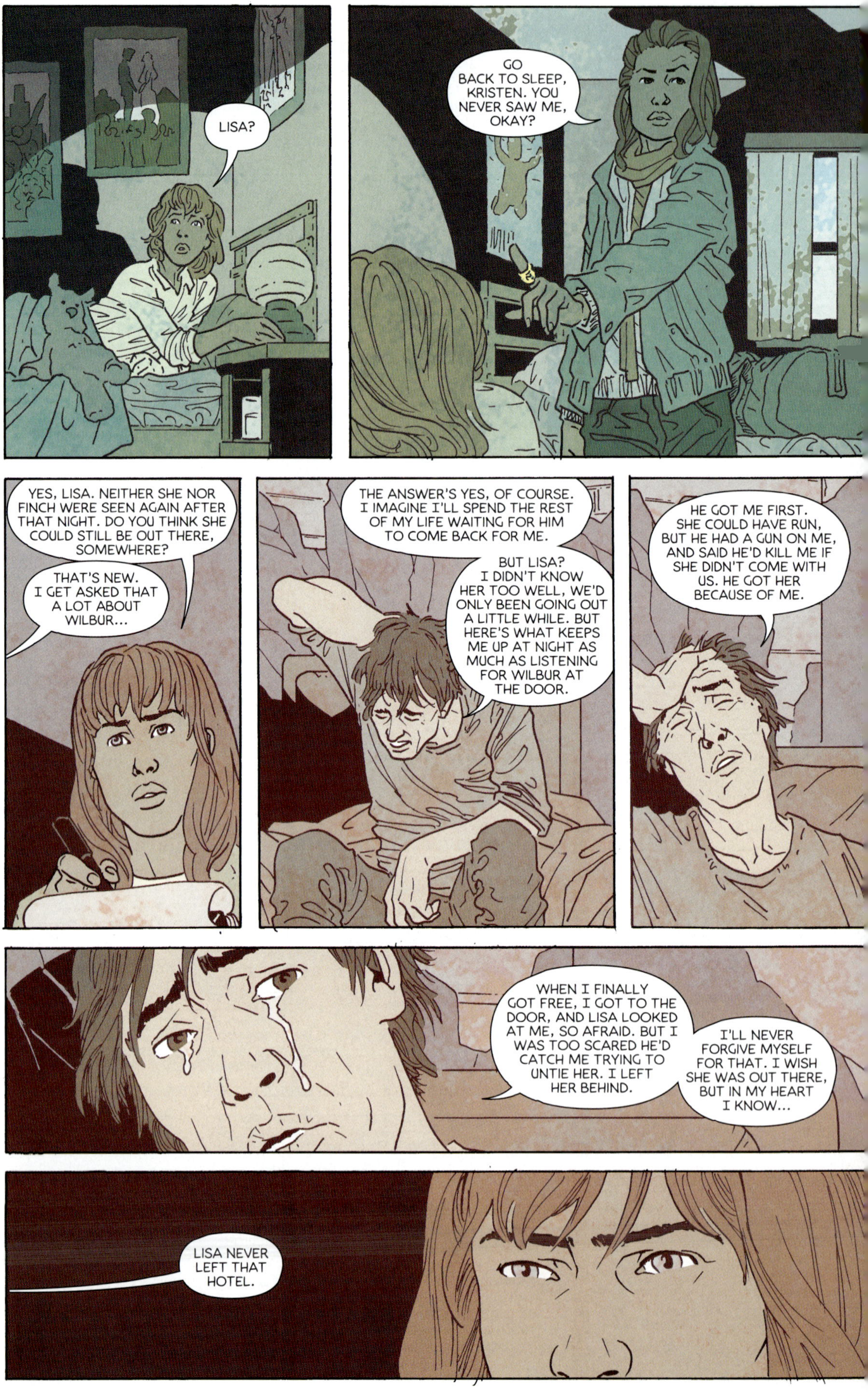
LISA?
GO BACK TO SLEEP, KRISTEN. YOU NEVER SAW ME, OKAY?
YES, LISA. NEITHER SHE NOR FINCH WERE SEEN AGAIN AFTER THAT NIGHT. DO YOU THINK SHE COULD STILL BE OUT THERE, SOMEWHERE?
THAT'S NEW. I GET ASKED THAT A LOT ABOUT WILBUR...
THE ANSWER'S YES, OF COURSE. I IMAGINE I'LL SPEND THE REST OF MY LIFE WAITING FOR HIM TO COME BACK FOR ME.
BUT LISA? I DIDN'T KNOW HER TOO WELL, WE'D ONLY BEEN GOING OUT A LITTLE WHILE. BUT HERE'S WHAT KEEPS ME UP AT NIGHT AS MUCH AS LISTENING FOR WILBUR AT THE DOOR.
HE GOT ME FIRST. SHE COULD HAVE RUN, BUT HE HAD A GUN ON ME, AND SAID HE'D KILL ME IF SHE DIDN'T COME WITH US. HE GOT HER BECAUSE OF ME.
WHEN I FINALLY GOT FREE, I GOT TO THE DOOR, AND LISA LOOKED AT ME, SO AFRAID. BUT I WAS TOO SCARED HE'D CATCH ME TRYING TO UNTIE HER. I LEFT HER BEHIND.
I'LL NEVER FORGIVE MYSELF FOR THAT. I WISH SHE WAS OUT THERE, BUT IN MY HEART I KNOW...
LISA NEVER LEFT THAT HOTEL.

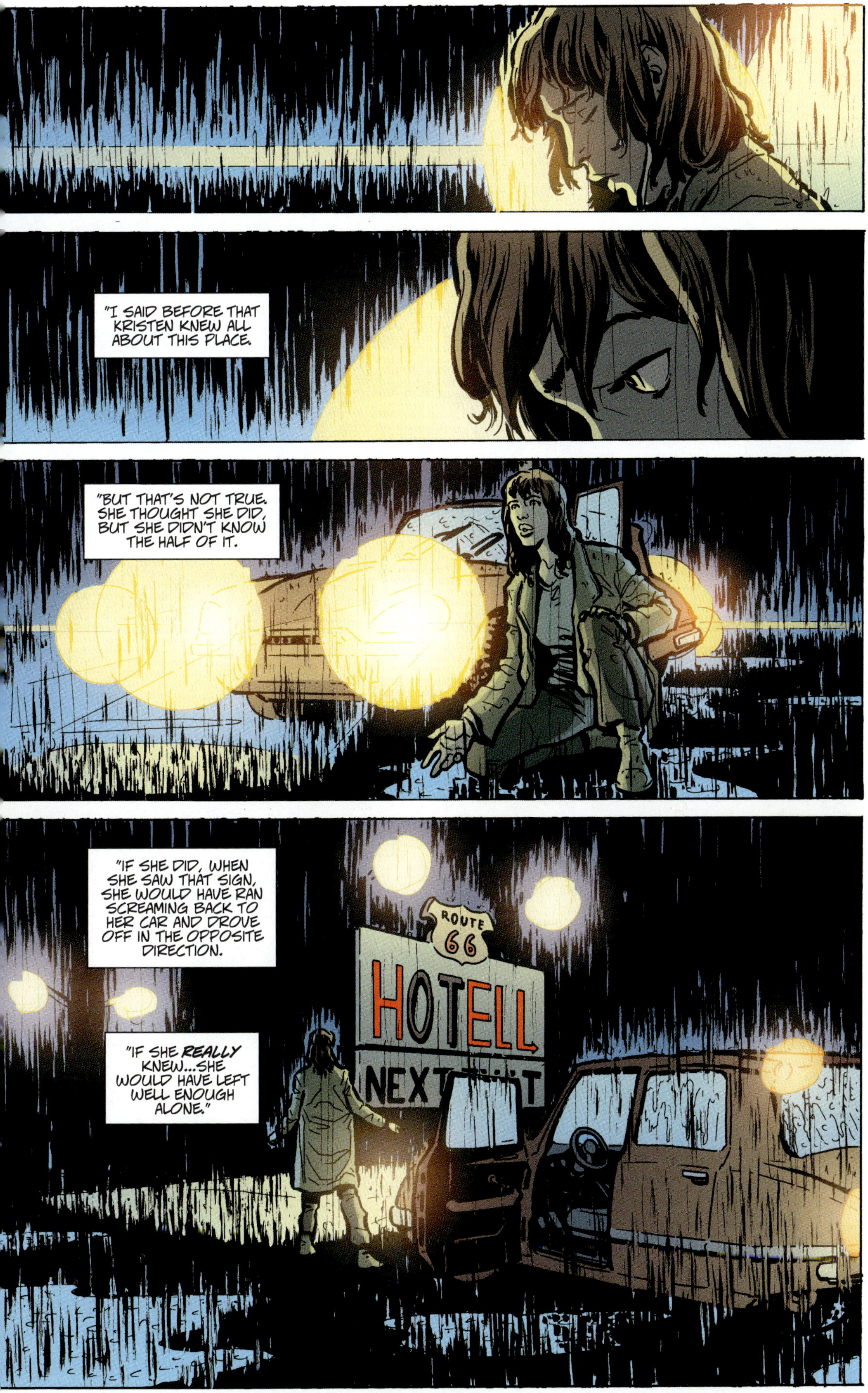
"I SAID BEFORE THAT KRISTEN KNEW ALL ABOUT THIS PLACE.
"BUT THAT'S NOT TRUE. SHE THOUGHT SHE DID, BUT SHE DIDN'T KNOW THE HALF OF IT.
"IF SHE DID, WHEN SHE SAW THAT SIGN, SHE WOULD HAVE RAN SCREAMING BACK TO HER CAR AND DROVE OFF IN THE OPPOSITE DIRECTION.
ROUTE 66
HOTELL
"IF SHE *REALLY* KNEW...SHE WOULD HAVE LEFT WELL ENOUGH ALONE."

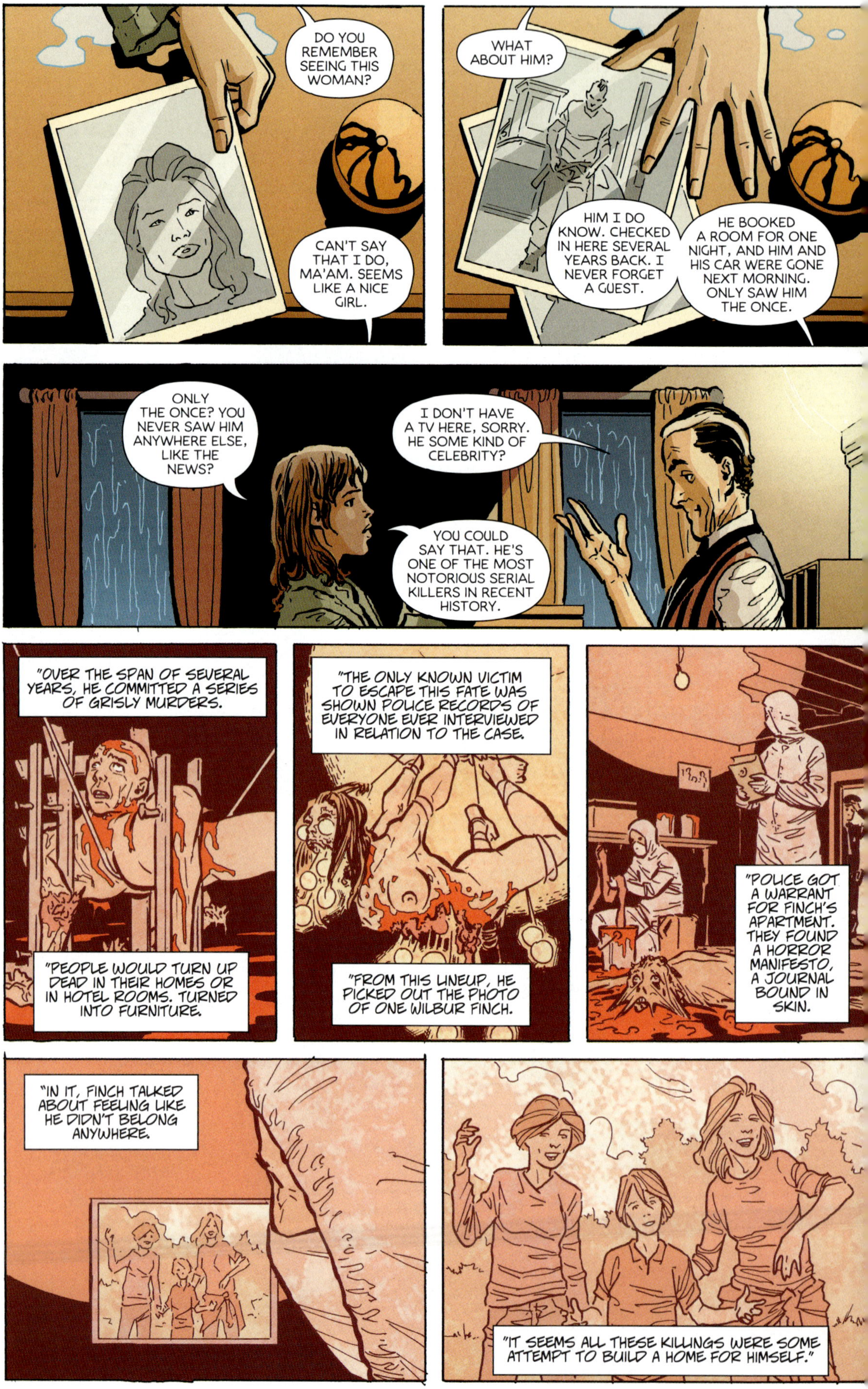
DO YOU REMEMBER SEEING THIS WOMAN?
CAN'T SAY THAT I DO, MA'AM. SEEMS LIKE A NICE GIRL.
WHAT ABOUT HIM?
HIM I DO KNOW. CHECKED IN HERE SEVERAL YEARS BACK. I NEVER FORGET A GUEST.
HE BOOKED A ROOM FOR ONE NIGHT, AND HIM AND HIS CAR WERE GONE NEXT MORNING. ONLY SAW HIM THE ONCE.
ONLY THE ONCE? YOU NEVER SAW HIM ANYWHERE ELSE, LIKE THE NEWS?
I DON'T HAVE A TV HERE, SORRY. HE SOME KIND OF CELEBRITY?
YOU COULD SAY THAT. HE'S ONE OF THE MOST NOTORIOUS SERIAL KILLERS IN RECENT HISTORY.
"OVER THE SPAN OF SEVERAL YEARS, HE COMMITTED A SERIES OF GRISLY MURDERS.
"PEOPLE WOULD TURN UP DEAD IN THEIR HOMES OR IN HOTEL ROOMS. TURNED INTO FURNITURE.
"THE ONLY KNOWN VICTIM TO ESCAPE THIS FATE WAS SHOWN POLICE RECORDS OF EVERYONE EVER INTERVIEWED IN RELATION TO THE CASE.
"FROM THIS LINEUP, HE PICKED OUT THE PHOTO OF ONE WILBUR FINCH.
"POLICE GOT A WARRANT FOR FINCH'S APARTMENT. THEY FOUND A HORROR MANIFESTO, A JOURNAL BOUND IN SKIN.
"IN IT, FINCH TALKED ABOUT FEELING LIKE HE DIDN'T BELONG ANYWHERE.
"IT SEEMS ALL THESE KILLINGS WERE SOME ATTEMPT TO BUILD A HOME FOR HIMSELF."

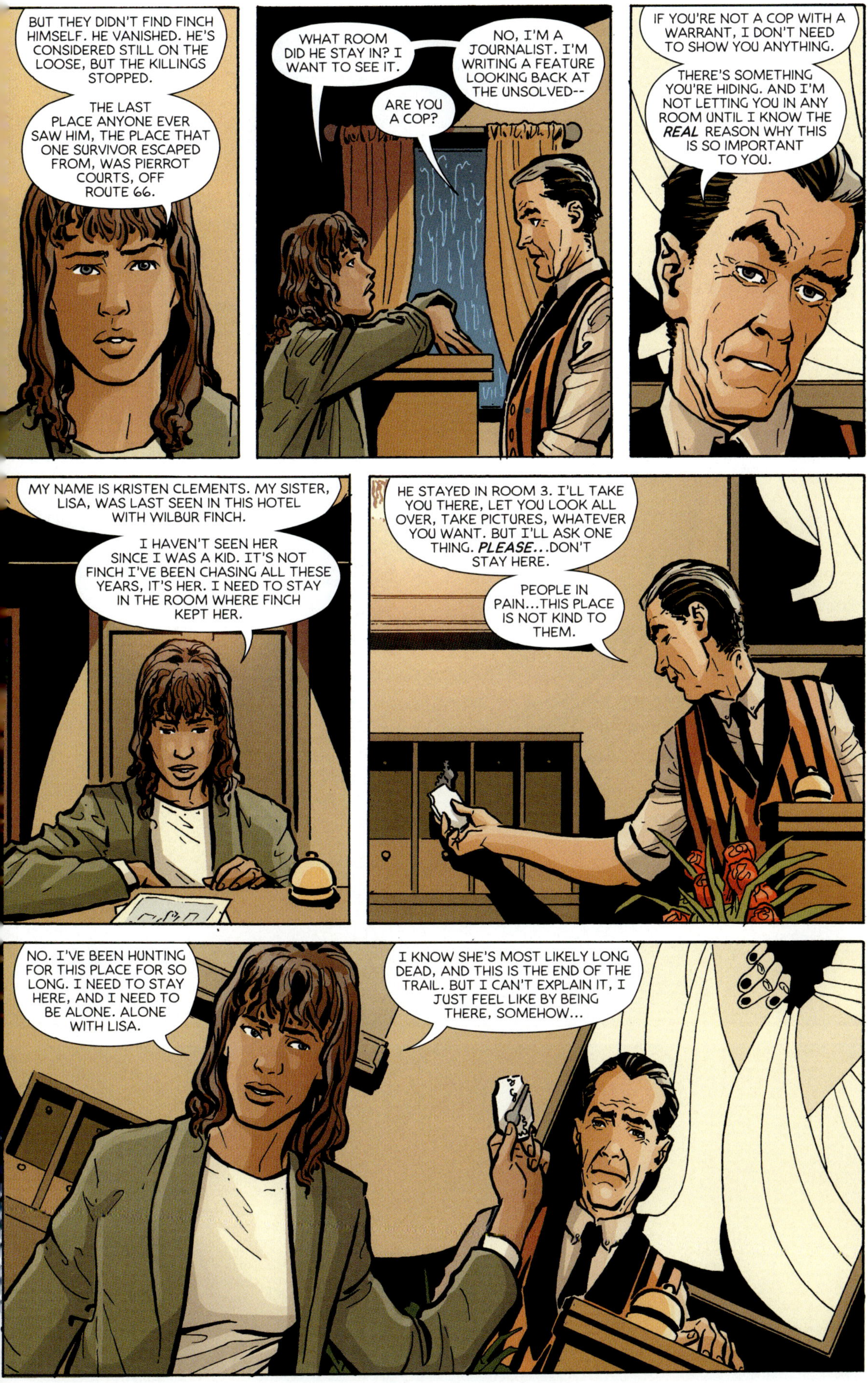
BUT THEY DIDN'T FIND FINCH HIMSELF. HE VANISHED. HE'S CONSIDERED STILL ON THE LOOSE, BUT THE KILLINGS STOPPED.
THE LAST PLACE ANYONE EVER SAW HIM, THE PLACE THAT ONE SURVIVOR ESCAPED FROM, WAS PIERROT COURTS, OFF ROUTE 66.
WHAT ROOM DID HE STAY IN? I WANT TO SEE IT.
ARE YOU A COP?
NO, I'M A JOURNALIST. I'M WRITING A FEATURE LOOKING BACK AT THE UNSOLVED--
IF YOU'RE NOT A COP WITH A WARRANT, I DON'T NEED TO SHOW YOU ANYTHING.
THERE'S SOMETHING YOU'RE HIDING. AND I'M NOT LETTING YOU IN ANY ROOM UNTIL I KNOW THE ***REAL*** REASON WHY THIS IS SO IMPORTANT TO YOU.
MY NAME IS KRISTEN CLEMENTS. MY SISTER, LISA, WAS LAST SEEN IN THIS HOTEL WITH WILBUR FINCH.
I HAVEN'T SEEN HER SINCE I WAS A KID. IT'S NOT FINCH I'VE BEEN CHASING ALL THESE YEARS, IT'S HER. I NEED TO STAY IN THE ROOM WHERE FINCH KEPT HER.
HE STAYED IN ROOM 3. I'LL TAKE YOU THERE, LET YOU LOOK ALL OVER, TAKE PICTURES, WHATEVER YOU WANT. BUT I'LL ASK ONE THING. ***PLEASE...***DON'T STAY HERE.
PEOPLE IN PAIN...THIS PLACE IS NOT KIND TO THEM.
NO. I'VE BEEN HUNTING FOR THIS PLACE FOR SO LONG. I NEED TO STAY HERE, AND I NEED TO BE ALONE. ALONE WITH LISA.
I KNOW SHE'S MOST LIKELY LONG DEAD, AND THIS IS THE END OF THE TRAIL. BUT I CAN'T EXPLAIN IT, I JUST FEEL LIKE BY BEING THERE, SOMEHOW...

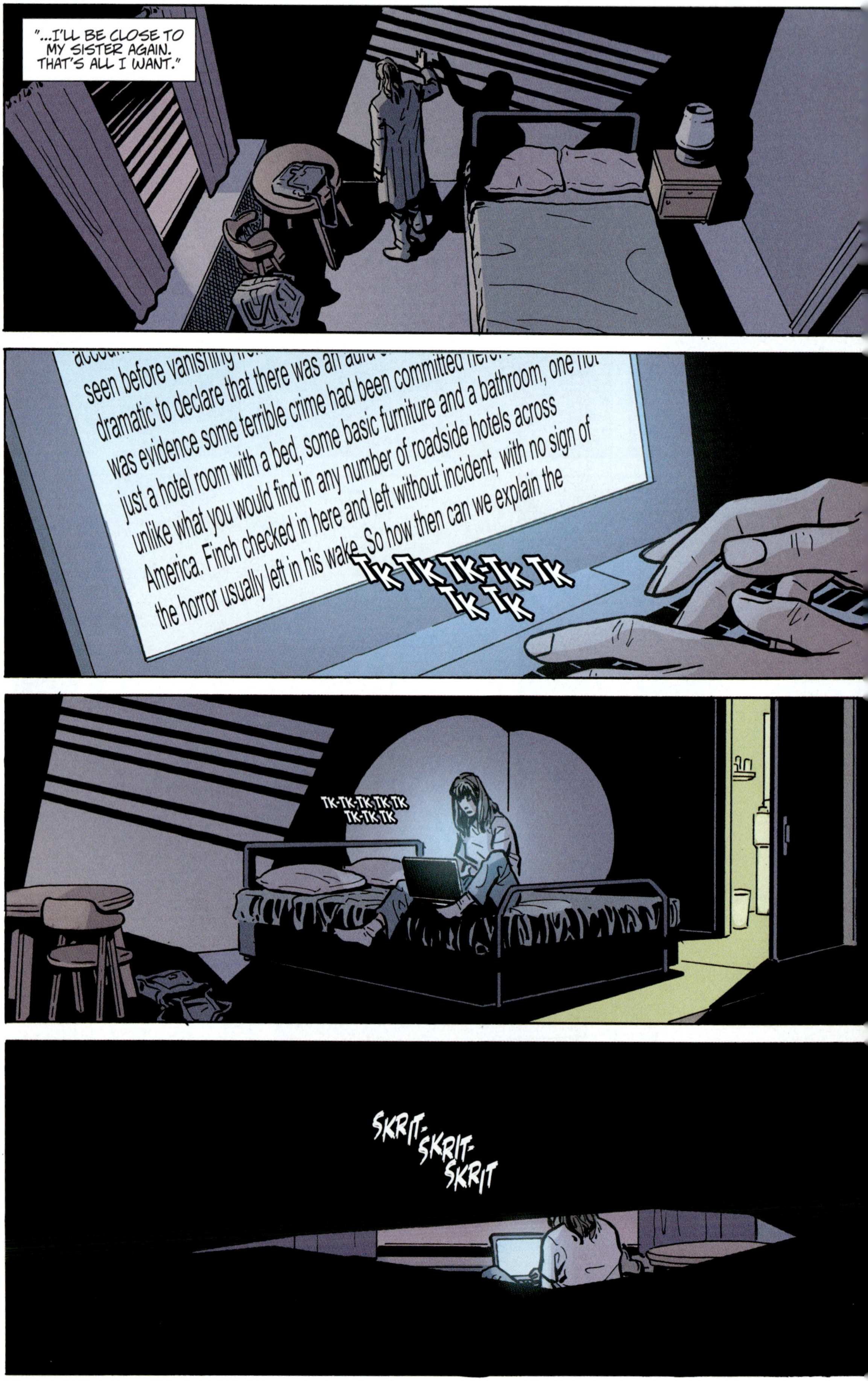
"...I'LL BE CLOSE TO MY SISTER AGAIN. THAT'S ALL I WANT."
seen before vanishing
dramatic to declare that there was an aura
was evidence some terrible crime had been committed
just a hotel room with a bed, some basic furniture and a bathroom, one not
unlike what you would find in any number of roadside hotels across
America. Finch checked in here and left without incident, with no sign of
the horror usually left in his wake. So how then can we explain the
TK TK TK-TK TK TK TK TK
TK-TK-TK TK TK TK-TK TK
SKRIT-SKRIT-SKRIT

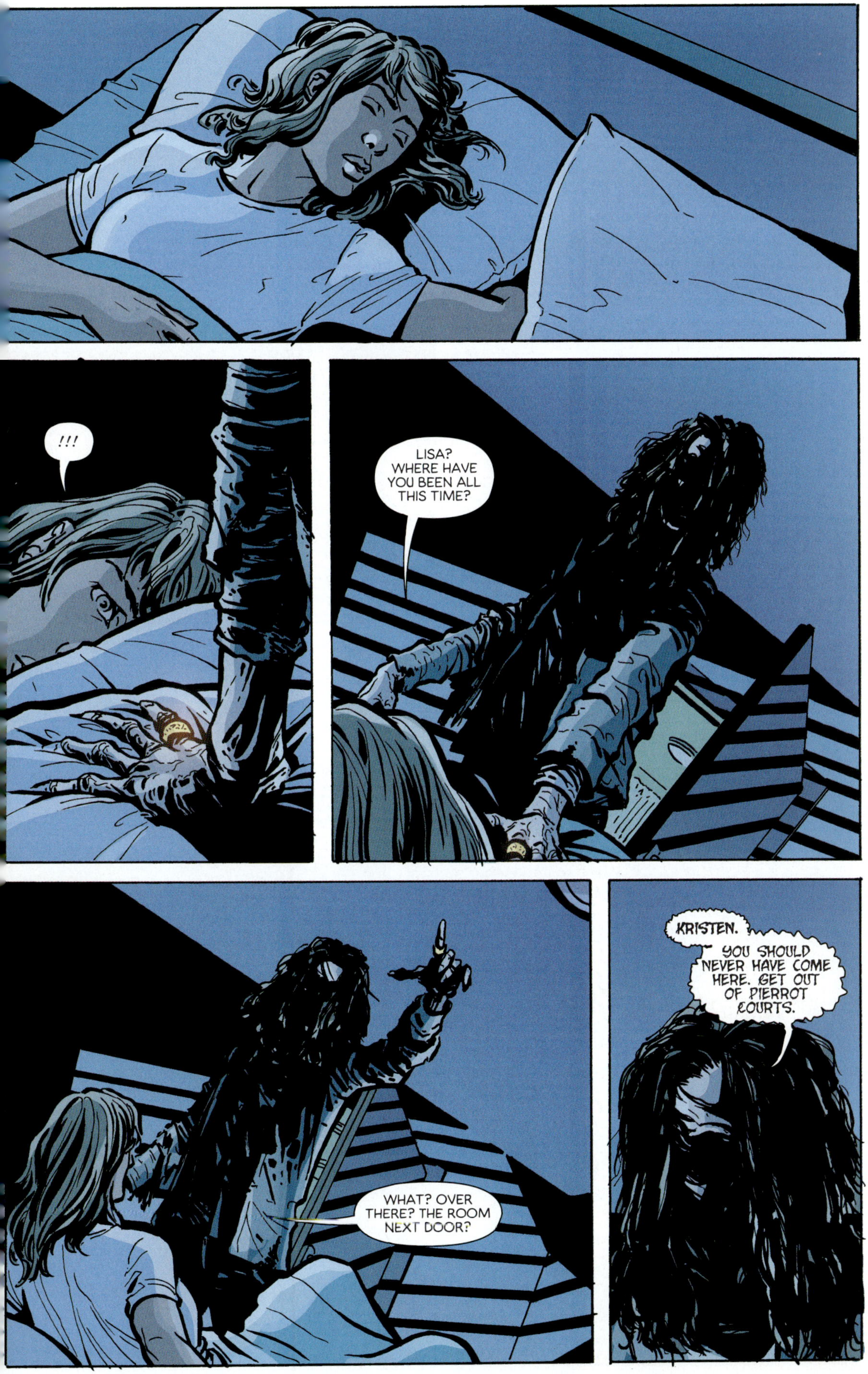
!!!
LISA? WHERE HAVE YOU BEEN ALL THIS TIME?
WHAT? OVER THERE? THE ROOM NEXT DOOR?
KRISTEN.
YOU SHOULD NEVER HAVE COME HERE. GET OUT OF PIERROT COURTS.

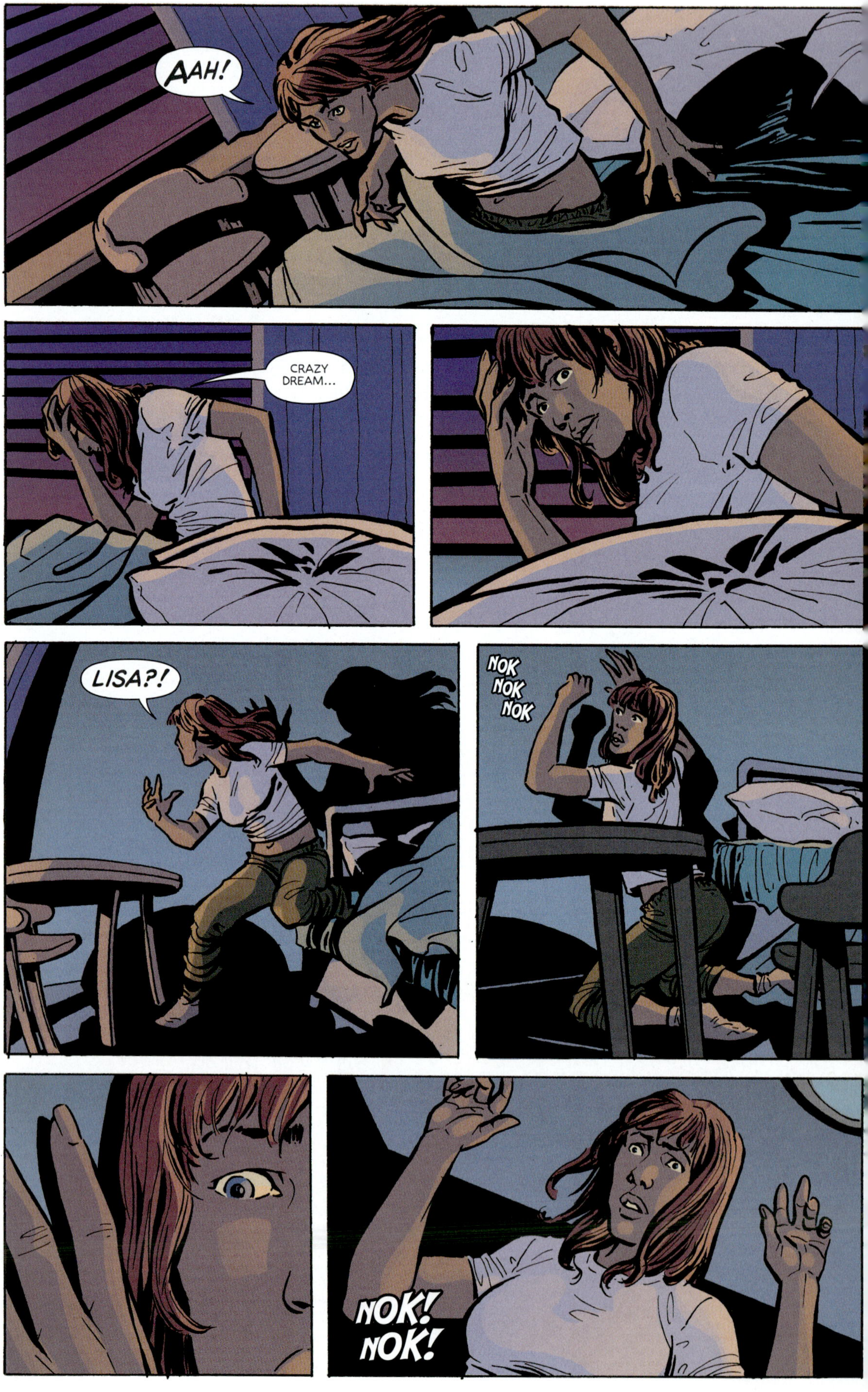
AAH!
CRAZY DREAM...
LISA?!
NOK NOK NOK
NOK! NOK!

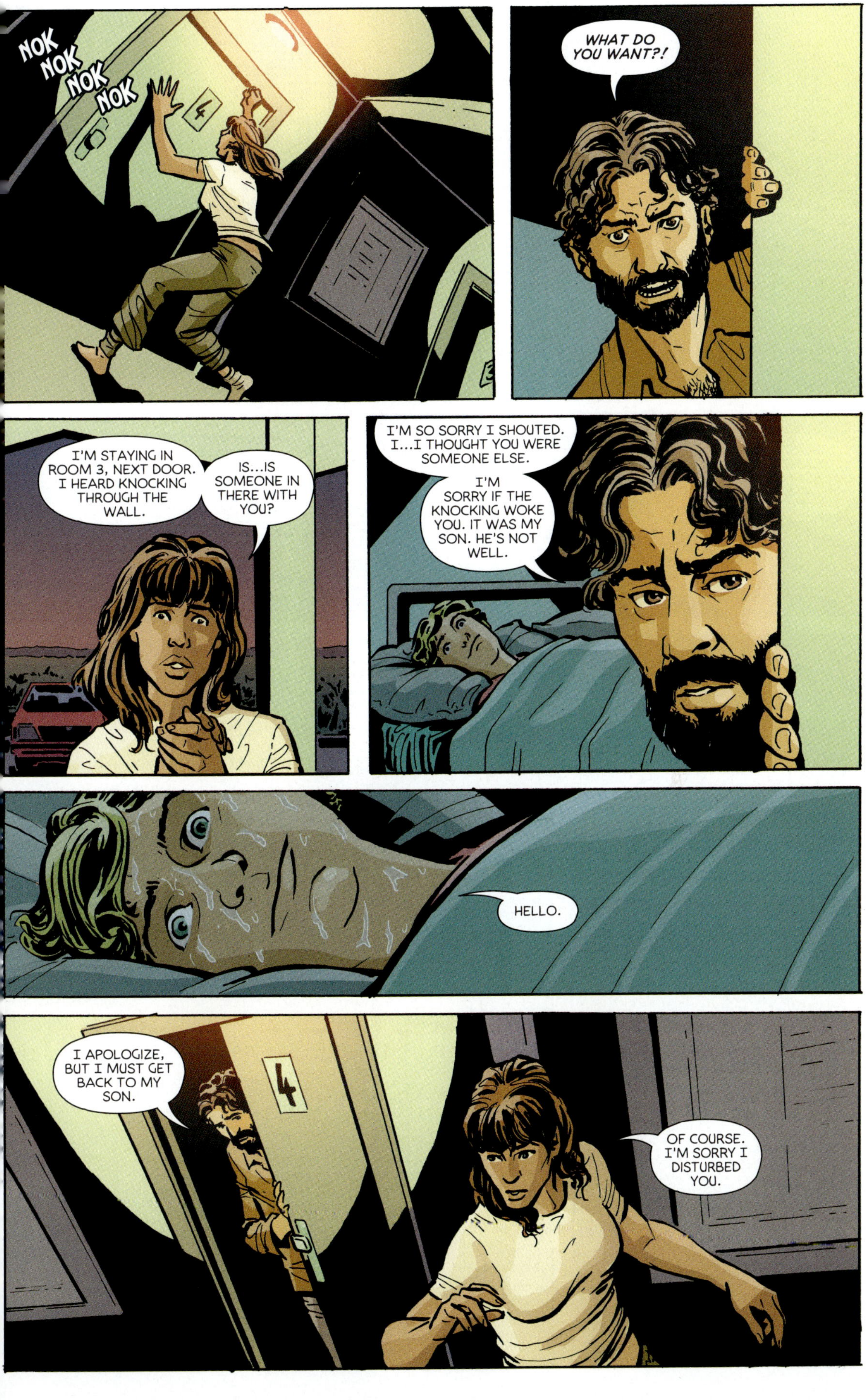
NOK NOK NOK NOK
WHAT DO YOU WANT?!
I'M STAYING IN ROOM 3, NEXT DOOR. I HEARD KNOCKING THROUGH THE WALL.
IS...IS SOMEONE IN THERE WITH YOU?
I'M SO SORRY I SHOUTED. I...I THOUGHT YOU WERE SOMEONE ELSE.
I'M SORRY IF THE KNOCKING WOKE YOU. IT WAS MY SON. HE'S NOT WELL.
HELLO.
I APOLOGIZE, BUT I MUST GET BACK TO MY SON.
OF COURSE. I'M SORRY I DISTURBED YOU.

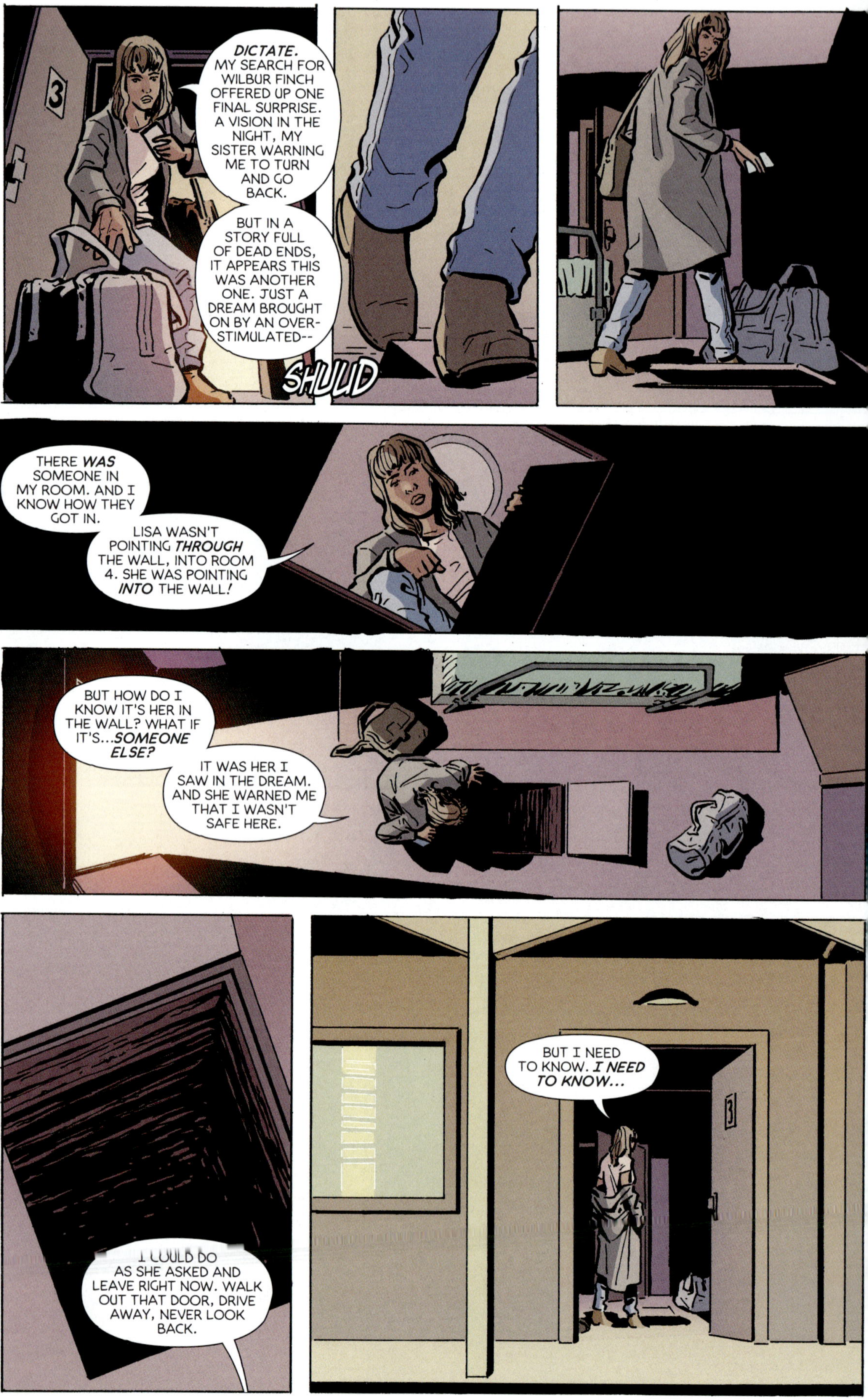

DICTATE. MY SEARCH FOR WILBUR FINCH OFFERED UP ONE FINAL SURPRISE. A VISION IN THE NIGHT, MY SISTER WARNING ME TO TURN AND GO BACK.
BUT IN A STORY FULL OF DEAD ENDS, IT APPEARS THIS WAS ANOTHER ONE. JUST A DREAM BROUGHT ON BY AN OVER-STIMULATED--
SHUUD
THERE WAS SOMEONE IN MY ROOM. AND I KNOW HOW THEY GOT IN.
LISA WASN'T POINTING THROUGH THE WALL, INTO ROOM 4. SHE WAS POINTING INTO THE WALL!
BUT HOW DO I KNOW IT'S HER IN THE WALL? WHAT IF IT'S...SOMEONE ELSE?
IT WAS HER I SAW IN THE DREAM. AND SHE WARNED ME THAT I WASN'T SAFE HERE.
I COULD DO AS SHE ASKED AND LEAVE RIGHT NOW. WALK OUT THAT DOOR, DRIVE AWAY, NEVER LOOK BACK.
BUT I NEED TO KNOW. I NEED TO KNOW...

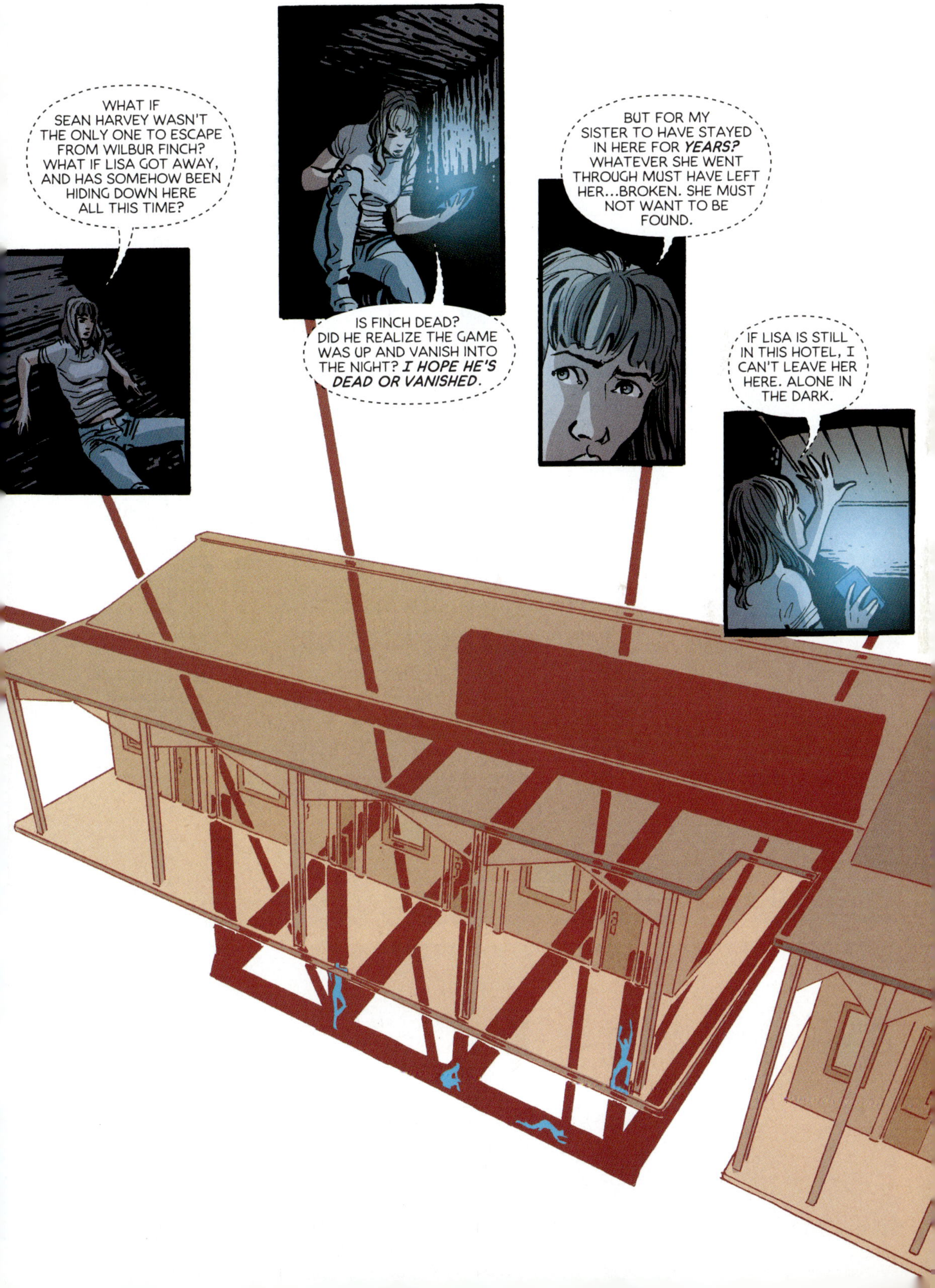
WHAT IF SEAN HARVEY WASN'T THE ONLY ONE TO ESCAPE FROM WILBUR FINCH? WHAT IF LISA GOT AWAY, AND HAS SOMEHOW BEEN HIDING DOWN HERE ALL THIS TIME?
IS FINCH DEAD? DID HE REALIZE THE GAME WAS UP AND VANISH INTO THE NIGHT? ***I HOPE HE'S DEAD OR VANISHED***.
BUT FOR MY SISTER TO HAVE STAYED IN HERE FOR ***YEARS?*** WHATEVER SHE WENT THROUGH MUST HAVE LEFT HER...BROKEN. SHE MUST NOT WANT TO BE FOUND.
IF LISA IS STILL IN THIS HOTEL, I CAN'T LEAVE HER HERE. ALONE IN THE DARK.

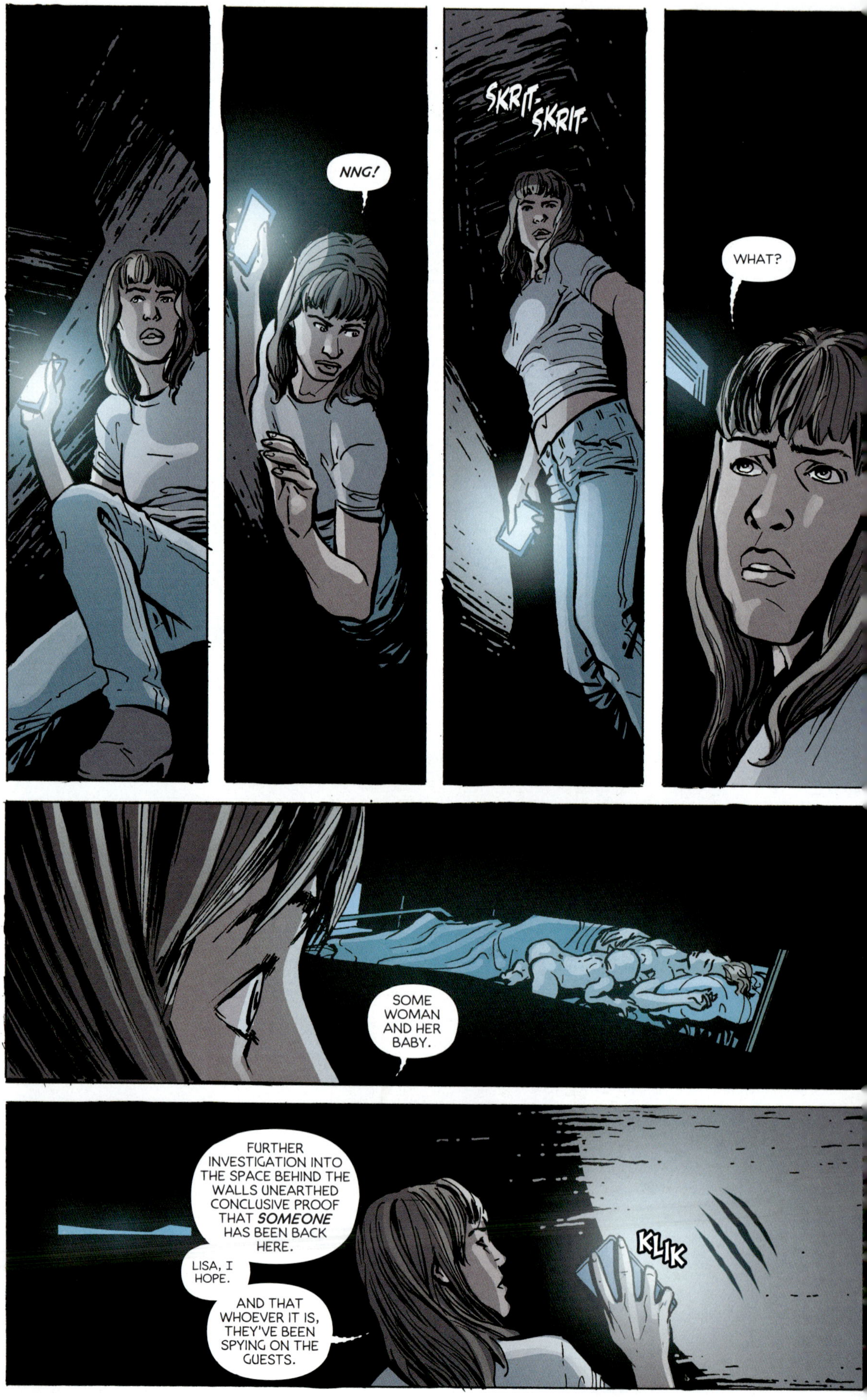
NNG!
SKRIT-
SKRIT-
WHAT?
SOME WOMAN AND HER BABY.
FURTHER INVESTIGATION INTO THE SPACE BEHIND THE WALLS UNEARTHED CONCLUSIVE PROOF THAT SOMEONE HAS BEEN BACK HERE.
LISA, I HOPE.
AND THAT WHOEVER IT IS, THEY'VE BEEN SPYING ON THE GUESTS.
KLIK

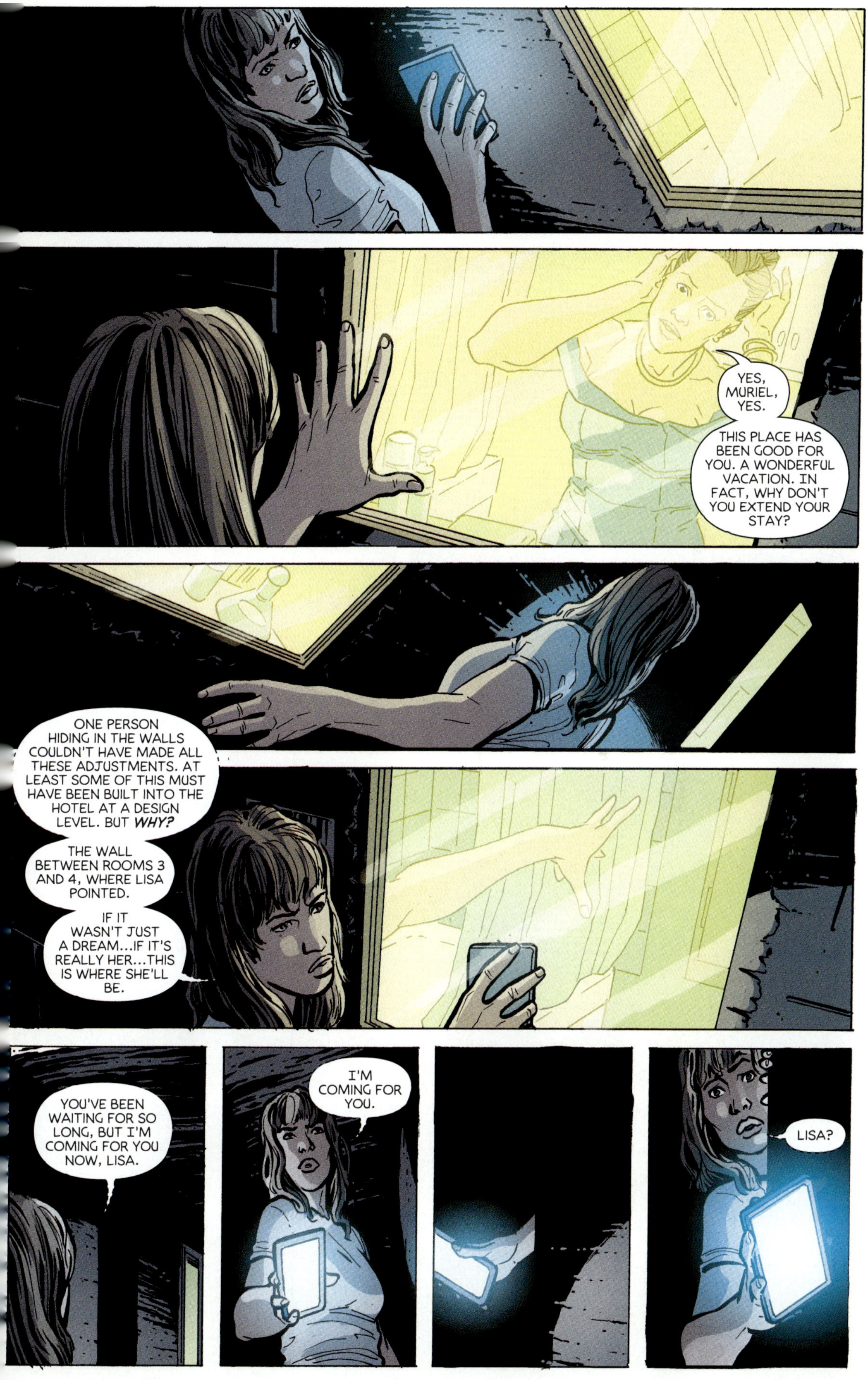
YES, MURIEL, YES.
THIS PLACE HAS BEEN GOOD FOR YOU. A WONDERFUL VACATION. IN FACT, WHY DON'T YOU EXTEND YOUR STAY?
ONE PERSON HIDING IN THE WALLS COULDN'T HAVE MADE ALL THESE ADJUSTMENTS. AT LEAST SOME OF THIS MUST HAVE BEEN BUILT INTO THE HOTEL AT A DESIGN LEVEL. BUT *WHY?*
THE WALL BETWEEN ROOMS 3 AND 4, WHERE LISA POINTED.
IF IT WASN'T JUST A DREAM...IF IT'S REALLY HER...THIS IS WHERE SHE'LL BE.
YOU'VE BEEN WAITING FOR SO LONG, BUT I'M COMING FOR YOU NOW, LISA.
I'M COMING FOR YOU.
LISA?

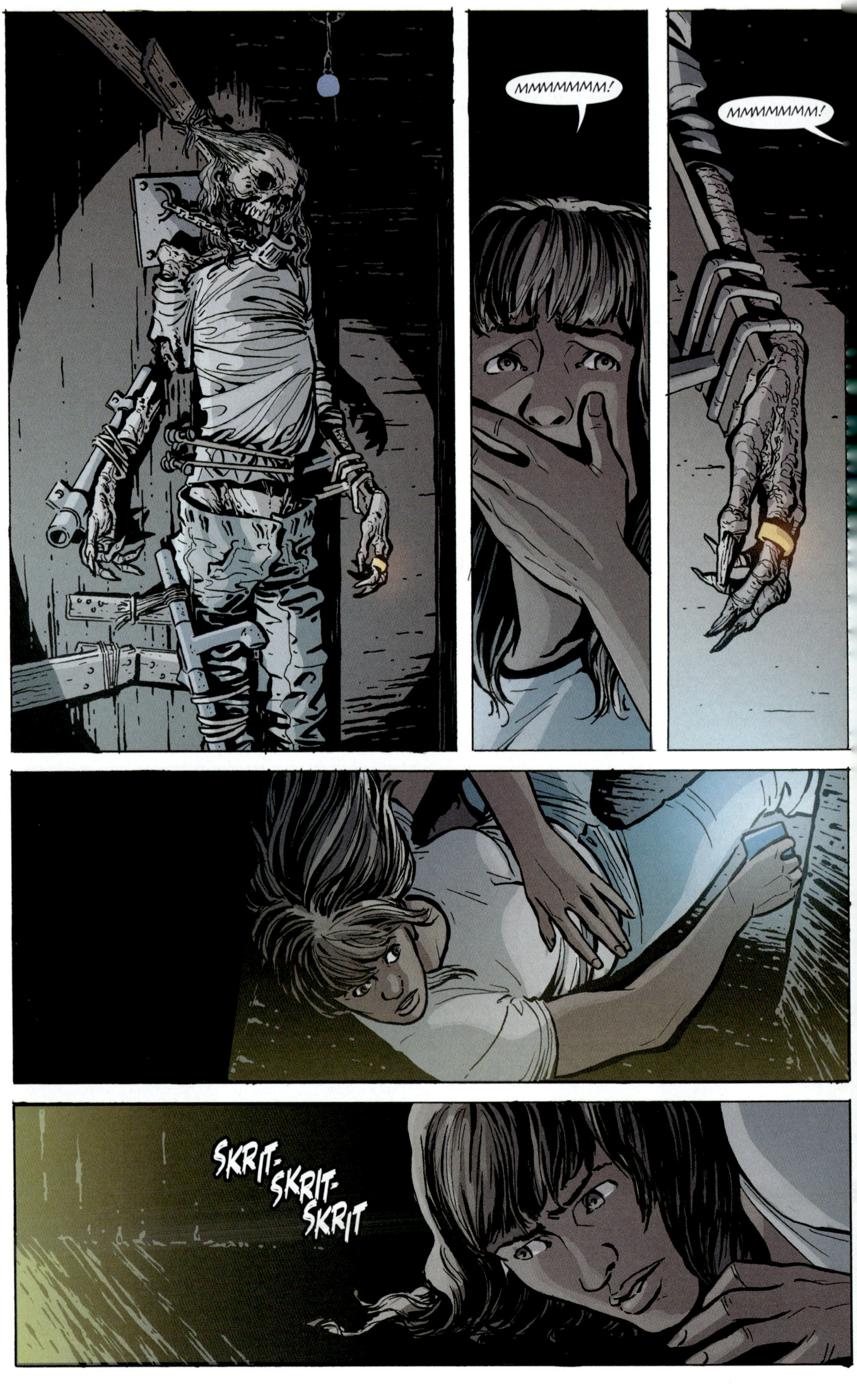
MMMMMMM!
MMMMMMM!
SKRIT-SKRIT-SKRIT

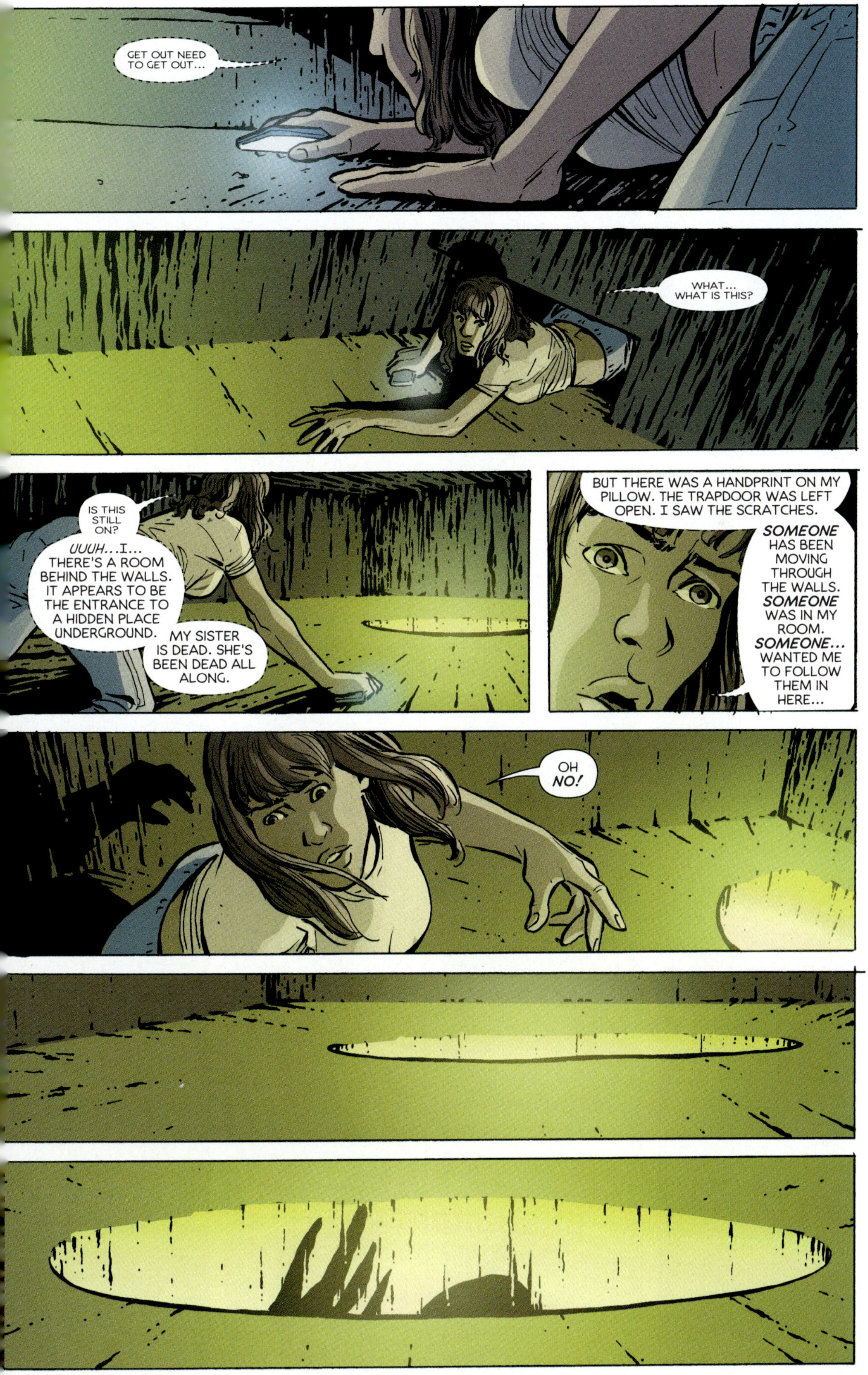
GET OUT NEED TO GET OUT...
WHAT... WHAT IS THIS?
IS THIS STILL ON?
UUUH...I... THERE'S A ROOM BEHIND THE WALLS. IT APPEARS TO BE THE ENTRANCE TO A HIDDEN PLACE UNDERGROUND.
MY SISTER IS DEAD. SHE'S BEEN DEAD ALL ALONG.
BUT THERE WAS A HANDPRINT ON MY PILLOW. THE TRAPDOOR WAS LEFT OPEN. I SAW THE SCRATCHES.
SOMEONE HAS BEEN MOVING THROUGH THE WALLS. SOMEONE WAS IN MY ROOM. SOMEONE... WANTED ME TO FOLLOW THEM IN HERE...
OH NO!

HFF!
HFF!
THUMM
THUMM
COME ON, COME ON!
IT'S FINCH!

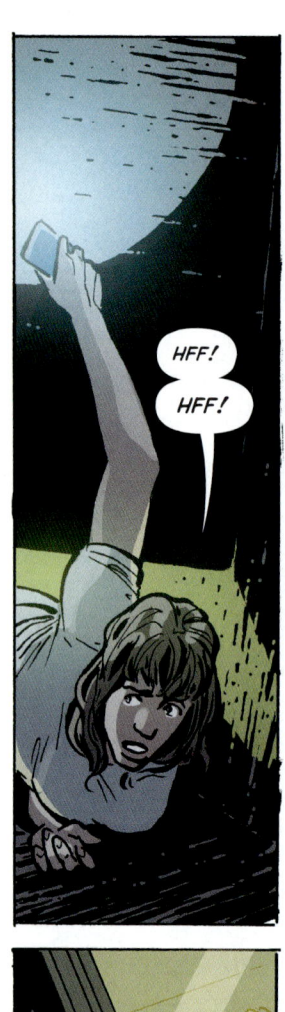

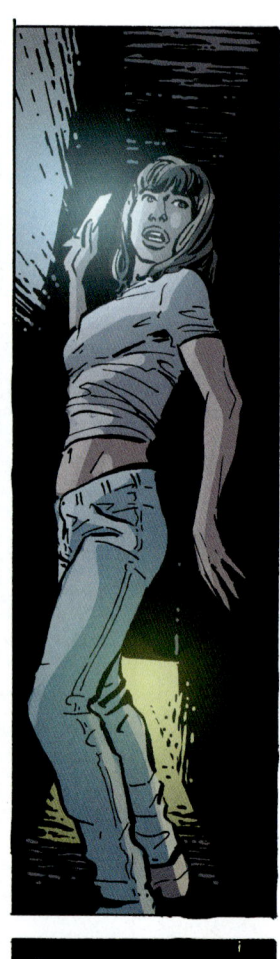

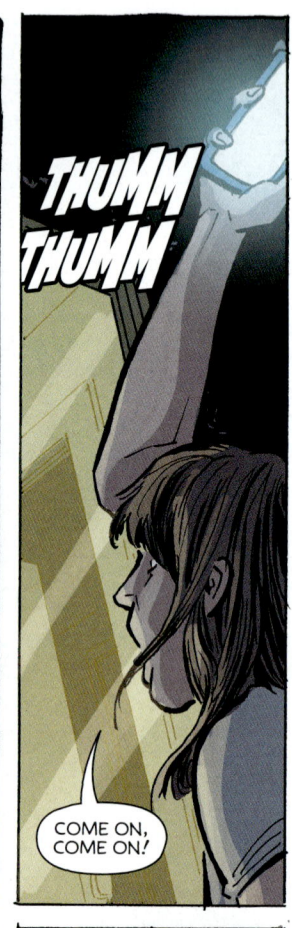

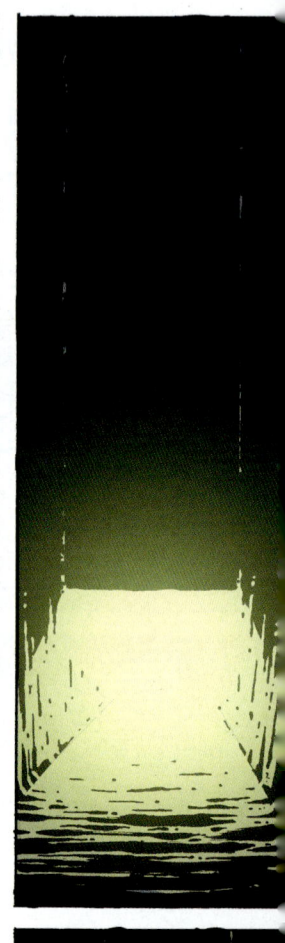

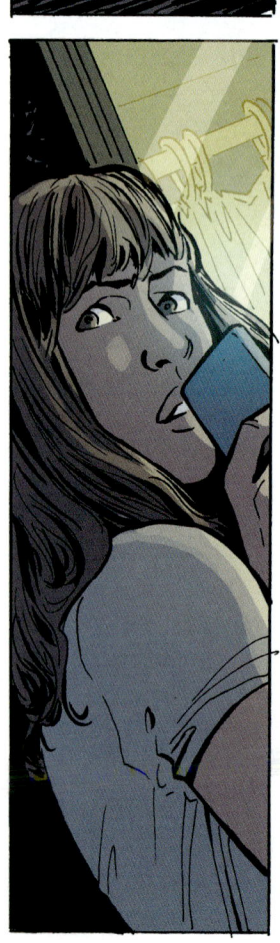

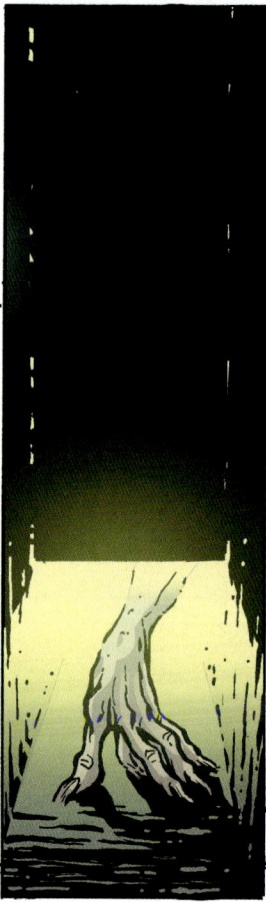

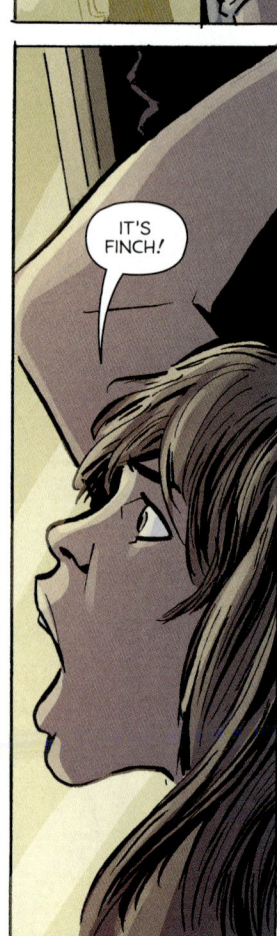

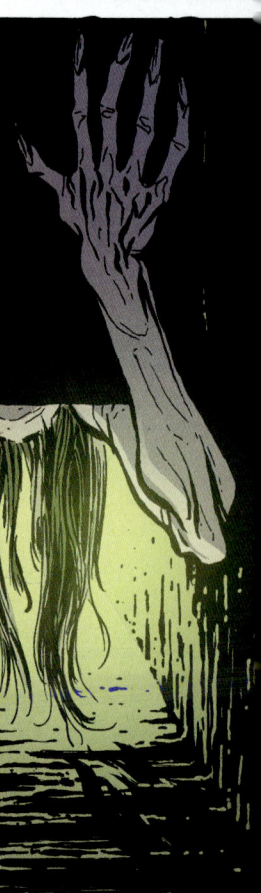

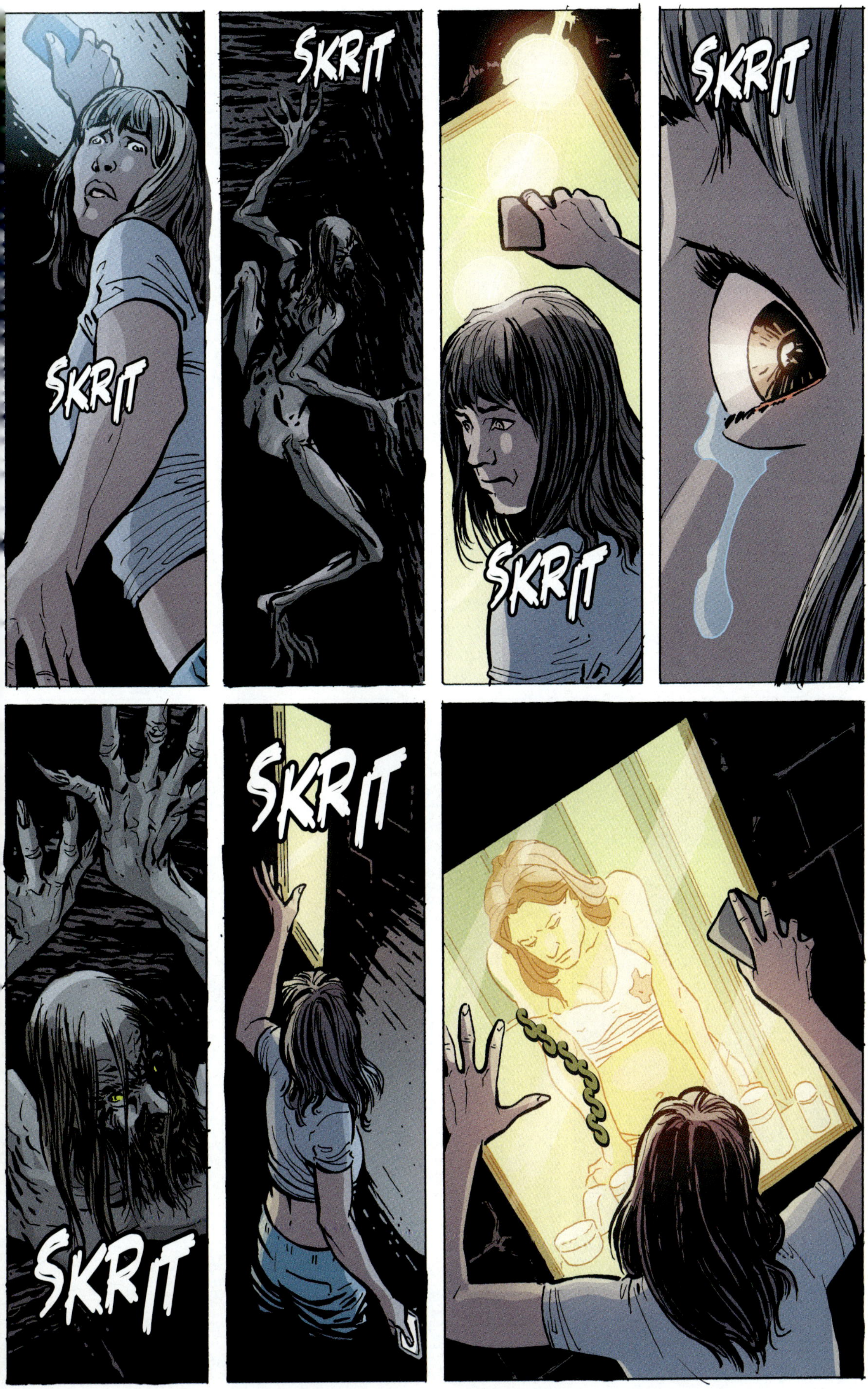
SKRIT
SKRIT
SKRIT
SKRIT
SKRIT
SKRIT

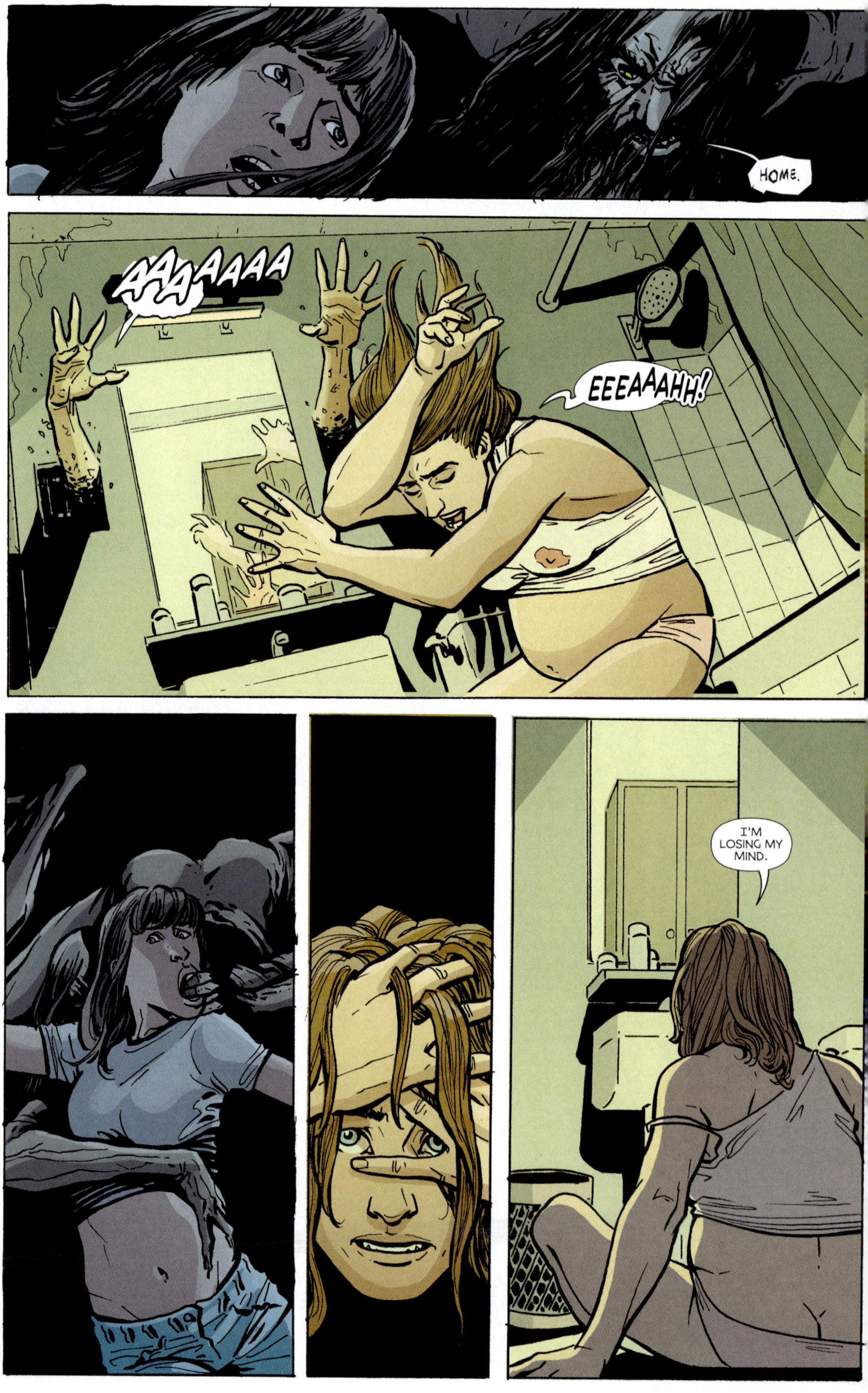
HOME.
AAAAAAA
EEEAAAHH!
I'M LOSING MY MIND.

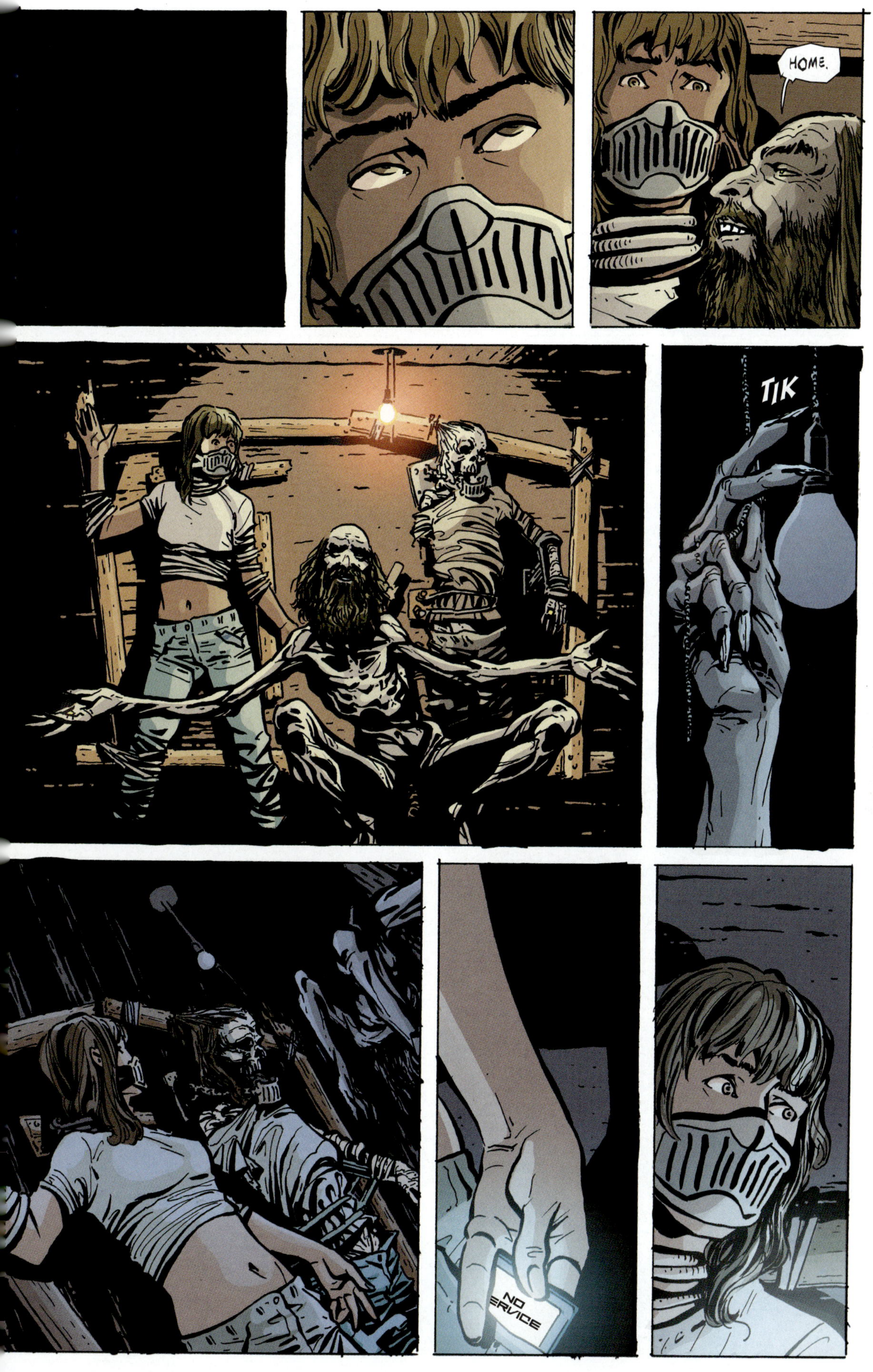
HOME.
TIK
NO SERVICE

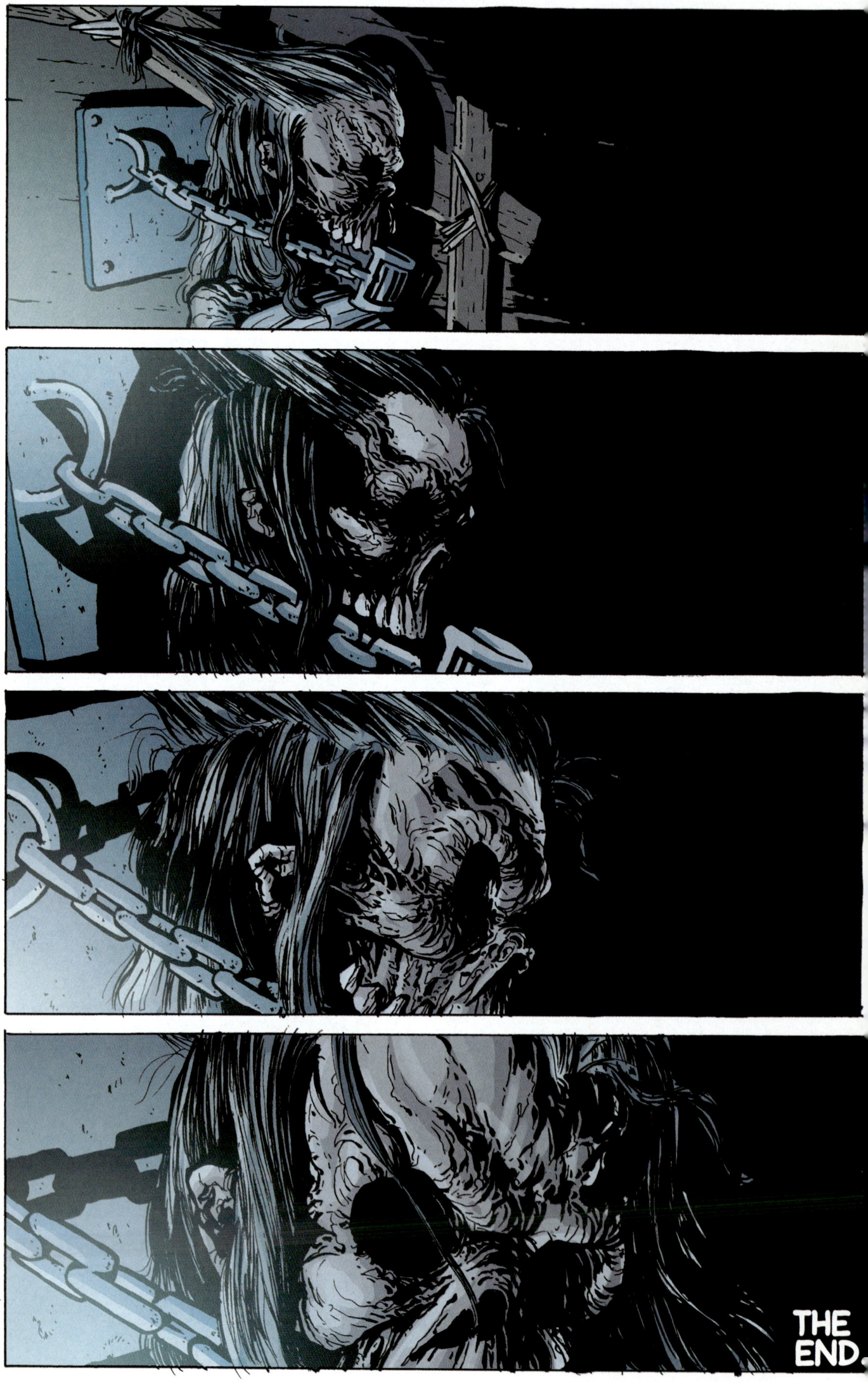
THE END.

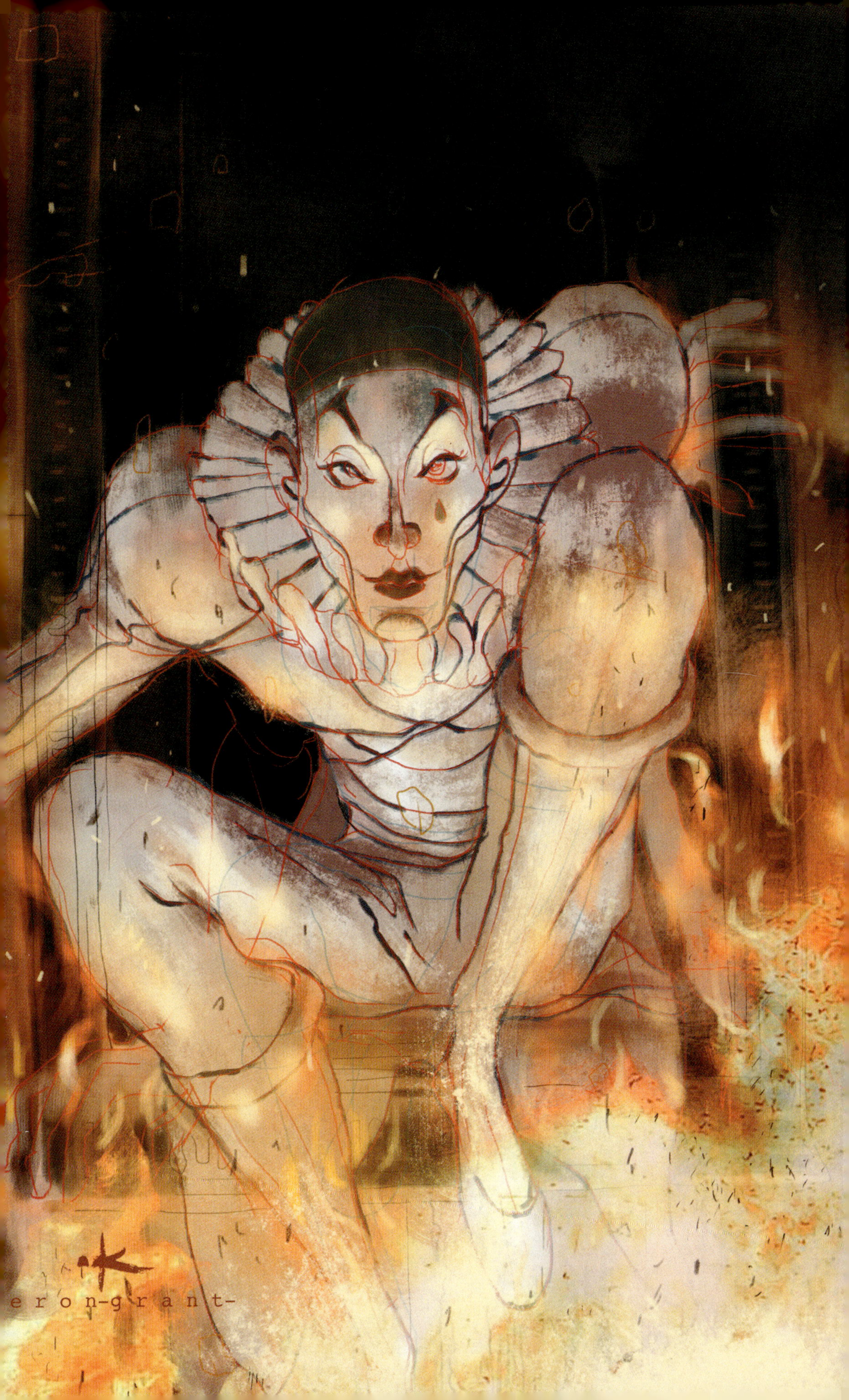
e r o n - g r a n t -

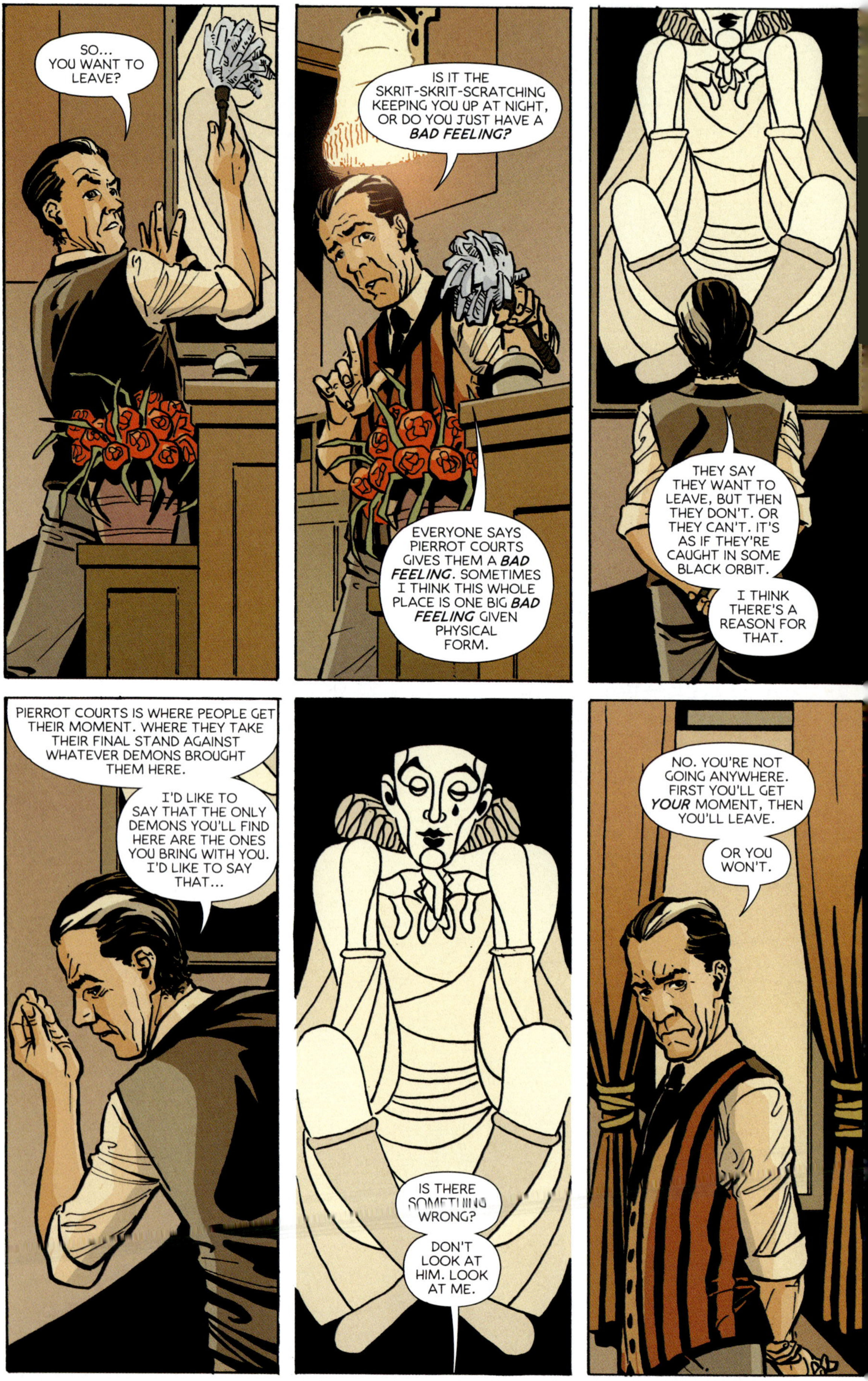
SO... YOU WANT TO LEAVE?
IS IT THE SKRIT-SKRIT-SCRATCHING KEEPING YOU UP AT NIGHT, OR DO YOU JUST HAVE A *BAD FEELING?*
EVERYONE SAYS PIERROT COURTS GIVES THEM A *BAD FEELING*. SOMETIMES I THINK THIS WHOLE PLACE IS ONE BIG *BAD FEELING* GIVEN PHYSICAL FORM.
THEY SAY THEY WANT TO LEAVE, BUT THEN THEY DON'T. OR THEY CAN'T. IT'S AS IF THEY'RE CAUGHT IN SOME BLACK ORBIT.
I THINK THERE'S A REASON FOR THAT.
PIERROT COURTS IS WHERE PEOPLE GET THEIR MOMENT. WHERE THEY TAKE THEIR FINAL STAND AGAINST WHATEVER DEMONS BROUGHT THEM HERE.
I'D LIKE TO SAY THAT THE ONLY DEMONS YOU'LL FIND HERE ARE THE ONES YOU BRING WITH YOU. I'D LIKE TO SAY THAT...
IS THERE SOMETHING WRONG?
DON'T LOOK AT HIM. LOOK AT ME.
NO. YOU'RE NOT GOING ANYWHERE. FIRST YOU'LL GET *YOUR* MOMENT, THEN YOU'LL LEAVE.
OR YOU WON'T.

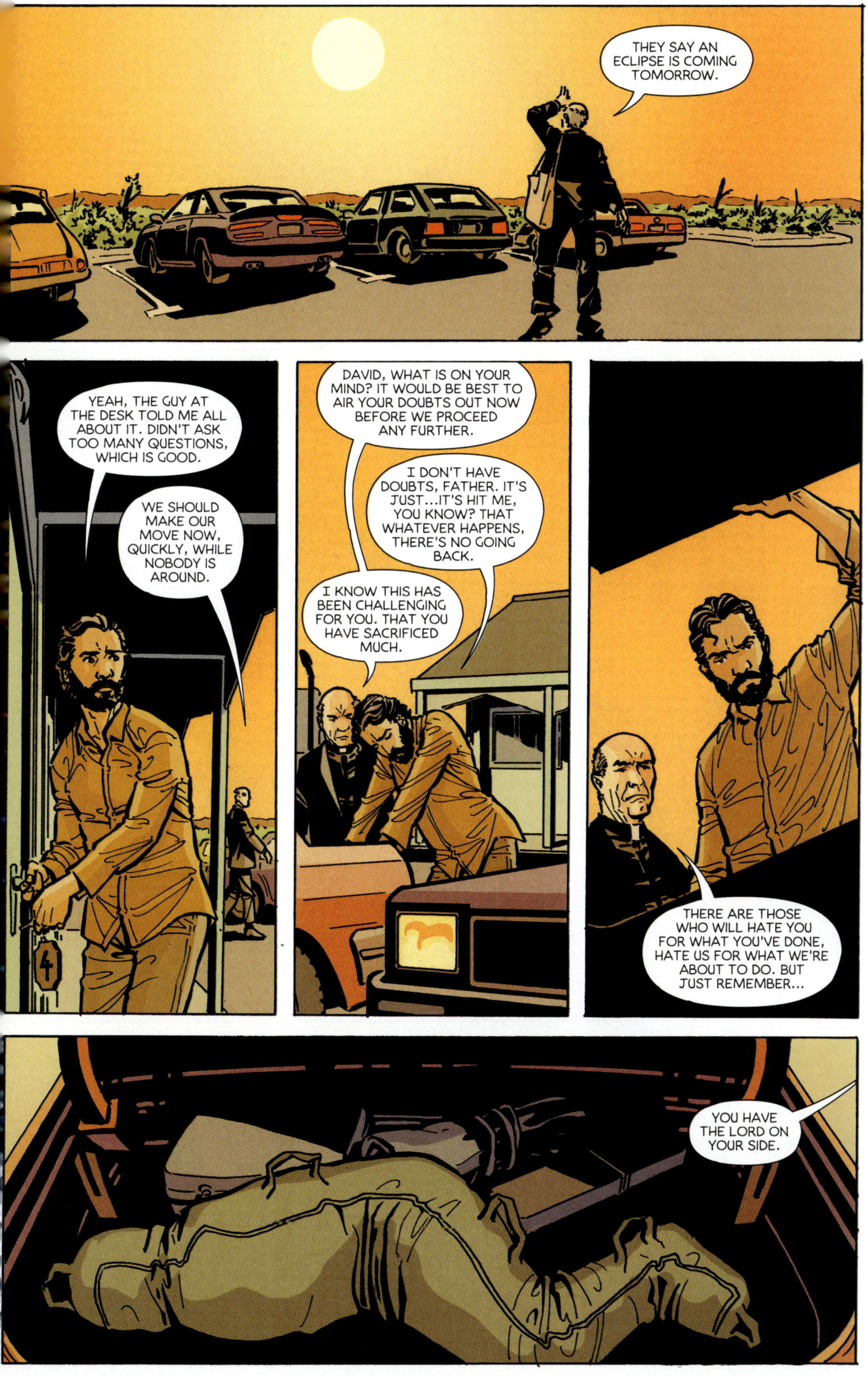
THEY SAY AN ECLIPSE IS COMING TOMORROW.
YEAH, THE GUY AT THE DESK TOLD ME ALL ABOUT IT. DIDN'T ASK TOO MANY QUESTIONS, WHICH IS GOOD.
WE SHOULD MAKE OUR MOVE NOW, QUICKLY, WHILE NOBODY IS AROUND.
DAVID, WHAT IS ON YOUR MIND? IT WOULD BE BEST TO AIR YOUR DOUBTS OUT NOW BEFORE WE PROCEED ANY FURTHER.
I DON'T HAVE DOUBTS, FATHER. IT'S JUST...IT'S HIT ME, YOU KNOW? THAT WHATEVER HAPPENS, THERE'S NO GOING BACK.
I KNOW THIS HAS BEEN CHALLENGING FOR YOU. THAT YOU HAVE SACRIFICED MUCH.
THERE ARE THOSE WHO WILL HATE YOU FOR WHAT YOU'VE DONE, HATE US FOR WHAT WE'RE ABOUT TO DO. BUT JUST REMEMBER...
YOU HAVE THE LORD ON YOUR SIDE.

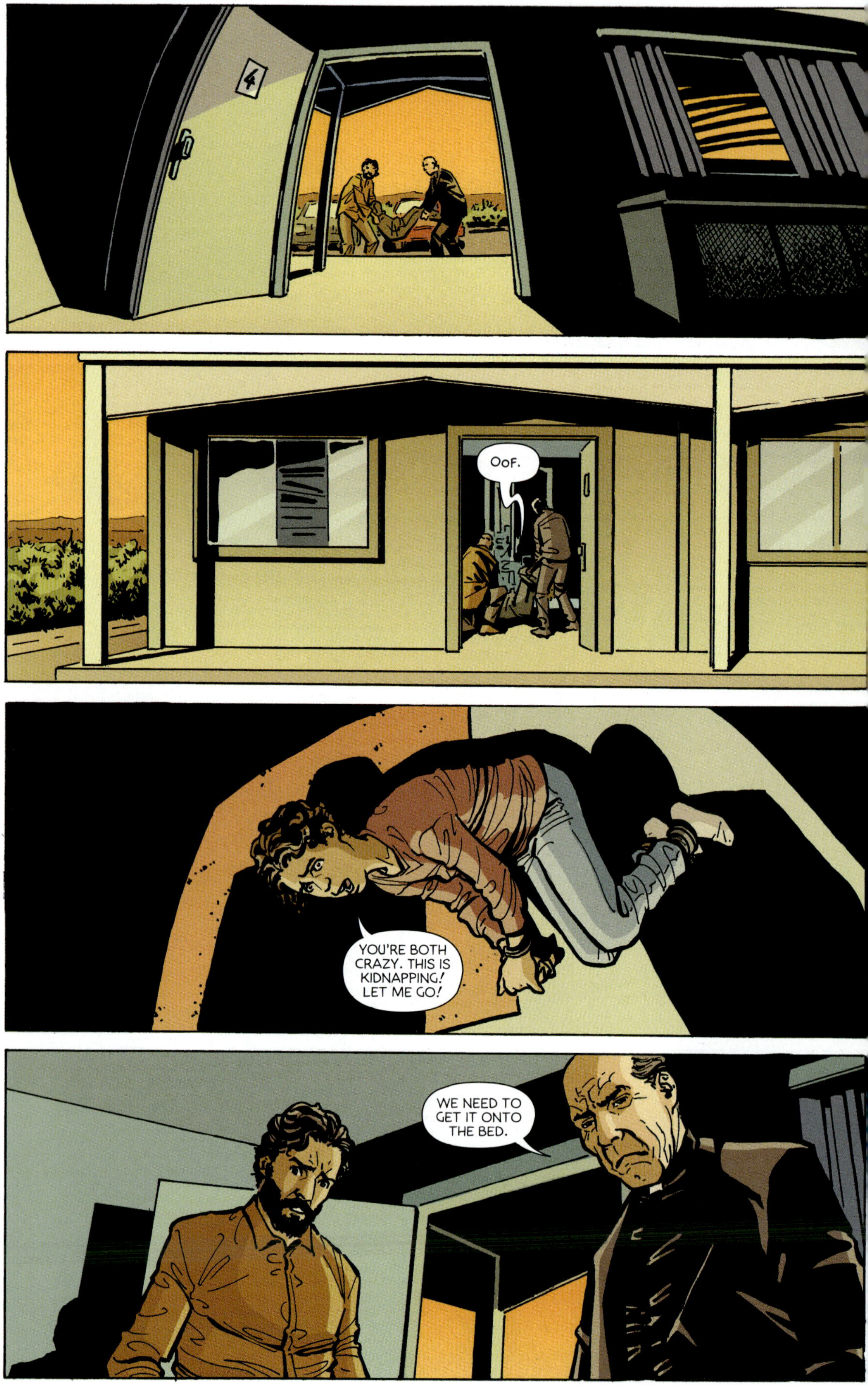
OoF.
YOU'RE BOTH CRAZY. THIS IS KIDNAPPING! LET ME GO!
WE NEED TO GET IT ONTO THE BED.

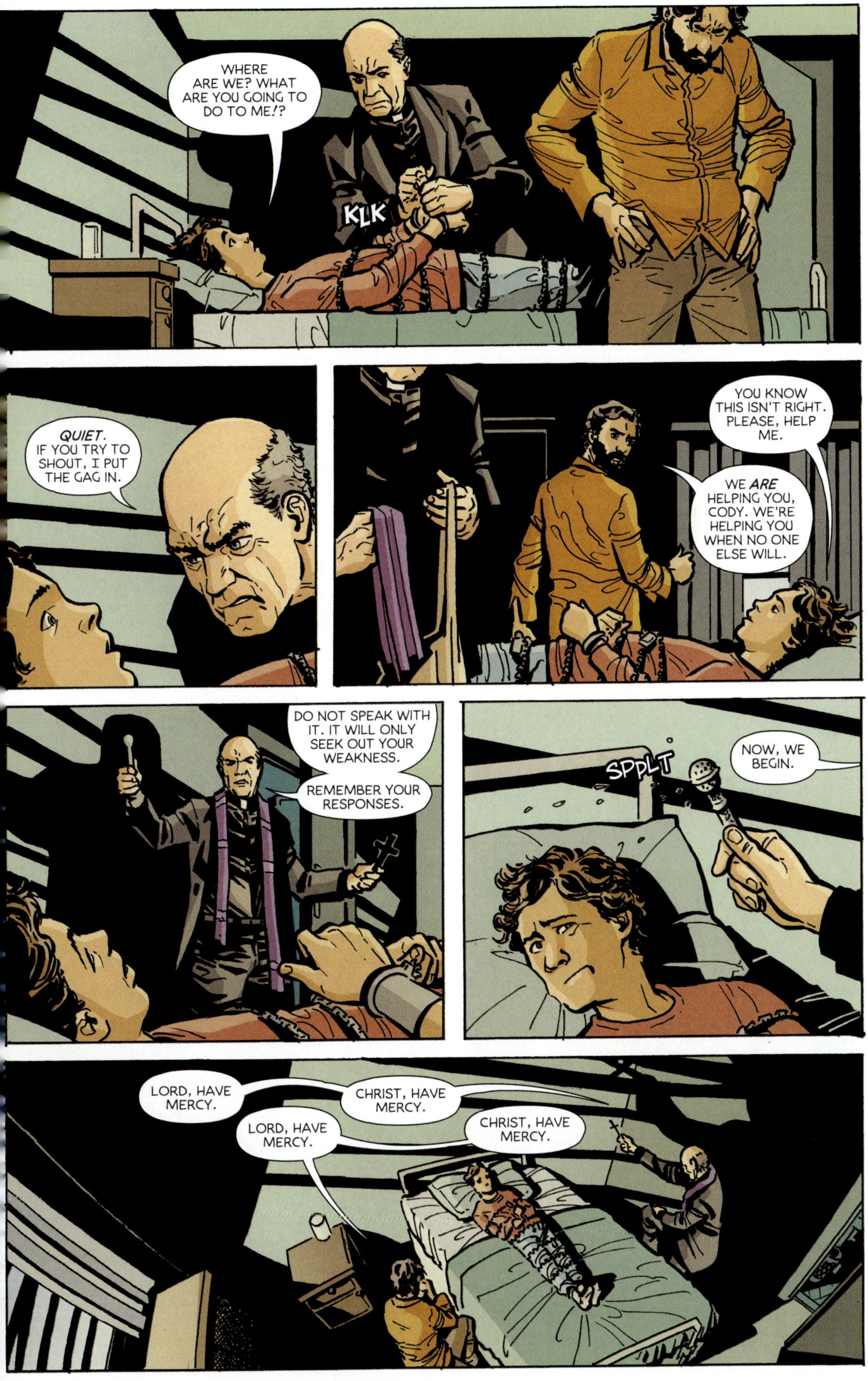

WHERE ARE WE? WHAT ARE YOU GOING TO DO TO ME!?
KLK
QUIET. IF YOU TRY TO SHOUT, I PUT THE GAG IN.
YOU KNOW THIS ISN'T RIGHT. PLEASE, HELP ME.
WE ARE HELPING YOU, CODY. WE'RE HELPING YOU WHEN NO ONE ELSE WILL.
DO NOT SPEAK WITH IT. IT WILL ONLY SEEK OUT YOUR WEAKNESS.
REMEMBER YOUR RESPONSES.
SPPLT
NOW, WE BEGIN.
LORD, HAVE MERCY.
LORD, HAVE MERCY.
CHRIST, HAVE MERCY.
CHRIST, HAVE MERCY.

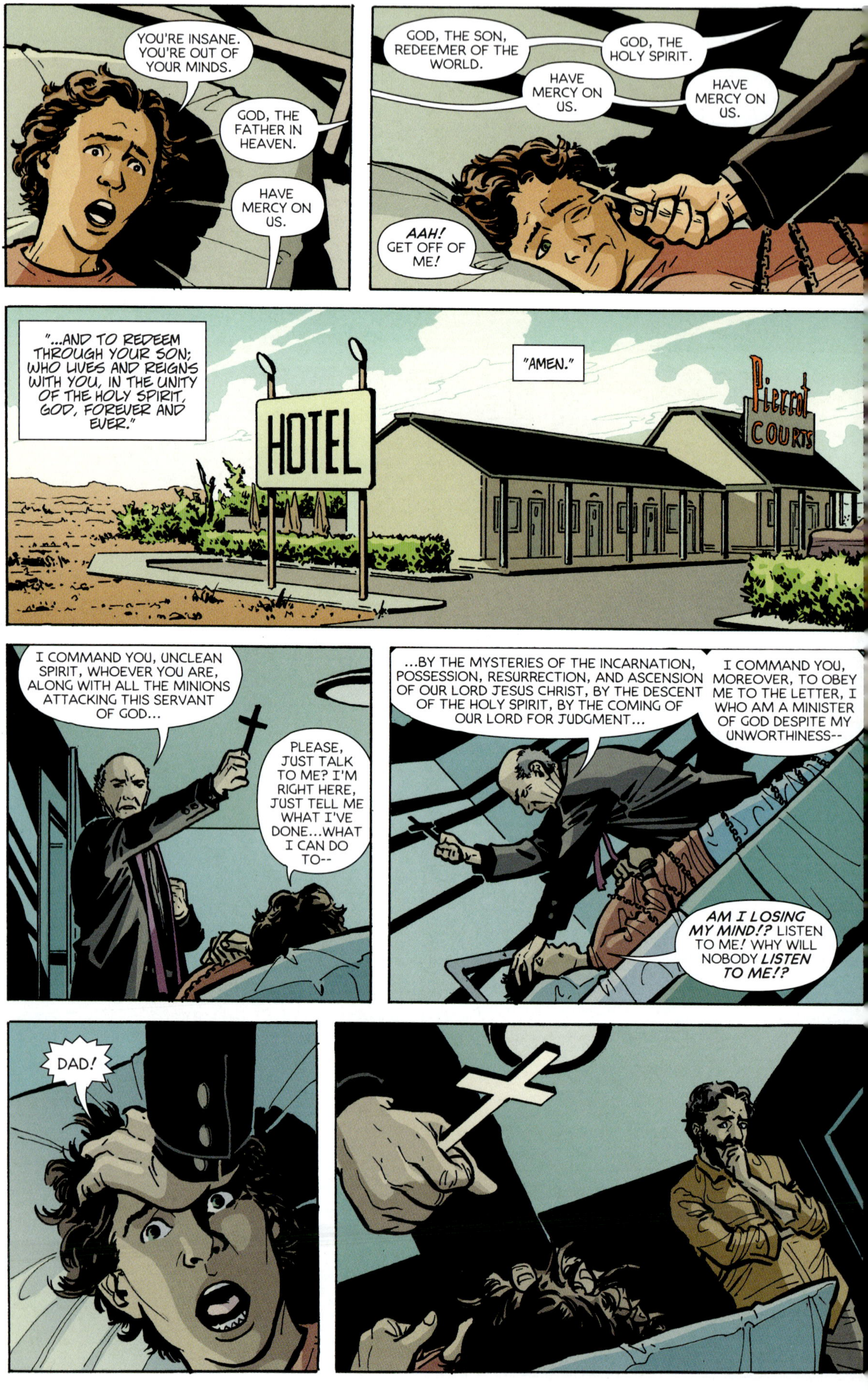
YOU'RE INSANE. YOU'RE OUT OF YOUR MINDS.
GOD, THE FATHER IN HEAVEN.
HAVE MERCY ON US.
GOD, THE SON, REDEEMER OF THE WORLD.
HAVE MERCY ON US.
GOD, THE HOLY SPIRIT.
HAVE MERCY ON US.
AAH! GET OFF OF ME!
"...AND TO REDEEM THROUGH YOUR SON; WHO LIVES AND REIGNS WITH YOU, IN THE UNITY OF THE HOLY SPIRIT, GOD, FOREVER AND EVER."
HOTEL
"AMEN."
Pierrot COURTS
I COMMAND YOU, UNCLEAN SPIRIT, WHOEVER YOU ARE, ALONG WITH ALL THE MINIONS ATTACKING THIS SERVANT OF GOD...
PLEASE, JUST TALK TO ME? I'M RIGHT HERE, JUST TELL ME WHAT I'VE DONE...WHAT I CAN DO TO--
...BY THE MYSTERIES OF THE INCARNATION, POSSESSION, RESURRECTION, AND ASCENSION OF OUR LORD JESUS CHRIST, BY THE DESCENT OF THE HOLY SPIRIT, BY THE COMING OF OUR LORD FOR JUDGMENT...
I COMMAND YOU, MOREOVER, TO OBEY ME TO THE LETTER, I WHO AM A MINISTER OF GOD DESPITE MY UNWORTHINESS--
AM I LOSING MY MIND!? LISTEN TO ME! WHY WILL NOBODY LISTEN TO ME!?
DAD!

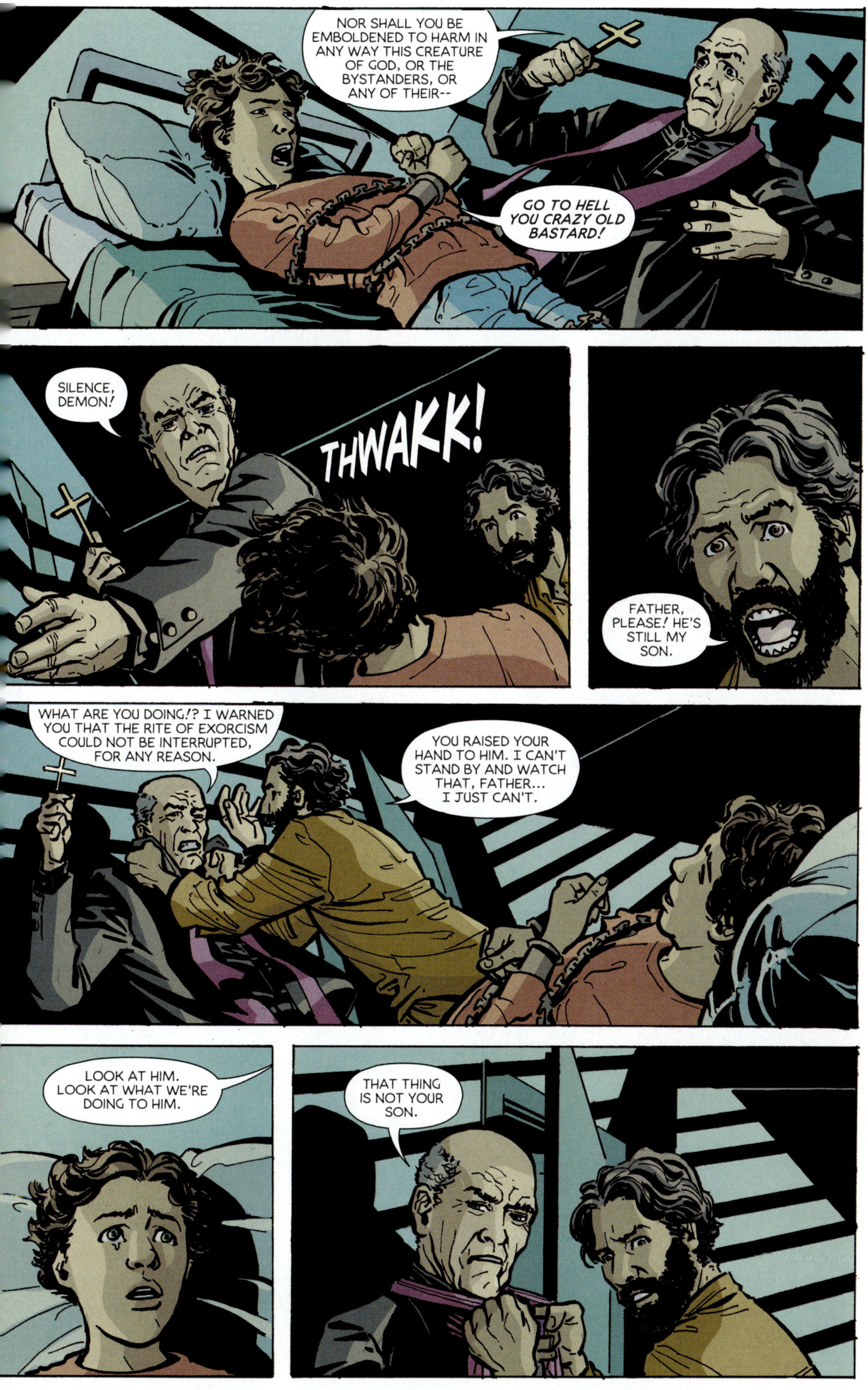
NOR SHALL YOU BE EMBOLDENED TO HARM IN ANY WAY THIS CREATURE OF GOD, OR THE BYSTANDERS, OR ANY OF THEIR--
GO TO HELL YOU CRAZY OLD BASTARD!
SILENCE, DEMON!
THWAKK!
FATHER, PLEASE! HE'S STILL MY SON.
WHAT ARE YOU DOING!? I WARNED YOU THAT THE RITE OF EXORCISM COULD NOT BE INTERRUPTED, FOR ANY REASON.
YOU RAISED YOUR HAND TO HIM. I CAN'T STAND BY AND WATCH THAT, FATHER... I JUST CAN'T.
LOOK AT HIM. LOOK AT WHAT WE'RE DOING TO HIM.
THAT THING IS NOT YOUR SON.

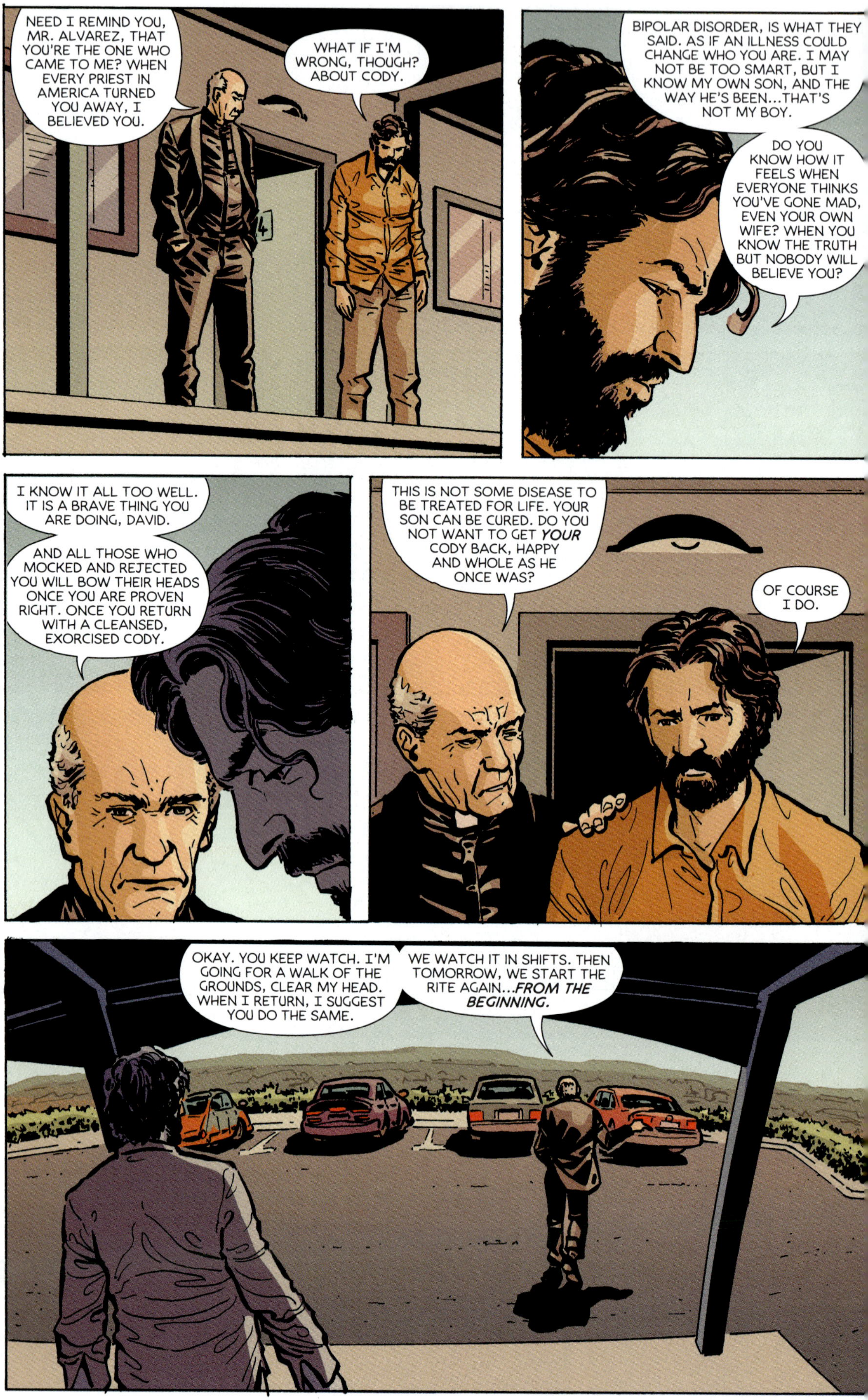
NEED I REMIND YOU, MR. ALVAREZ, THAT YOU'RE THE ONE WHO CAME TO ME? WHEN EVERY PRIEST IN AMERICA TURNED YOU AWAY, I BELIEVED YOU.
WHAT IF I'M WRONG, THOUGH? ABOUT CODY.
BIPOLAR DISORDER, IS WHAT THEY SAID. AS IF AN ILLNESS COULD CHANGE WHO YOU ARE. I MAY NOT BE TOO SMART, BUT I KNOW MY OWN SON, AND THE WAY HE'S BEEN...THAT'S NOT MY BOY.
DO YOU KNOW HOW IT FEELS WHEN EVERYONE THINKS YOU'VE GONE MAD, EVEN YOUR OWN WIFE? WHEN YOU KNOW THE TRUTH BUT NOBODY WILL BELIEVE YOU?
I KNOW IT ALL TOO WELL. IT IS A BRAVE THING YOU ARE DOING, DAVID.
AND ALL THOSE WHO MOCKED AND REJECTED YOU WILL BOW THEIR HEADS ONCE YOU ARE PROVEN RIGHT. ONCE YOU RETURN WITH A CLEANSED, EXORCISED CODY.
THIS IS NOT SOME DISEASE TO BE TREATED FOR LIFE. YOUR SON CAN BE CURED. DO YOU NOT WANT TO GET *YOUR* CODY BACK, HAPPY AND WHOLE AS HE ONCE WAS?
OF COURSE I DO.
OKAY. YOU KEEP WATCH. I'M GOING FOR A WALK OF THE GROUNDS, CLEAR MY HEAD. WHEN I RETURN, I SUGGEST YOU DO THE SAME.
WE WATCH IT IN SHIFTS. THEN TOMORROW, WE START THE RITE AGAIN...***FROM THE BEGINNING.***

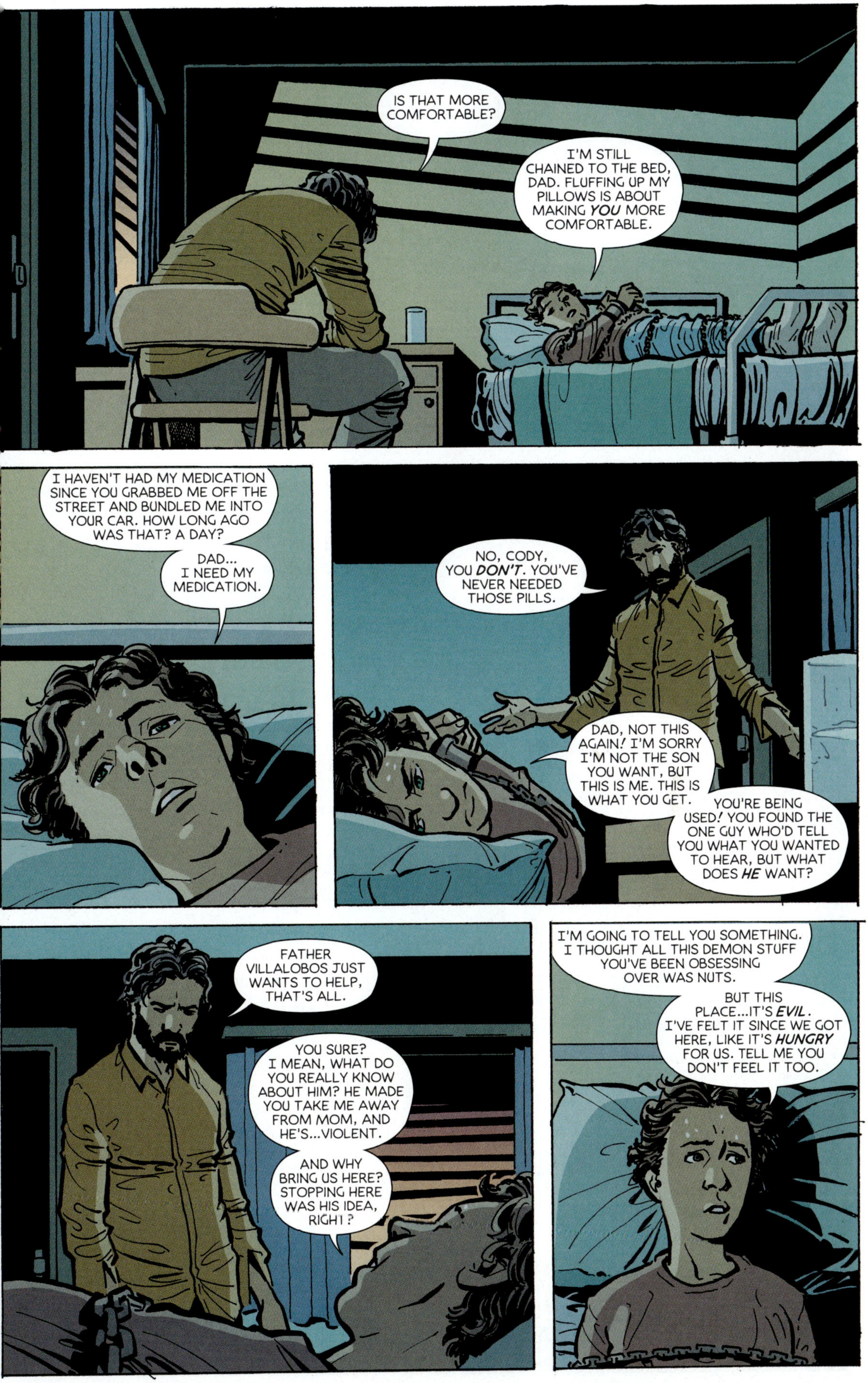
IS THAT MORE COMFORTABLE?
I'M STILL CHAINED TO THE BED, DAD. FLUFFING UP MY PILLOWS IS ABOUT MAKING *YOU* MORE COMFORTABLE.
I HAVEN'T HAD MY MEDICATION SINCE YOU GRABBED ME OFF THE STREET AND BUNDLED ME INTO YOUR CAR. HOW LONG AGO WAS THAT? A DAY?
DAD... I NEED MY MEDICATION.
NO, CODY, YOU ***DON'T***. YOU'VE NEVER NEEDED THOSE PILLS.
DAD, NOT THIS AGAIN! I'M SORRY I'M NOT THE SON YOU WANT, BUT THIS IS ME. THIS IS WHAT YOU GET.
YOU'RE BEING USED! YOU FOUND THE ONE GUY WHO'D TELL YOU WHAT YOU WANTED TO HEAR, BUT WHAT DOES *HE* WANT?
FATHER VILLALOBOS JUST WANTS TO HELP, THAT'S ALL.
YOU SURE? I MEAN, WHAT DO YOU REALLY KNOW ABOUT HIM? HE MADE YOU TAKE ME AWAY FROM MOM, AND HE'S...VIOLENT.
AND WHY BRING US HERE? STOPPING HERE WAS HIS IDEA, RIGHT?
I'M GOING TO TELL YOU SOMETHING. I THOUGHT ALL THIS DEMON STUFF YOU'VE BEEN OBSESSING OVER WAS NUTS.
BUT THIS PLACE...IT'S *EVIL*. I'VE FELT IT SINCE WE GOT HERE, LIKE IT'S *HUNGRY* FOR US. TELL ME YOU DON'T FEEL IT TOO.

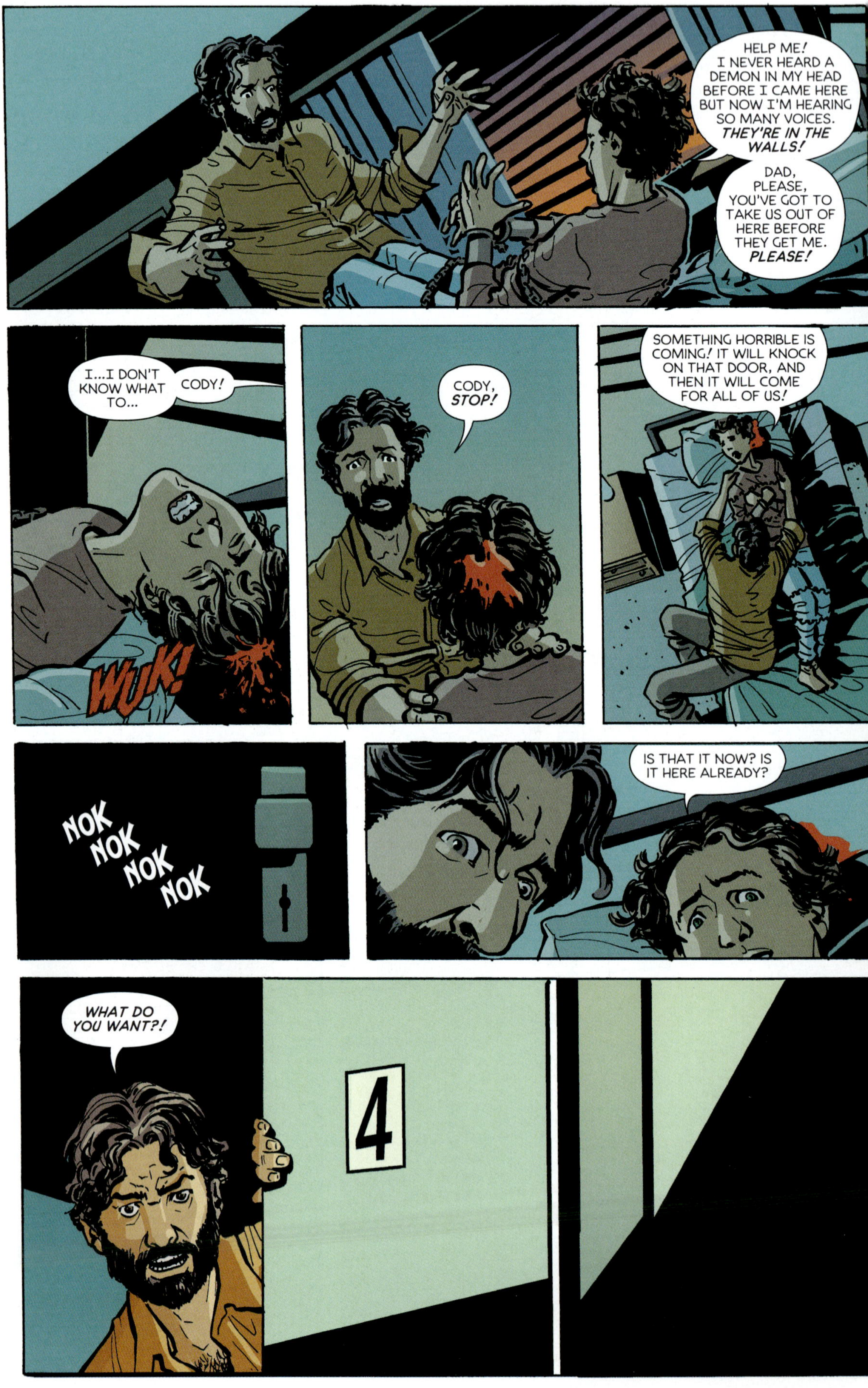
HELP ME! I NEVER HEARD A DEMON IN MY HEAD BEFORE I CAME HERE BUT NOW I'M HEARING SO MANY VOICES. THEY'RE IN THE WALLS!
DAD, PLEASE, YOU'VE GOT TO TAKE US OUT OF HERE BEFORE THEY GET ME. PLEASE!
I...I DON'T KNOW WHAT TO...
CODY!
WUK!
CODY, STOP!
SOMETHING HORRIBLE IS COMING! IT WILL KNOCK ON THAT DOOR, AND THEN IT WILL COME FOR ALL OF US!
NOK NOK NOK NOK
IS THAT IT NOW? IS IT HERE ALREADY?
WHAT DO YOU WANT?!
4

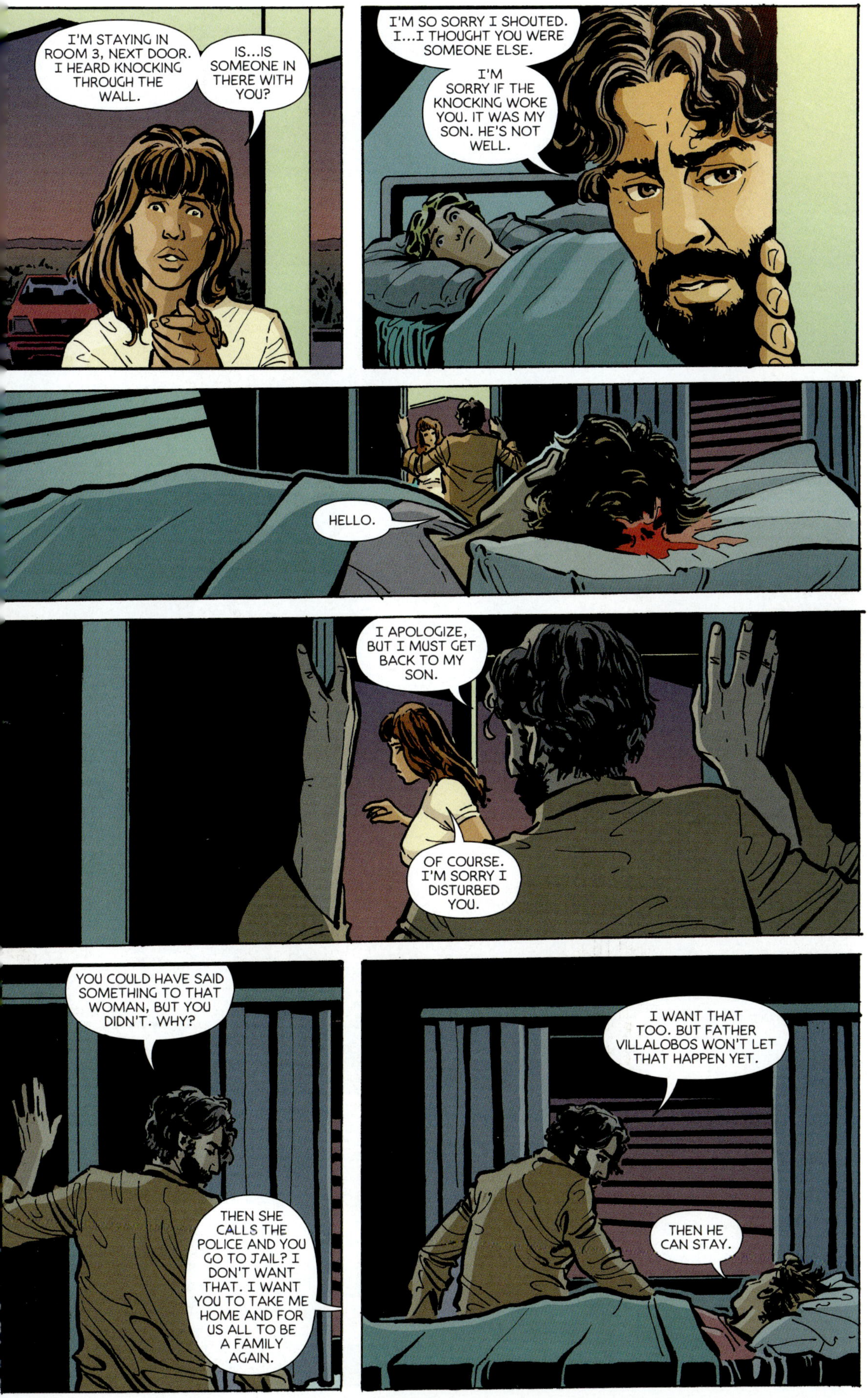
I'M STAYING IN ROOM 3, NEXT DOOR. I HEARD KNOCKING THROUGH THE WALL.
IS...IS SOMEONE IN THERE WITH YOU?
I'M SO SORRY I SHOUTED. I...I THOUGHT YOU WERE SOMEONE ELSE.
I'M SORRY IF THE KNOCKING WOKE YOU. IT WAS MY SON. HE'S NOT WELL.
HELLO.
I APOLOGIZE, BUT I MUST GET BACK TO MY SON.
OF COURSE. I'M SORRY I DISTURBED YOU.
YOU COULD HAVE SAID SOMETHING TO THAT WOMAN, BUT YOU DIDN'T. WHY?
THEN SHE CALLS THE POLICE AND YOU GO TO JAIL? I DON'T WANT THAT. I WANT YOU TO TAKE ME HOME AND FOR US ALL TO BE A FAMILY AGAIN.
I WANT THAT TOO. BUT FATHER VILLALOBOS WON'T LET THAT HAPPEN YET.
THEN HE CAN STAY.

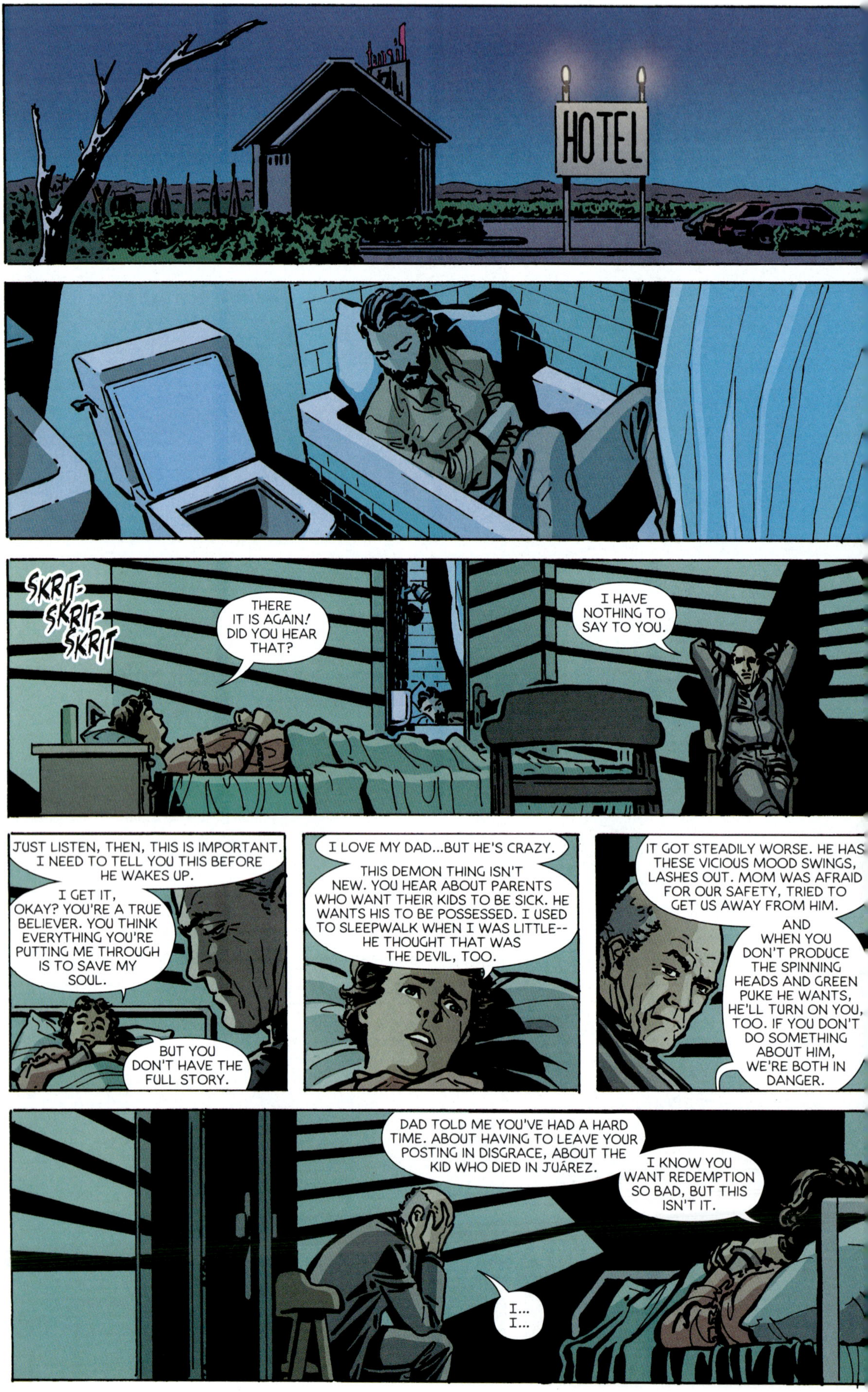
HOTEL
SKRIT-SKRIT-SKRIT
THERE IT IS AGAIN! DID YOU HEAR THAT?
I HAVE NOTHING TO SAY TO YOU.
JUST LISTEN, THEN, THIS IS IMPORTANT. I NEED TO TELL YOU THIS BEFORE HE WAKES UP.
I GET IT, OKAY? YOU'RE A TRUE BELIEVER. YOU THINK EVERYTHING YOU'RE PUTTING ME THROUGH IS TO SAVE MY SOUL.
BUT YOU DON'T HAVE THE FULL STORY.
I LOVE MY DAD...BUT HE'S CRAZY.
THIS DEMON THING ISN'T NEW. YOU HEAR ABOUT PARENTS WHO WANT THEIR KIDS TO BE SICK. HE WANTS HIS TO BE POSSESSED. I USED TO SLEEPWALK WHEN I WAS LITTLE-- HE THOUGHT THAT WAS THE DEVIL, TOO.
IT GOT STEADILY WORSE. HE HAS THESE VICIOUS MOOD SWINGS, LASHES OUT. MOM WAS AFRAID FOR OUR SAFETY, TRIED TO GET US AWAY FROM HIM.
AND WHEN YOU DON'T PRODUCE THE SPINNING HEADS AND GREEN PUKE HE WANTS, HE'LL TURN ON YOU, TOO. IF YOU DON'T DO SOMETHING ABOUT HIM, WE'RE BOTH IN DANGER.
DAD TOLD ME YOU'VE HAD A HARD TIME. ABOUT HAVING TO LEAVE YOUR POSTING IN DISGRACE, ABOUT THE KID WHO DIED IN JUÁREZ.
I KNOW YOU WANT REDEMPTION SO BAD, BUT THIS ISN'T IT.
I... I...

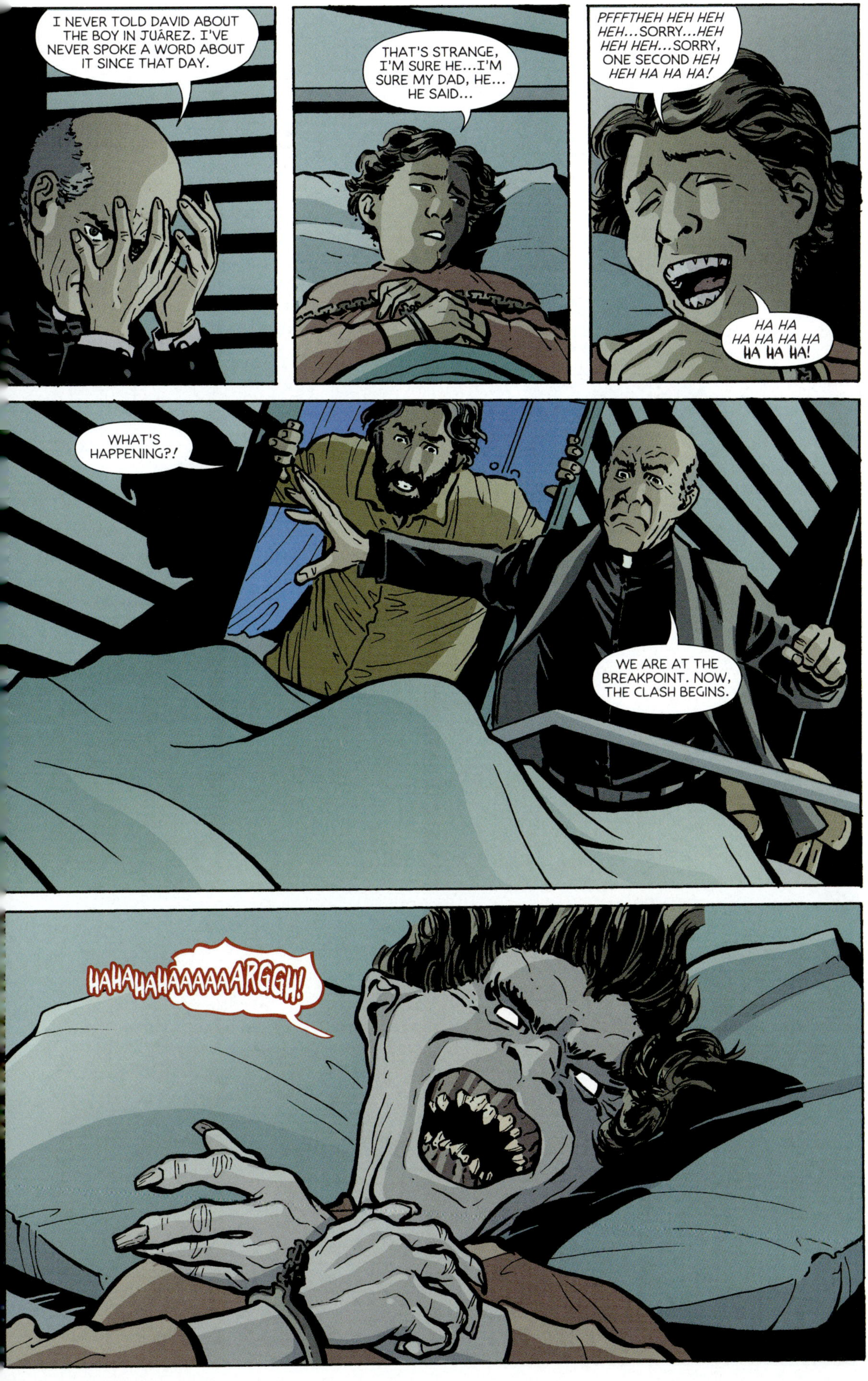
I NEVER TOLD DAVID ABOUT THE BOY IN JUÁREZ. I'VE NEVER SPOKE A WORD ABOUT IT SINCE THAT DAY.
THAT'S STRANGE, I'M SURE HE...I'M SURE MY DAD, HE... HE SAID...
PFFFTHEH HEH HEH HEH...SORRY...HEH HEH HEH...SORRY, ONE SECOND HEH HEH HA HA HA!
HA HA HA HA HA HA HA HA HA!
WHAT'S HAPPENING?!
WE ARE AT THE BREAKPOINT. NOW, THE CLASH BEGINS.
HAHAHAHAAAAAARGGH!

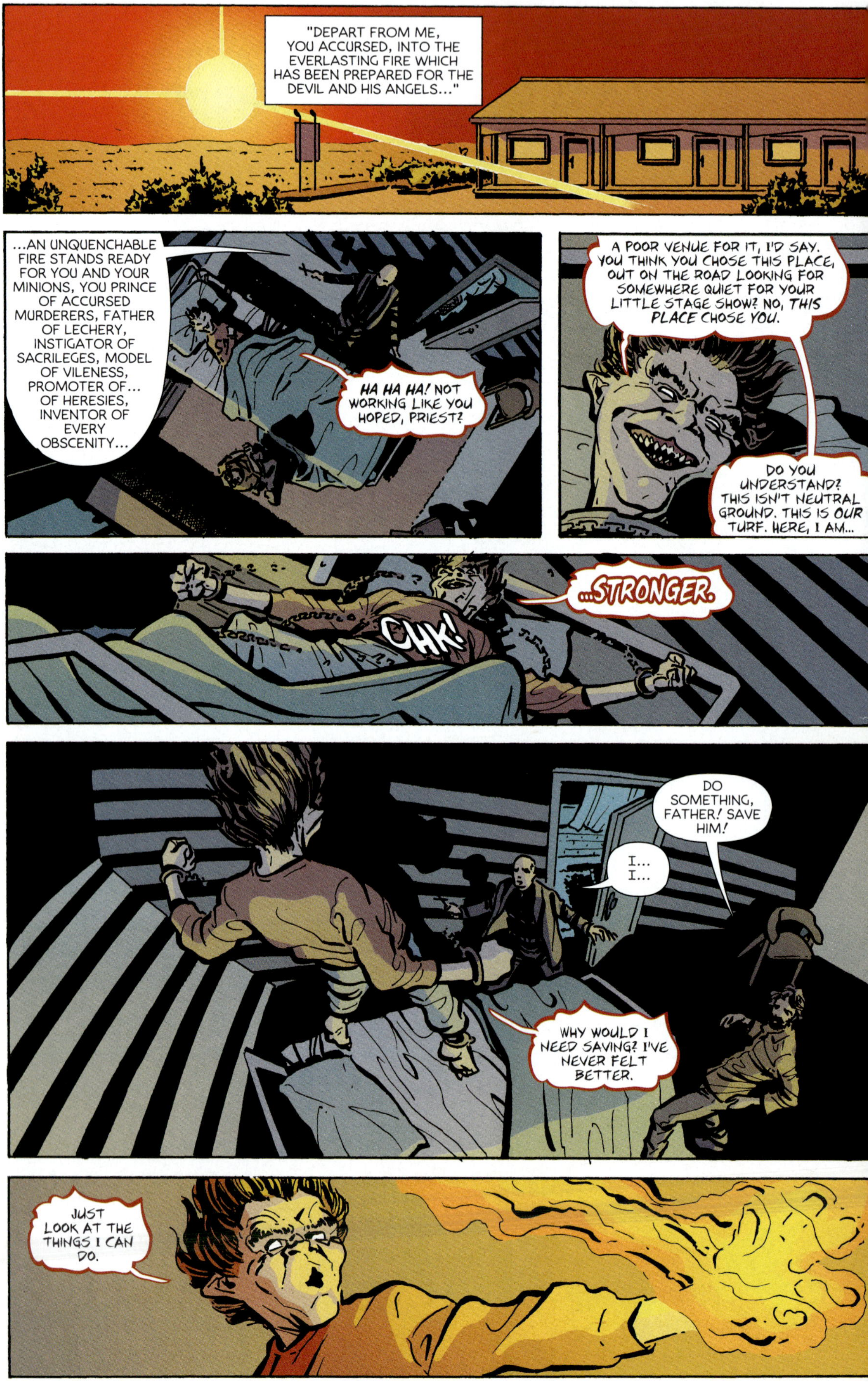
"DEPART FROM ME, YOU ACCURSED, INTO THE EVERLASTING FIRE WHICH HAS BEEN PREPARED FOR THE DEVIL AND HIS ANGELS..."
...AN UNQUENCHABLE FIRE STANDS READY FOR YOU AND YOUR MINIONS, YOU PRINCE OF ACCURSED MURDERERS, FATHER OF LECHERY, INSTIGATOR OF SACRILEGES, MODEL OF VILENESS, PROMOTER OF... OF HERESIES, INVENTOR OF EVERY OBSCENITY...
HA HA HA! NOT WORKING LIKE YOU HOPED, PRIEST?
A POOR VENUE FOR IT, I'D SAY. YOU THINK YOU CHOSE THIS PLACE, OUT ON THE ROAD LOOKING FOR SOMEWHERE QUIET FOR YOUR LITTLE STAGE SHOW? NO, THIS PLACE CHOSE YOU.
DO YOU UNDERSTAND? THIS ISN'T NEUTRAL GROUND. THIS IS OUR TURF. HERE, I AM...
...STRONGER.
CHK!
DO SOMETHING, FATHER! SAVE HIM!
I... I...
WHY WOULD I NEED SAVING? I'VE NEVER FELT BETTER.
JUST LOOK AT THE THINGS I CAN DO.

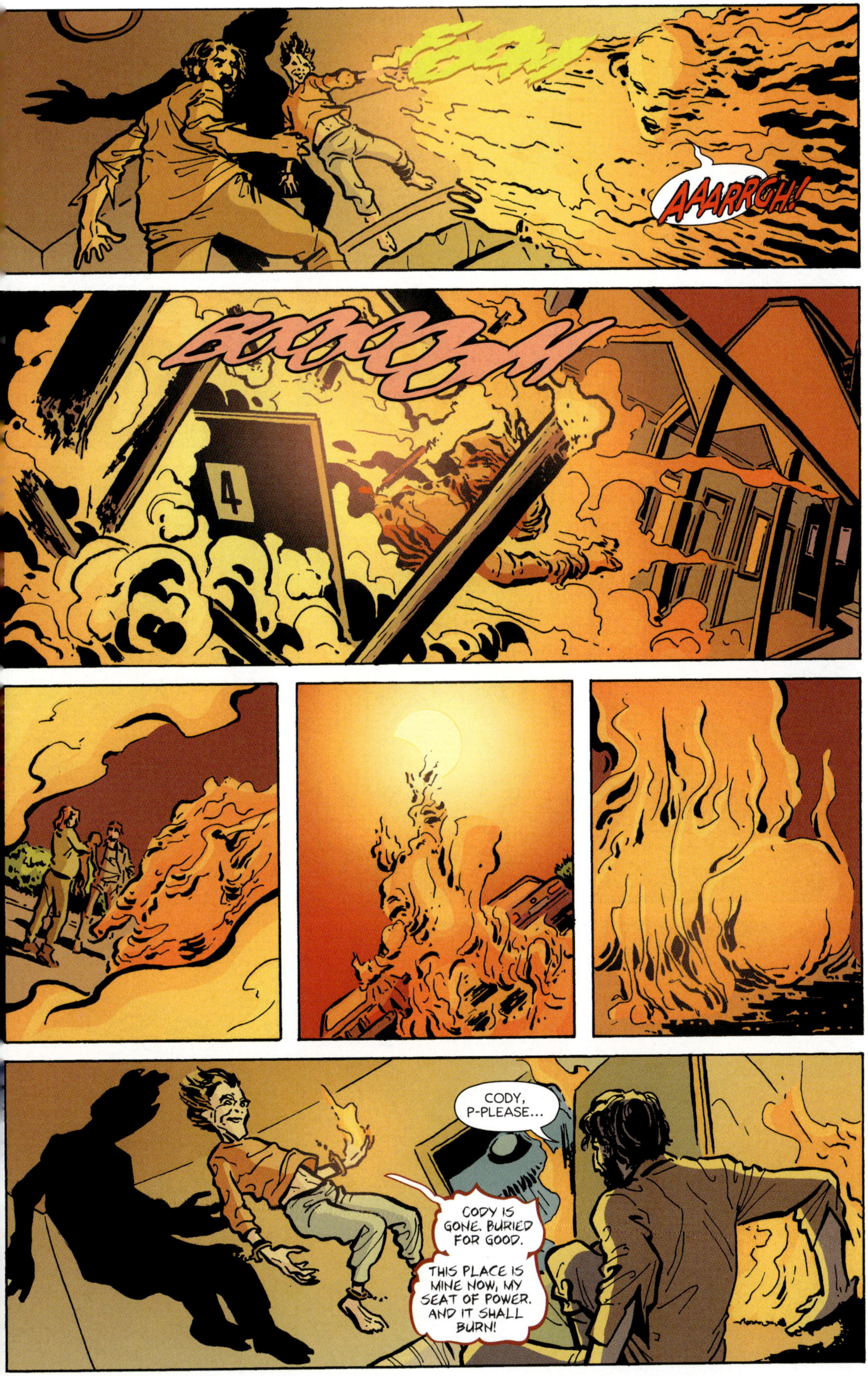
FOOM
AAARRGH!
BOOOOOM
4
CODY, P-PLEASE...
CODY IS GONE. BURIED FOR GOOD.
THIS PLACE IS MINE NOW, MY SEAT OF POWER. AND IT SHALL BURN!

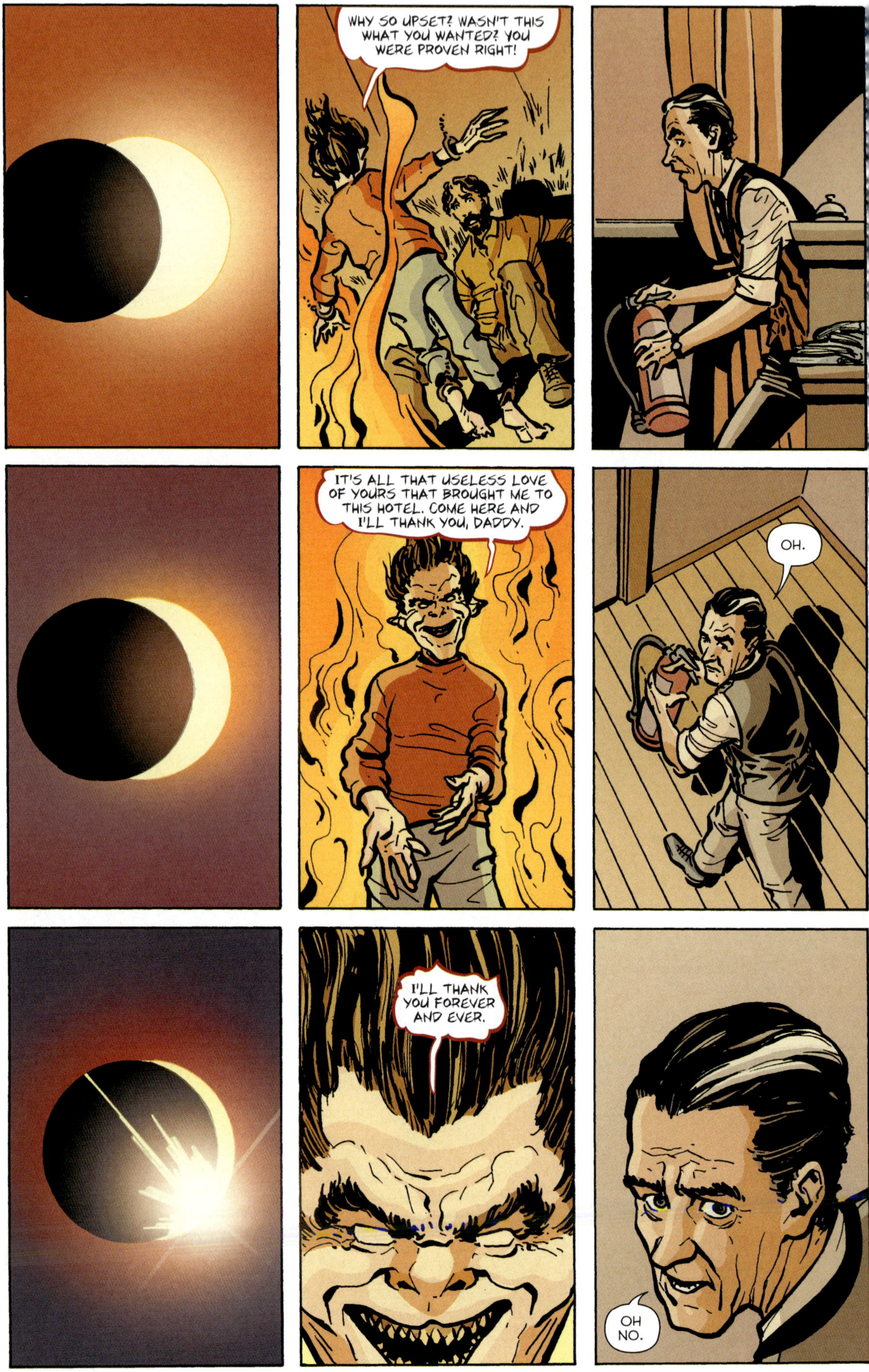
WHY SO UPSET? WASN'T THIS WHAT YOU WANTED? YOU WERE PROVEN RIGHT!
IT'S ALL THAT USELESS LOVE OF YOURS THAT BROUGHT ME TO THIS HOTEL. COME HERE AND I'LL THANK YOU, DADDY.
OH.
I'LL THANK YOU FOREVER AND EVER.
OH NO.

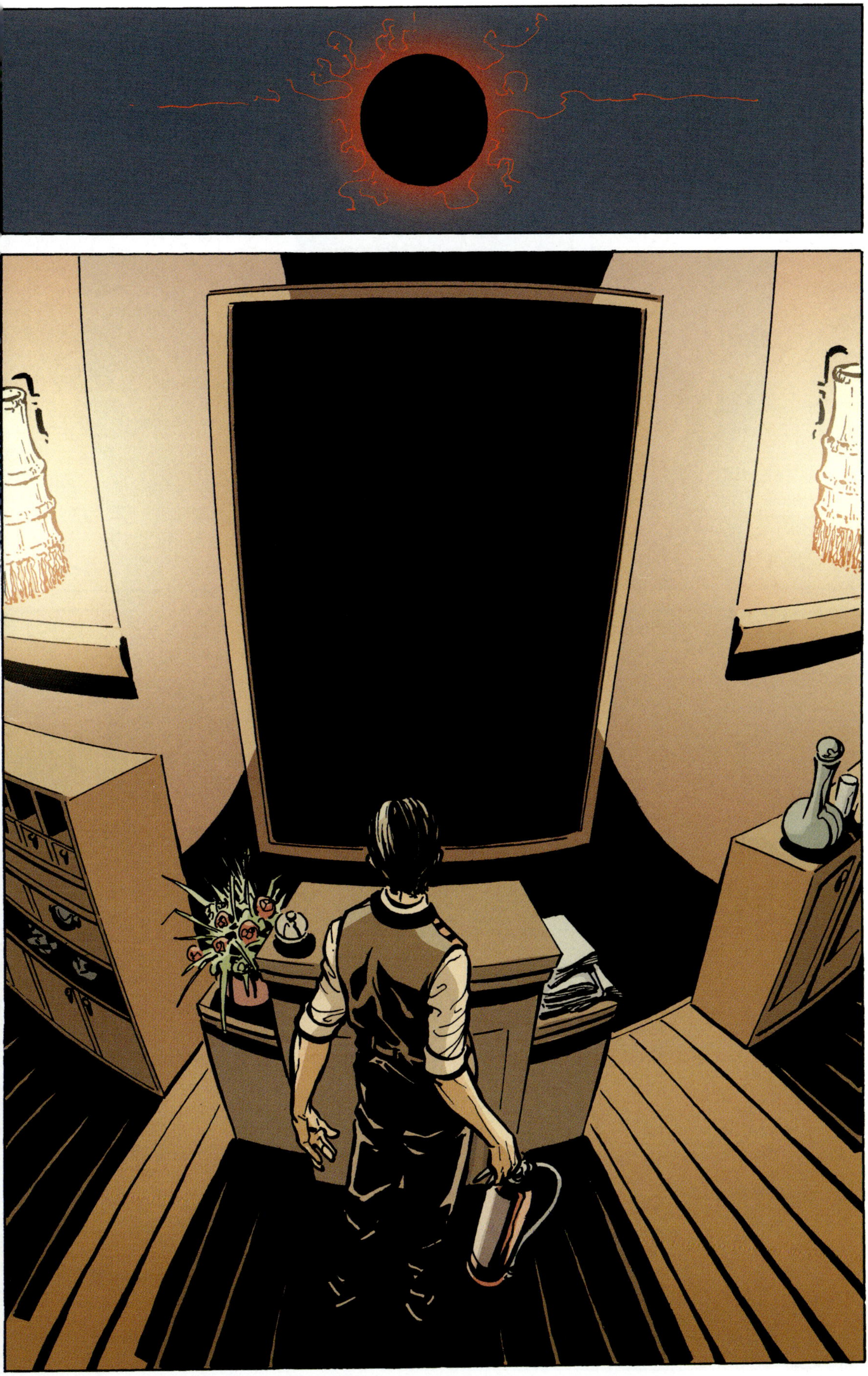

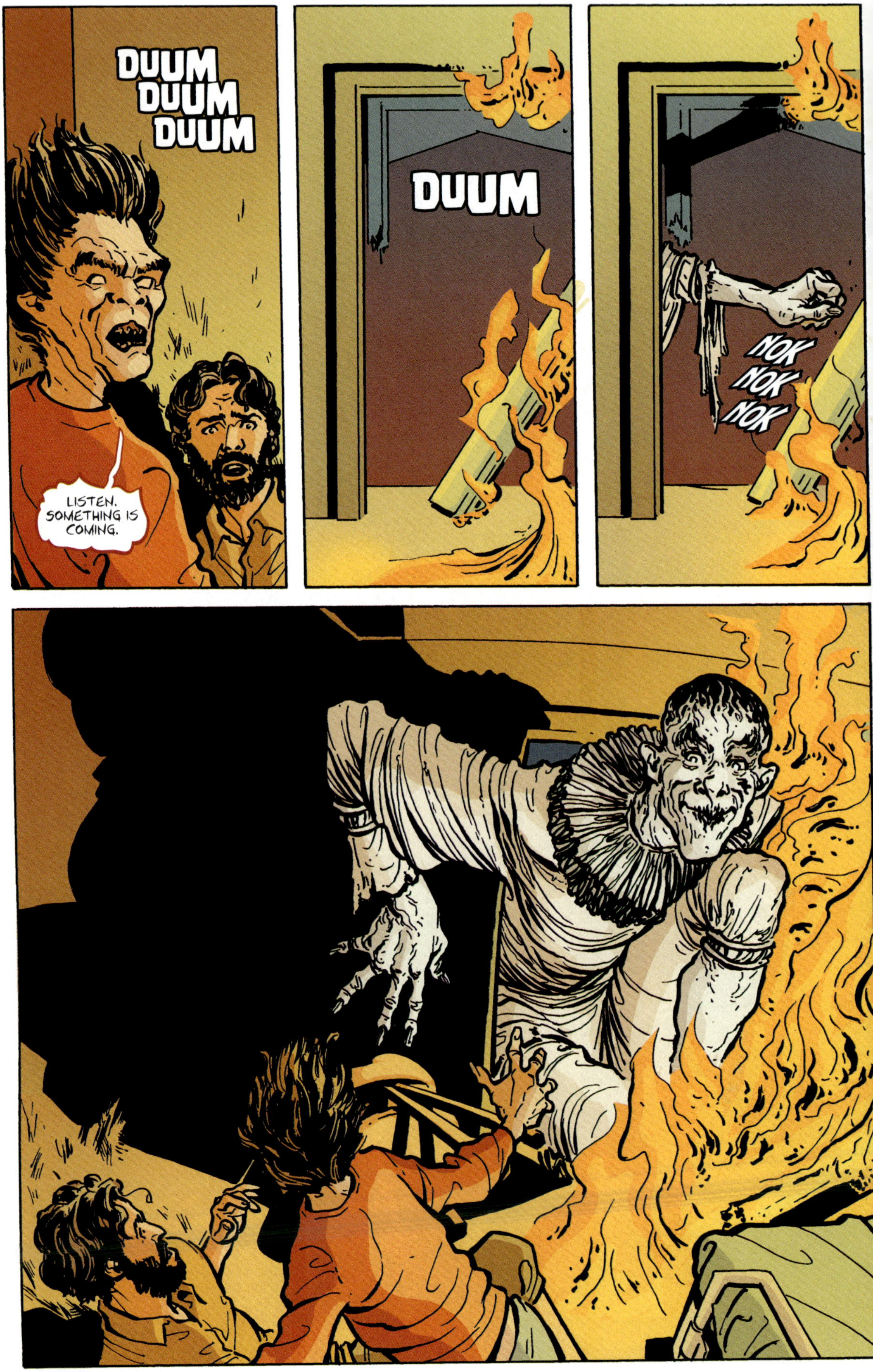
DUUM
DUUM
DUUM
LISTEN. SOMETHING IS COMING.
DUUM
NOK
NOK
NOK

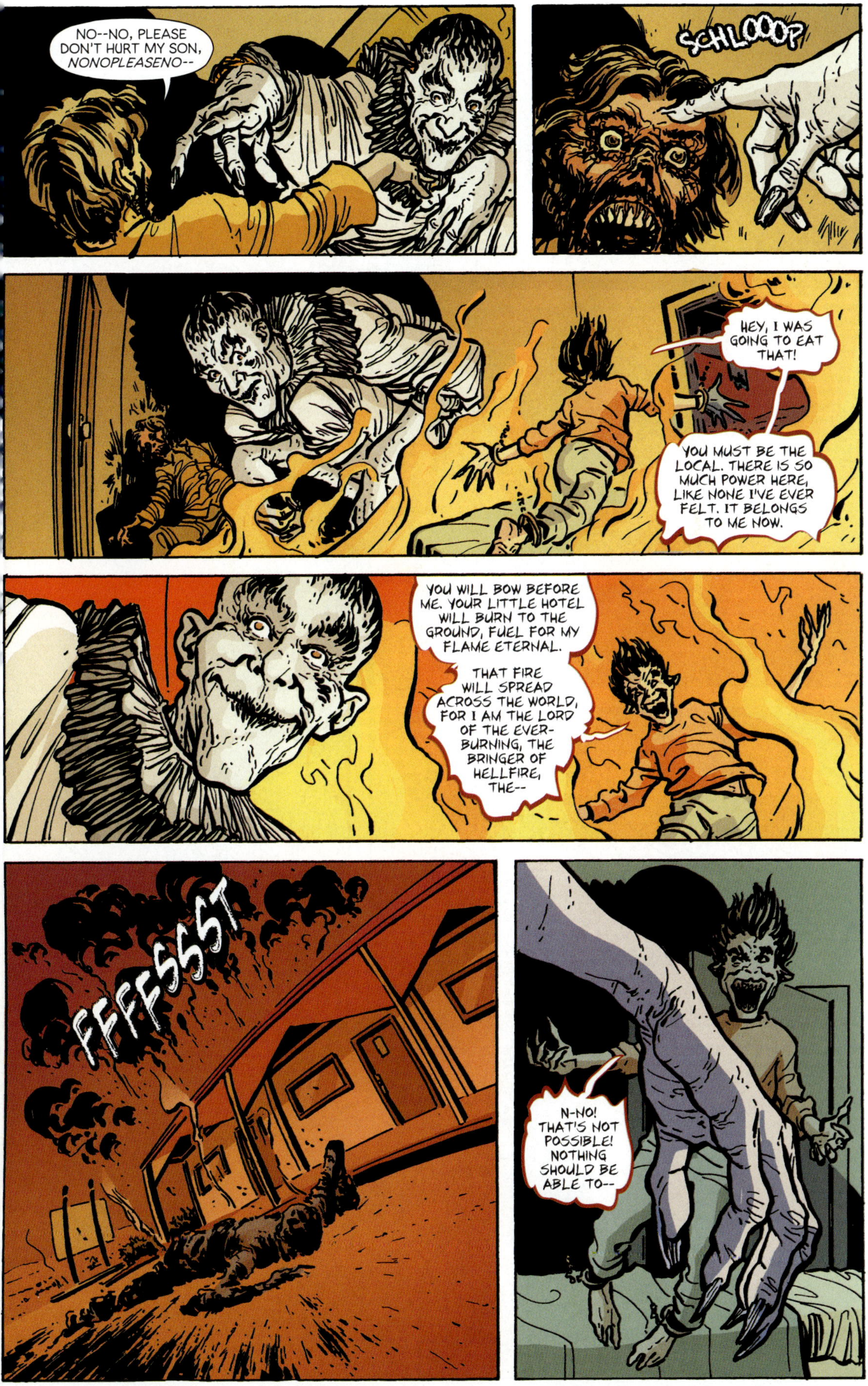
NO--NO, PLEASE DON'T HURT MY SON, *NONOPLEASENO--*
SCHLOOOP
HEY, I WAS GOING TO EAT THAT!
YOU MUST BE THE LOCAL. THERE IS SO MUCH POWER HERE, LIKE NONE I'VE EVER FELT. IT BELONGS TO ME NOW.
YOU WILL BOW BEFORE ME. YOUR LITTLE HOTEL WILL BURN TO THE GROUND, FUEL FOR MY FLAME ETERNAL.
THAT FIRE WILL SPREAD ACROSS THE WORLD, FOR I AM THE LORD OF THE EVER-BURNING, THE BRINGER OF HELLFIRE, THE--
FFFFSSST
N-NO! THAT'S NOT POSSIBLE! NOTHING SHOULD BE ABLE TO--

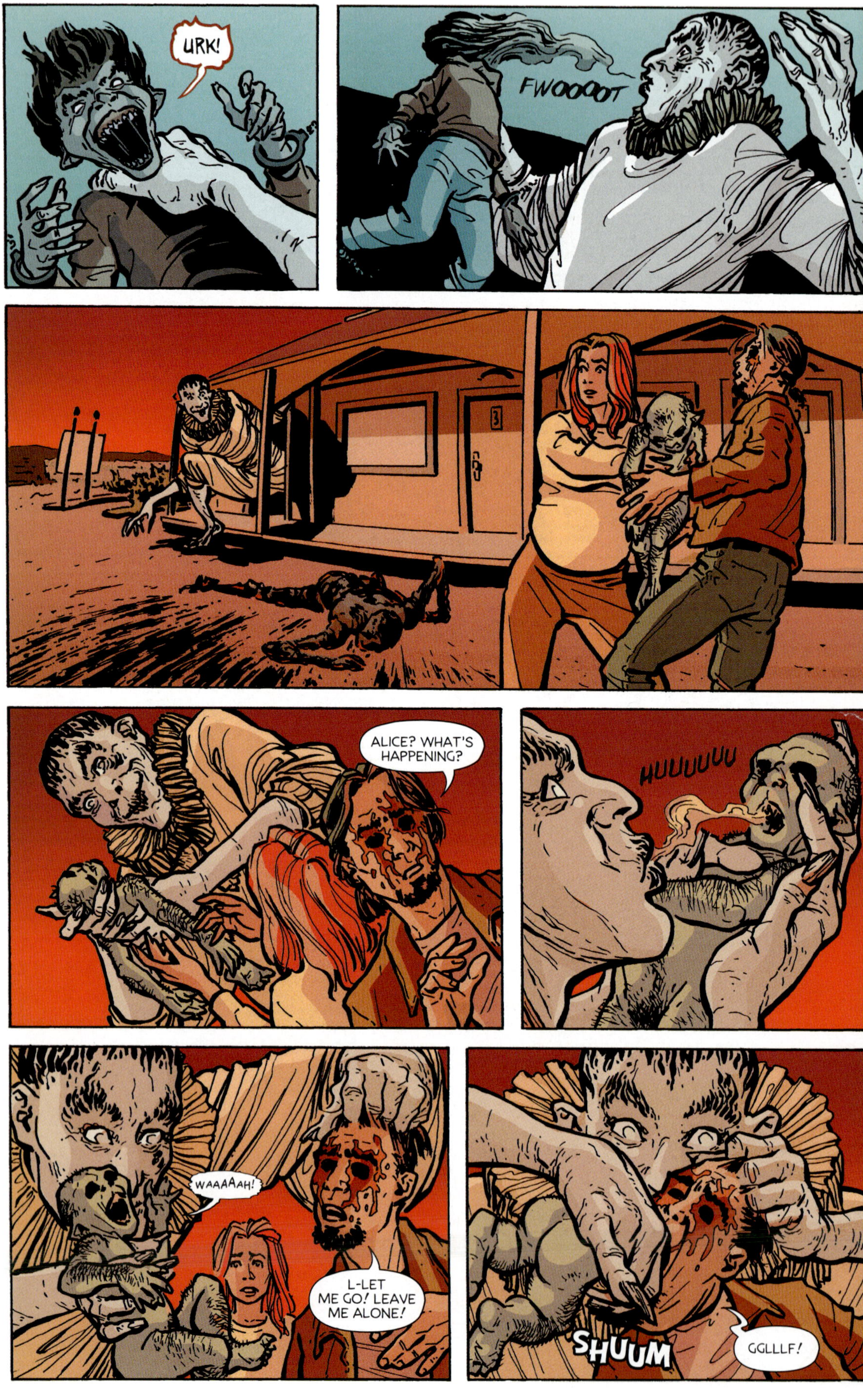
URK!
FWOOOOT
ALICE? WHAT'S HAPPENING?
HUUUUUU
WAAAAAH!
L-LET ME GO! LEAVE ME ALONE!
SHUUM
GGLLLF!

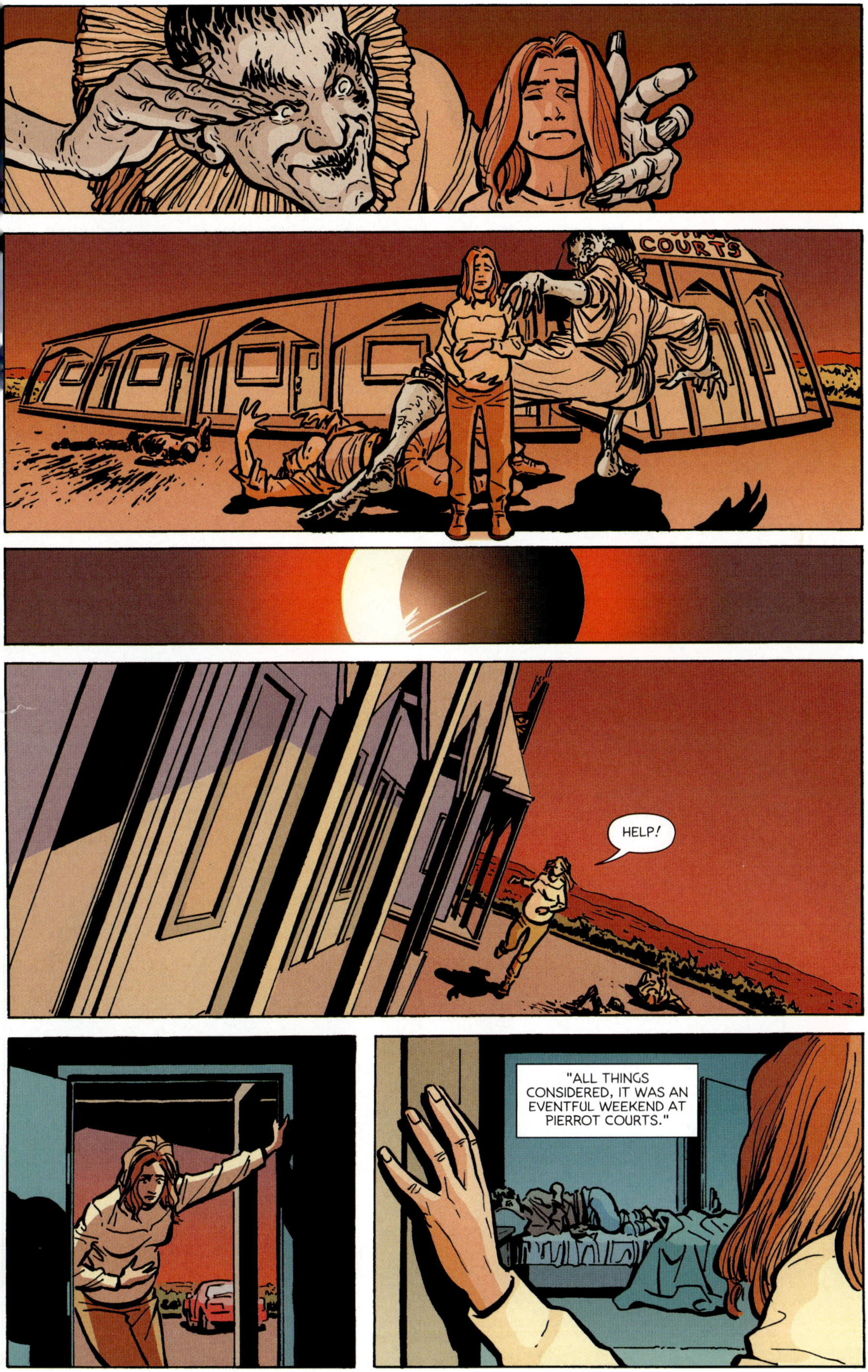
COURTS
HELP!
"ALL THINGS CONSIDERED, IT WAS AN EVENTFUL WEEKEND AT PIERROT COURTS."

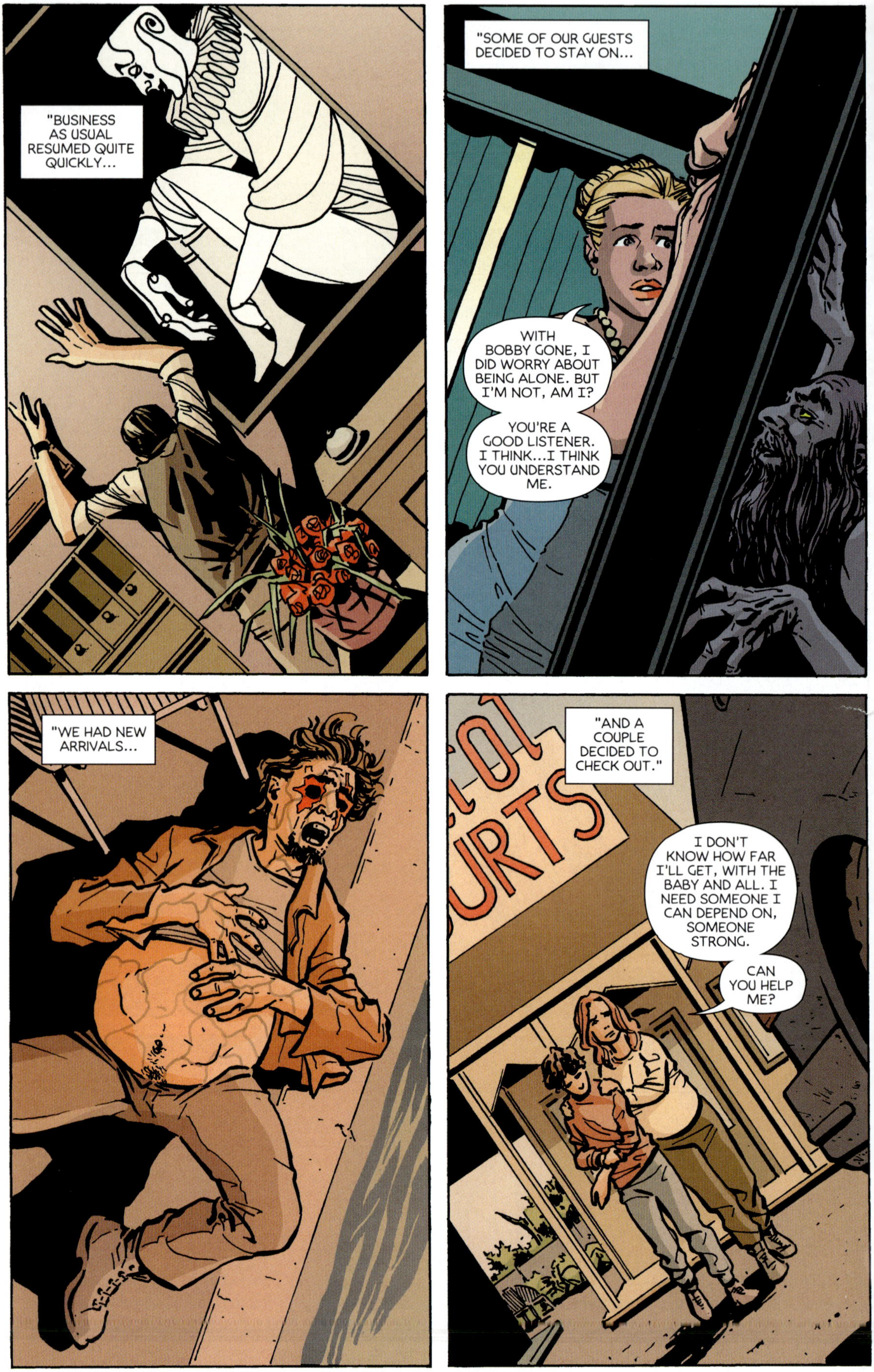
"BUSINESS AS USUAL RESUMED QUITE QUICKLY...
"SOME OF OUR GUESTS DECIDED TO STAY ON...
WITH BOBBY GONE, I DID WORRY ABOUT BEING ALONE. BUT I'M NOT, AM I?
YOU'RE A GOOD LISTENER. I THINK...I THINK YOU UNDERSTAND ME.
"WE HAD NEW ARRIVALS...
"AND A COUPLE DECIDED TO CHECK OUT."
URTS
I DON'T KNOW HOW FAR I'LL GET, WITH THE BABY AND ALL. I NEED SOMEONE I CAN DEPEND ON, SOMEONE STRONG.
CAN YOU HELP ME?

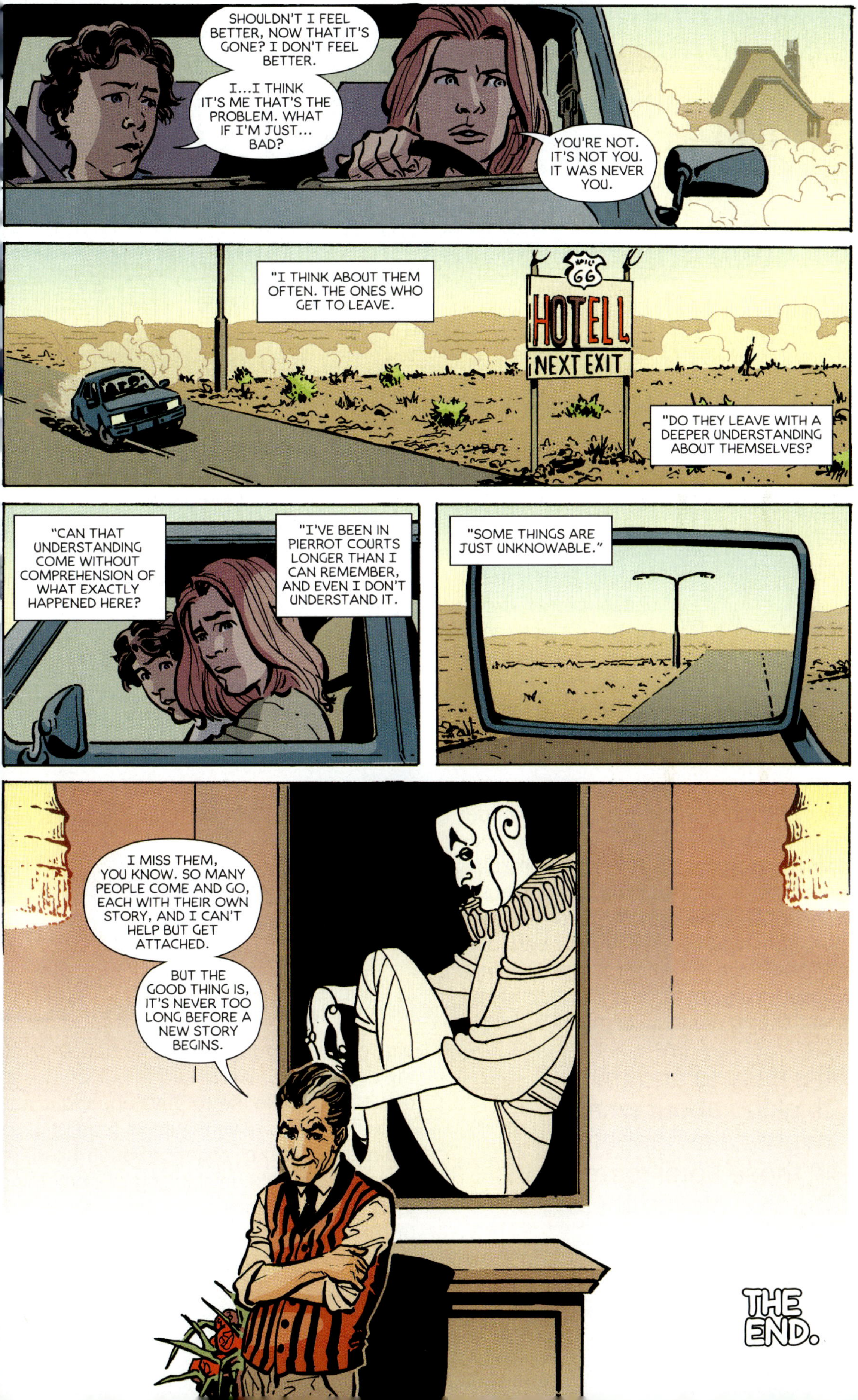
SHOULDN'T I FEEL BETTER, NOW THAT IT'S GONE? I DON'T FEEL BETTER.
I...I THINK IT'S ME THAT'S THE PROBLEM. WHAT IF I'M JUST... BAD?
YOU'RE NOT. IT'S NOT YOU. IT WAS NEVER YOU.
"I THINK ABOUT THEM OFTEN. THE ONES WHO GET TO LEAVE.
66
HOTELL
NEXT EXIT
"DO THEY LEAVE WITH A DEEPER UNDERSTANDING ABOUT THEMSELVES?
"CAN THAT UNDERSTANDING COME WITHOUT COMPREHENSION OF WHAT EXACTLY HAPPENED HERE?
"I'VE BEEN IN PIERROT COURTS LONGER THAN I CAN REMEMBER, AND EVEN I DON'T UNDERSTAND IT.
"SOME THINGS ARE JUST UNKNOWABLE."
I MISS THEM, YOU KNOW. SO MANY PEOPLE COME AND GO, EACH WITH THEIR OWN STORY, AND I CAN'T HELP BUT GET ATTACHED.
BUT THE GOOD THING IS, IT'S NEVER TOO LONG BEFORE A NEW STORY BEGINS.
THE END.

A LETTER FROM THE WRITER OF HOTELL

WE HOPE YOU ENJOY YOUR STAY...

Being a comic creator who travels to conventions on both sides of the Atlantic, I've spent a fair amount of time staying in hotels. Because of my creative streak, it's easy to find myself thinking about what might have happened in those hotel rooms before I stayed there. And because that creative streak of mine has always manifested itself in grim, mordant ways going way back to my days as a ghoulish, horror-loving child, inevitably these thoughts would turn to, "I wonder if anyone ever died in here?" In one particularly vivid daydream, I was in my room's bathroom, and looked out the open bathroom door to the full-length mirror on the wardrobe, from which I could see my bed reflected. I could see the empty space underneath the bed from there, and I got to thinking about seeing some awful figure lurking under my bed. Perhaps they would be waiting in eager silence, believing themselves to still be hidden, waiting until the lights were off and I was lying on the bed. Or perhaps they would turn towards the mirror and see me standing in the bathroom, reflected back...

> It's easy to find myself thinking about what might have happened in those hotel rooms before I stayed there

But let's jump from my imagination to the real world. A nice little Italian restaurant in New York City in October 2018, to be precise. It was here I had my first meeting with Axel Alonso, who of course I was already well familiar with as a hugely significant figure in the comics industry. He told me about his exciting vision for AWA Studios, and then asked me if I would like to be a

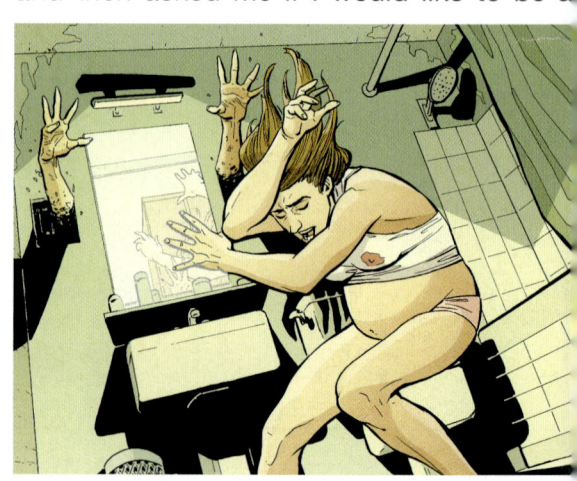

part of it, citing how much he had enjoyed my comic, *Sink*. We talked about what kind of story he'd like me to develop, and it was actually he who gave the initial prompt of an old roadside hotel setting, though I believe he might have been thinking of something more along the lines of the crime genre. But my mind immediately went to horror.

Hotell is a haunted house story, of sorts. But when you say "haunted house," often there is an expectation of grand old manors. And when something falls into familiar tropes, it becomes less frightening. But I hoped that by taking the hidden rooms and monstrous visions and cries in the dark and instead placing them in a crummy dive off Route 66, it would render them unfamiliar once more. I thought of *Psycho*, and what makes that image of the house looming over the Bates Motel so enduring: the intersection of modern Americana with the Gothic.

> By taking the hidden rooms and monstrous visions and cries in the dark and instead placing them in a crummy dive off Route 66, it would render them unfamiliar once more.

Now that this first issue is in your hands, I have a lot of people to thank. First, Axel Alonso, for bringing me onboard. Finding people who believe in you and champion you can be rare in comics, and I will forever appreciate the faith Axel has shown in me. Joining Axel are Mike, Dulce, Jaime, and all the rest of the brilliant team at AWA, working tirelessly to make these comics better. Sal Cipriano is a respected industry veteran for a reason, bringing clever insight to his letters. Lee Loughridge is a genius colorist, drawing out new dimensions in the art. And then there's the fantastic Dalibor Talajić, artist extraordinaire, producing some gruesome tableaus but also knowing when to go quiet, to underplay and let the dread simmer. I first met Dalibor at New York Comic Con last year, and we hit it off right away, sharing the same easy rapport we'd developed over e-mail. I can't wait to work with him again.

Finally, I want to thank *you*, reading this comic now. It meant so much to be included in AWA Upshot's launch lineup, but there's pressure there, too. Even with the impressive pedigree behind this publisher, any new venture is still an unknown commodity. But you still took a chance on us. I hope that you are happy with that decision. And with three more issues on the way, I hope you'll extend your stay a little longer. Just don't look under the bed...

-John Lees
Glasgow, Scotland, February 2020

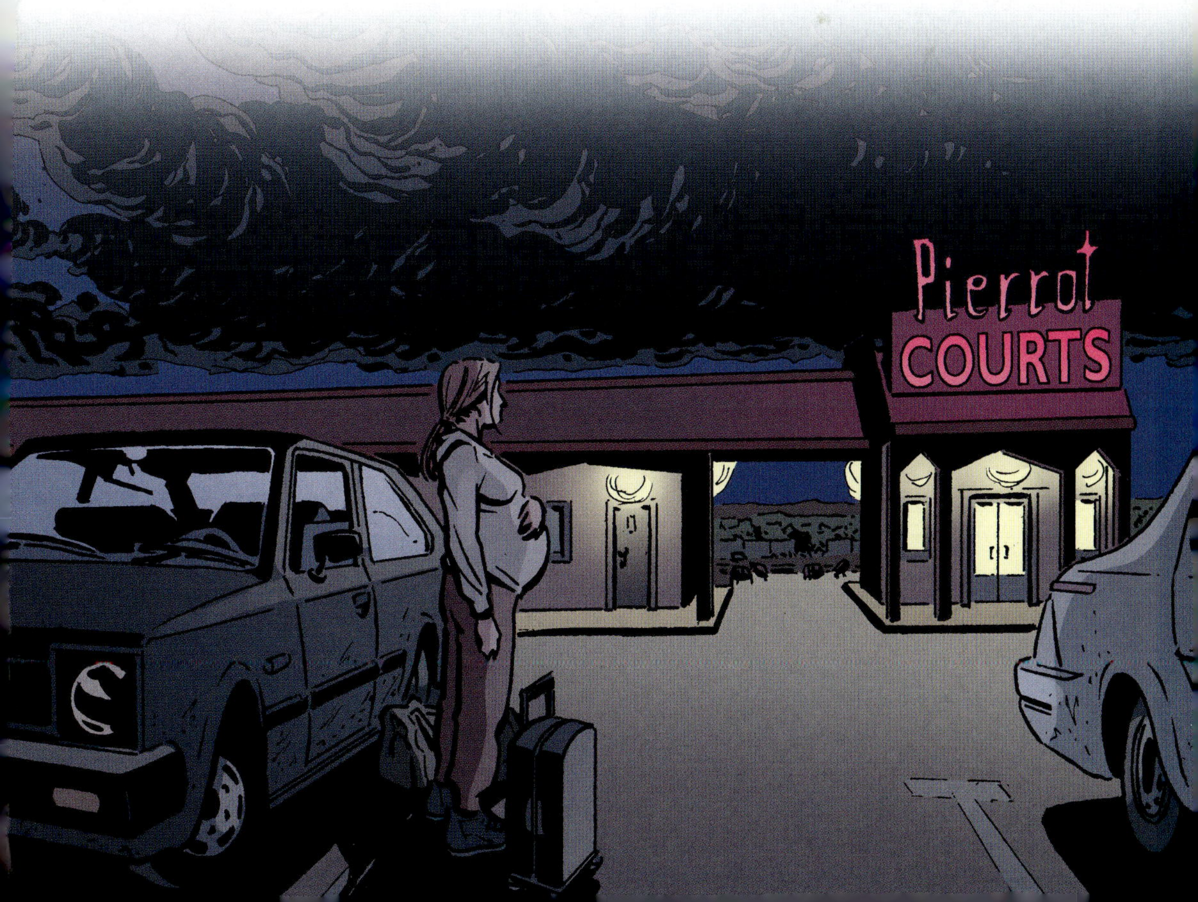
Pierrot
COURTS

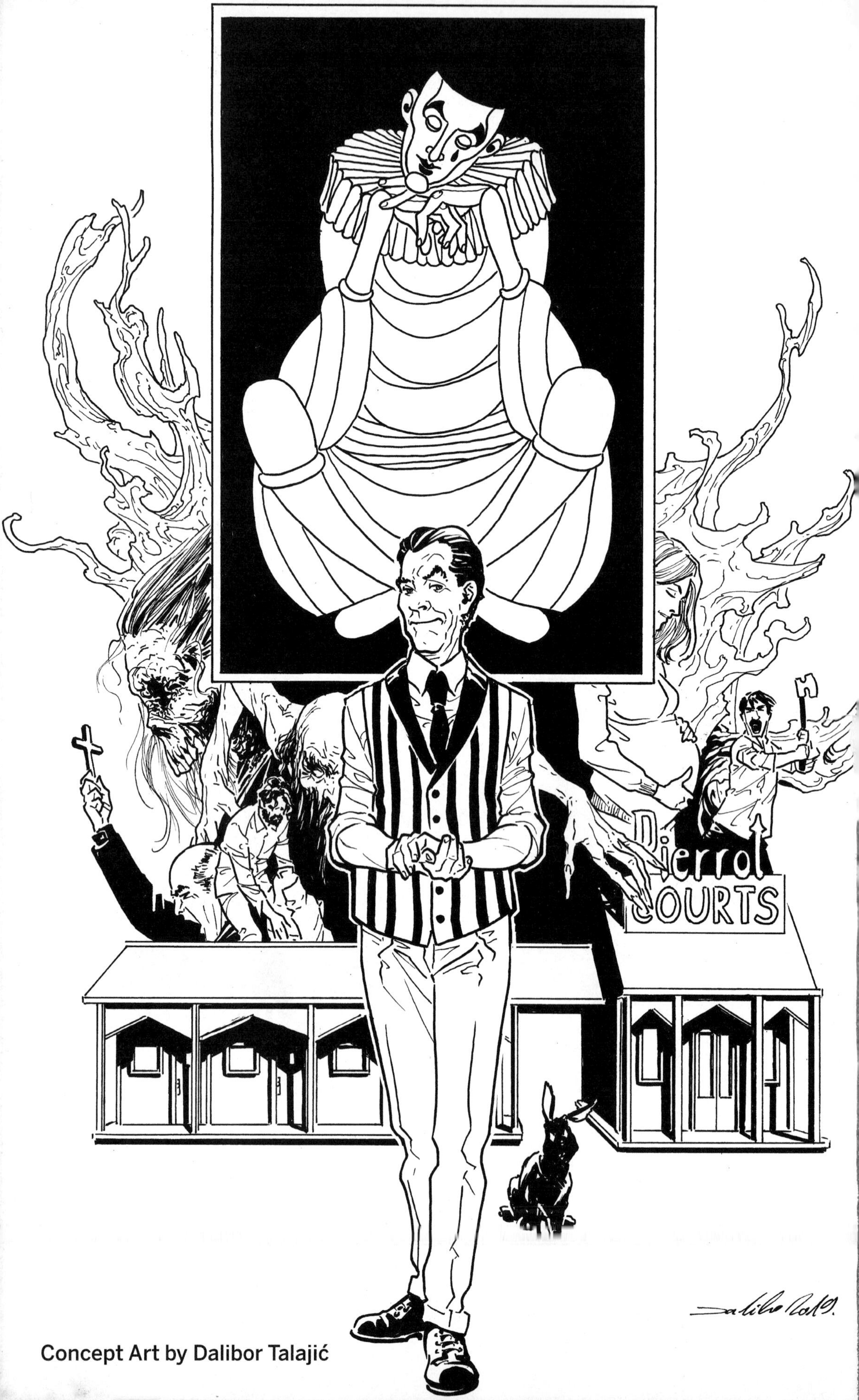
Pierrot
COURTS

Concept Art by Dalibor Talajić